The United States Expands West: 1785-1842

⊗⊗

Teachers Guide

A Supplemental Teaching Unit
from the Records of the National Archives

National Archives Trust Fund Board
National Archives and Records Administration

A B C ⊜ C L I O

ABC – CLIO, Inc
130 Cremona Drive, P.O. Box 1911
Santa Barbara, CA 93116-1911
ISBN 1-57607-780-2

Other Units in this Series:

Table of Contents

Foreword

In its efforts to make the historical records of the federal government available nationally, the National Archives began a program in 1970 to introduce these vast resources to upper elementary and secondary school students. School classes visiting the National Archives in Washington were given the opportunity to examine and interpret original sources as historians use them. Teachers and students responded enthusiastically and encouraged the development of a series of supplemental teaching units.

The United States Expands West: 1785-1842 is the eleventh unit in the series. It, like those that have preceded and will follow, is intended to bring you and your students the excitement and satisfaction of working with primary sources and to enhance your instructional program.

DON W. WILSON
Archivist of the United States
1990

...to bring you and your students the excitement and satisfaction of working with primary sources and to enhance your instructional program

Preface

The *United States Expands West: 1785-1842* is a teaching unit designed to supplement your students' study of the first phase of westward expansion; *Westward Expansion: 1842-1912* illustrates the second phase. The unit is made up of 10 exercises. Each exercise includes reproductions of documents from the National Archives and suggests classroom activities based on these documents. The documents include official correspondence, petitions, artwork, broadsides, newspapers, maps, and court decisions. Students practice the historian's skills as they complete exercises, using these documents to gather information, identify points of view, evaluate evidence, form hypotheses, and draw conclusions.

> ◆ This unit is made up of 10 exercises.
>
> ◆ Each exercise includes reproductions of documents from the National Archives and suggests classroom activities based on these documents.

The documents in this unit do not reflect every topic usually included in a history or government textbook. In some instances, the federal government had no interest in or authority over a given event and therefore created no records on it. In other cases, documents in the National Archives on several historic topics proved to be difficult to use in the classroom due to problems with legibility, length, or format.

The documents in this unit show a side of western history not commonly portrayed, that of the very significant commitment of the federal government to westward expansion at every phase of settlement. They also highlight the international character of life in the American West and the tenuousness of the nation's supposed Manifest Destiny. Because settlement of the western lands is so colored by myth, extra time is devoted in this unit to developing skills to separate the mythology of the west from its history.

Because the records in the National Archives demonstrate government involvement, the experience of the individual can be elusive. In particular, federal documentation of women's experiences in the West is very weak during this time period; to provide balance, the teacher should seek out information in state and local historical societies.

This unit departs from the previous format for the time line and bibliography. The time line for this unit does not list landmark dates in U.S. history from 1785-1842. Rather, the documents are listed in chronological order. This format emphasizes the sequence of and relationship between documents. In an effort to suggest more titles, we have dropped annotations from the bibliography. All recommended books are good sources of background information for the teacher; many are suitable and stimulating to students as well. The year 1842 was selected as a cutoff since the boundaries of the United States east of the Mississippi assumed their current configuration with the ratification of the Webster-Ashburton treaty.

Many textbooks treat the post-Revolutionary period as a whole, so teachers may find it useful to use some documents from *The Constitution: Evolution of a Government*, along with this one. *The United States Expands West: 1785-1842* is useful in classrooms other than the history classroom. Exercises contain activities suitable for use by government, civics, geography, economics, English, art, and science teachers.

National Archives education specialists Jean M. West and Wynell B. Schamel and education branch chief Elsie Freeman Finch developed this publication. We are pleased to issue a revised and updated set of these documentary teaching materials.

WYNELL B. SCHAMEL
LEE ANN POTTER
Education Specialists
2001

*A*cknowledgments

Many people helped in the original production of this unit. They included National Archives staff members John Butler, Dale Connelley, Richard Crawford, Mark Fischer, Nola Freeman, Robert Fowler, Cynthia Hightower, Michael Knapp, Susan Karren, Elizabeth Lockwood, Nancy Malan, Sally Marks, Mike Musick, Cathy Nicastro, Connie Potter, Mary Ronan, Jimmy Rush, and Reggie Washington.

James Percoco, a classroom teacher in Fairfax County, VA, and other social studies teachers reviewed elements of this unit. Their reactions and comments shaped and improved the document selection and the teaching exercises.

Ron Lucero, a National Archives volunteer, assisted in the development of the bibliography, in the document search, and in reviewing the manuscript. Linda N. Brown, Assistant Archivist of the Office of Public Programs; Robert E. Richardson, reference chief in the Cartographic Branch; Richard H. Smith, reference archivist in the Cartographic Branch; Edith James, Director of the Exhibits and Educational Programs Division; William T. Hagan, The University of Oklahoma; and Lawana Trout, Central State University, reviewed the unit for historical content. [Positions held at time of original publication.]

Special thanks go to Tom Gray, a classroom teacher in De Ruyter, NY, for his assistance throughout this project. He outlined content areas the unit needed to address in its formative stages. He scanned numerous rolls of microfilmed records of the State Department and Bureau of Indian Affairs. Later on, he enlisted fellow teachers to evaluate the documents and helped to critique the rough and final drafts. Finally, he tested the materials in his classroom.

During the republication process, we were ably assisted by George Mason University intern Adam Jevec; volunteers Elizabeth S. Lourie, Jane Douma Pearson, and Donald Alderson; and National Archives staff members Michael Hussey, A.J. Daverede, Patrick Osborn, Amy Patterson, Kate Flaherty, Donald Roe, and Charles Mayn.

 # Publisher's Note

Primary source documents have long been a cornerstone of ABC-CLIO's commitment to producing high-quality, learner-centered history and social studies resources. When our nation's students have the opportunity to interact with the undiluted artifacts of the past, they can better understand the breadth of the human experience and the present state of affairs.

It is with great enthusiasm that we celebrate the release of this series of teaching units designed in partnership with the National Archives—materials that we hope will bring historical context and deeper knowledge to U.S. middle and high school students. Each unit has been revised and updated, including new bibliographic references. Each teaching unit has been correlated to the curriculum standards for the teaching of social studies and history developed by the National Council for the Social Studies and the National Center for History in the Schools.

For more effective use of these teaching units in the classroom, each booklet is accompanied by an interactive CD-ROM which includes exercise worksheets, digital images of original documents, and, for four titles, sound recordings. A videocassette of motion pictures accompanies the teaching unit *The United States At War: 1944*. For those who would like to order facsimiles of primary source documents in their original sizes, or additional titles in this series, we have included an order form to make it easy for you to do so.

These units go a long way toward fulfilling that mission, helping the next generation of American citizens develop a clear understanding of the nation's past and a firm grasp of the role of the individual in guiding the nation's future. ABC-CLIO is honored to be part of this process.

BECKY SNYDER
Publisher & Vice President
ABC-CLIO Schools

The mission of the National Archives is "to ensure ready access to the essential evidence that documents the rights of American citizens, the actions of Federal officials, and the national experience."

Teaching With Documents Curriculum Standards Correlations

The National Council for the Social Studies and the National Center for History in the Schools have developed a set of comprehensive curriculum standards for the teaching of social studies and history. Take a look at how thoroughly the Teaching With Documents series supports the curriculum.

	The Constitution: Evolution of a Government	The Bill of Rights: Evolution of Personal Liberties	The United States Expands West: 1785–1842	Westward Expansion: 1842–1912	The Civil War: Soldiers and Civilians	The Progressive Years: 1898–1917	World War I: The Home Front	The 1920's	The Great Depression and The New Deal World	War II: The Home Front	The United States At War: 1944	The Truman Years: 1945–1953	Peace and Prosperity: 1953–1961
National Council for the Social Studies													
CULTURE—should provide for the study of culture and cultural diversity	●			●				●		●			●
TIME, CONTINUITY & CHANGE—should provide for the study of the ways people view themselves in and over time	●	●	●			●	●	●	●	●			
PEOPLE, PLACES & ENVIRONMENT—should provide for the study of people, places, and environments	●	●	●	●	●	●		●	●		●		
INDIVIDUAL DEVELOPMENT & IDENTITY—should provide for the study of individual development and identity	●	●	●	●	●	●	●	●	●				●
INDIVIDUALS, GROUPS & INSTITUTIONS—should provide for the study of interactions among individuals, groups, and institutions	●	●	●	●	●	●		●	●		●	●	●
POWER, AUTHORITY & GOVERNANCE—should provide for the study of how structures of power are created and changed	●	●	●	●	●	●		●	●			●	●
PRODUCTION, DISTRIBUTION & CONSUMPTION—should provide for the study of the usage of goods and services	●		●	●	●	●		●	●		●	●	●
SCIENCE, TECHNOLOGY & SOCIETY—should provide for the study of relationships among science, technology, and society			●	●	●	●		●			●	●	
GLOBAL CONNECTIONS—should provide for the study of global connections and interdependence	●		●			●		●				●	●
CIVIC IDEALS & PRACTICES—should provide for the study of the ideals, principles, and practices of citizenship	●	●						●			●		
National Center for History in the Schools													
CHRONOLOGICAL THINKING	●	●	●	●	●	●	●	●	●	●	●	●	●
HISTORICAL COMPREHENSION	●	●	●	●	●	●	●	●	●	●	●	●	●
HISTORICAL ANALYSIS & INTERPRETATION	●	●	●	●	●	●	●	●	●	●	●	●	●
HISTORICAL RESEARCH CAPABILITIES	●	●	●	●	●	●	●	●	●	●	●	●	●
HISTORICAL ISSUES-ANALYSIS & DECISION-MAKING	●	●	●	●	●	●	●	●	●	●	●	●	●

Introduction

This unit contains two elements: 1) a book, which contains a teachers guide and a set of reproductions of print documents and slides, and 2) a CD-ROM, which contains the exercise worksheets from the teachers guide and a set of reproductions of documents and slides in electronic format. In selecting the documents, we applied three standards. First, the documents had to be entirely from the holdings of the National Archives and had to reflect the actions of the federal government or citizens' responses to those actions. Second, each document had to be typical of the hundreds of records of its kind relating to its particular topic. Third, the documents had to be legible and potentially useful for vocabulary development. In selecting documents, we have tried to choose those having appeal to young people.

UNIT CONTAINS:

♦ **1)** a book, which contains a teachers guide and a set of reproductions of print documents and slides, and

♦ **2)** a CD-ROM, which contains the exercise worksheets from the teachers guide and a set of reproductions of documents and slides in electronic format.

Objectives

We have provided an outline of the general objectives for the unit. You will be able to achieve these objectives by completing several, if not all, of the exercises in the unit. Because each exercise aims to develop skills defined in the general objectives, you may be selective and still develop those skills. In addition, each exercise has its own specific objectives.

Outline

This unit on westward expansion includes 10 exercises. The first exercise provides an overview of all the documents, introducing students to the federal role in western life, in the nature of documentation, and how documentation impacts on interpretation. Exercises 2, 3, and 4 introduce three major themes that emerge from government documents and provide students with a large number of documents to interpret. The remaining exercises, 5 through 10, concentrate on particular topics in western history, focusing on a small number of documents. The structure and relation of the exercises are presented in the Unit Outline, p. 4.

List of Documents

The list of documents gives specific information (e.g., date and name of author) and record group number for each document. Records in the National Archives are arranged in record groups. A typical record group (RG) consists of the records created or accumulated by a department, agency, bureau, or other administrative unit of the federal government. Each record group is identified for retrieval purposes by a record group number; for example, RG 59 (Department of State) or RG 75 (Bureau of Indian Affairs). Complete archival citations of all documents are listed in the appendix, p. 69.

Exercise Summary Chart

The chart shows the organization of the 10 exercises. For each exercise the chart outlines the materials needed, the document content, the student activities that are emphasized, and the number of class periods needed. Review the chart carefully and decide which exercises to use based on your objectives for the students, their ability levels, and the content you wish to teach. The exercises may be adapted to fit your objectives and teaching style.

Introductory Exercises

Before starting exercises 1-10, it is important to familiarize students with documents and their importance to the historian who interprets them and writes history from them. We suggest that you direct students to do one or all of the introductory exercises. Introduction to Documents, p. 11, is designed to increase students' awareness of documents in their environment and is suitable for all secondary students. The Historian's Tools, p. 12, is designed to increase students' awareness of the process of analyzing historical information and is most appropriate for students working at or above ninth grade reading level. The Written Document Analysis, p. 14, is designed to help students analyze systematically any written document in this unit. The Map Analysis, p. 15, can be used similarly with any map.

Classroom Exercises

This unit contains 10 suggested exercises. Within the explanatory material for each of the exercises, you will find the following information:

- ➤ Note to the teacher
- ➤ Classroom time required
- ➤ Objectives (specific)
- ➤ Materials needed
- ➤ Procedures
- ➤ Student worksheets

You may choose to combine several exercises on a topic within the unit. In some instances, a document is used in more than one exercise when appropriate to the skill or content objectives. We encourage you to select and adapt the exercises and documents that best suit your own teaching style.

Ability Levels

As in our other units, we have developed exercises for students of different abilities. For some topics, we have designed two or more procedures, tailored to different student needs. Throughout the unit we have made an effort to provide exercises in which students use a variety of skills, including reading for understanding, interpreting maps and posters, and analyzing legislation and court cases. All lessons have procedures for ability levels one, two, and three. Procedures begin with strategies designed for level three students, continue with level two strategies, and conclude with level one strategies. Our definition of student ability at each ability level is as follows:

Level One: Good reading skills, ability to organize and interpret information from several sources with minimal direction from teacher, and ability to complete assignments independently;

Level Two: Average reading skills, ability to organize and interpret information from several sources with general direction from teacher, and ability to complete assignments with some assistance from teacher;

Level Three: Limited reading skills, ability to organize and interpret information from several sources with step-by-step direction from teacher, and ability to complete assignments with close supervision from teacher.

These ability levels are merely guides. We recognize that you will adapt the exercises to suit your students' needs and your own teaching style.

Time Line

A time line is included for use by your students. You may want to reproduce it for each student or display it. It is also appropriate to use it in conjunction with procedures in Exercise 1.

Bibliography

As students work with the documents, they should be assigned appropriate readings from their textbooks and other secondary sources. Also, they should be encouraged to use the resources of school and public libraries. To guide them, a bibliography appears at the end of the Teachers Guide.

General Objectives

Upon successfully completing the exercises in this unit, students should be able to demonstrate the following skills using a single document:

➤ Identify factual evidence

➤ Identify points of view (bias and/or prejudice)

➤ Collect, reorder, and weigh the significance of evidence

➤ Develop defensible inferences, conclusions, and generalizations from factual information

Using several documents from this unit, students should be able to:

➤ Analyze the documents to compare and contrast evidence

➤ Evaluate and interpret evidence drawn from the documents

Outline of Classroom Exercises

The United States Expands West: 1785-1842

Exercise 1
Western Expansion: An Overview

Exercise 2
The Role of the Federal Government

Exercise 3
Government Motivations and the West: Louisiana, A Case Study

Exercise 4
Formulating and Changing Government Policy:
The Cherokee Nation, A Case Study

Exercise 5
Mythmaking and the West

Exercise 6
The West of Opportunity

Exercise 7
Western Waterways

Exercise 8
The Romantic Worldview and the West

Exercise 9
The International West

Exercise 10
The Forgotten West

List of Documents

Following the identifying information for each document reproduced in the unit, we have given the record group (RG) number in which the original can be found. Should you want copies of these documents or wish to refer to them in correspondence with us, give the complete archival citation, which is found in the appendix on page 69. **You may duplicate any of the documents in this unit for use with your students.**

Documents in *The United States Expands West: 1785-1842* are taken from the following record groups: General Records of the U.S. Government (RG 11), U.S. Postal Service (RG 28), U.S. Senate (RG 46), Bureau of Land Management (RG 49), Department of the Treasury (RG 56), Department of State (RG 59), Department of Justice (RG 60), Bureau of Indian Affairs (RG 75), Office of the Chief of Engineers (RG 77), National Park Service (RG 79), Adjutant General's Office (RG 94), Smithsonian Institution (RG 106), Office of the Secretary of War (RG 107), Office of the Chief Signal Officer (RG 111), Solicitor of the Treasury (RG 206), U.S. House of Representatives (RG 233), Patent Office (RG 241), Supreme Court of the United States (RG 267), and Continental and Confederation Congresses and the Constitutional Convention (RG 360).

1. Land Ordinance of 1785, May 20, 1785 (RG 233).
2. Address by Governor Arthur St. Clair at his inauguration, July 9, 1788 (RG 59).
3. Land certificate, December 27, 1811 (RG 49).
4. Petition of Ohioans regarding land sale policy, January 10, 1810 (RG 233).
5. The *Kentucky Gazette*, newspaper, October 8, 1819 (RG 107).
6. Zebulon Pike's exploration notebook, 1805-1807 (RG 94).
7. Instructions from John C. Calhoun to Major Stephen Long, March 30, 1819 (RG 107).
8. Chart of Chesapeake and Ohio Canal toll rates, July 1, 1857 (RG 79).
9. Act authorizing road construction, January 23, 1822 (RG 233).
10. Letter from H. Dearborn to Thomas Peterkin, July 28, 1802 (RG 75).
11. Memorial of Eli Whitney, April 16, 1812 (RG 233).
12. Letter from Joseph Barrett to Captain John Kendrick, ca. 1786-1787(RG 59).
13. Court injunction in *Gibbons v. Ogden*, October 21, 1818 (RG 267).
14. Letter from John Chisholm to Colonel Meigs, January 25, 1807 (RG 75).
15. Letter from the War Department to various territorial governors, June 11, 1814 (RG 75).
16. Letter from Thomas Forsyth to Governor Howard, February 18, 1812 (RG 233).
17. Letter from Judge Rufus Putnam to President George Washington, July 24, 1790 (RG 59).
18. Message from President Thomas Jefferson to Congress, February 19, 1806 (RG 46).
19. Packing list for pelts, July 30, 1818 (RG 75).
20. The Louisiana Purchase, April 30, 1803 (RG 11).
21. Authorization from President Thomas Jefferson to Secretary of the Treasury Gallatin, January 16, 1804 (RG 56).
22. Proposed amendment to Louisiana territorial organization to restrict slavery, December 30, 1803 (RG 46).
23. Letter from Louisiana District Attorney John Dick to Governor Claiborne about Jean Lafitte, February 10, 1815 (RG 60).
24. Proclamation about territorial elections, July 26, 1805 (RG 59).
25. General Orders from General Wilkinson's letterbook, October 28, 1806 (RG 94).
26. Private Land Claim, January 10, 1831 (RG 49).

27. Land sale notice, May 28, 1810 (RG 206).

28. Letter from Joseph St. Marie to Territorial Secretary Sargent, July 29, 1790 (RG 59).

29. Letter from Governor Claiborne to Secretary of State Madison, January 24, 1806 (RG 59).

30. Letter from Secretary of State Madison to Robert Livingston and James Monroe, July 29, 1803 (RG 59).

31. The Missouri Compromise, March 6, 1820 (RG 11).

32. Committee draft report on Indian affairs, October 15, 1783 (RG 360).

33. Address from Confederated Tribes to the Confederation Congress, December 18, 1786 (RG 46).

34. Choctaw factory daybook, July 10, 1811 (RG 75).

35. Letter from chiefs of the Cherokee Nation to President James Monroe, March 5, 1819 (RG 75).

36. Letter from President Andrew Jackson to Secretary of War Eaton, November 18, 1830 (RG 75).

37. Court order in *Worcester v. Georgia*, January 1832 (RG 267).

38. Statement of the Protestant Episcopal Mission at Green Bay, September 30, 1833 (RG 75).

39. Letter from Governor Gilmer to Colonel Sanford, April 20, 1831 (RG 75).

40. Enrolled Cherokee immigrants, March 31, 1832 (RG 75).

41. Cherokee mortality schedule, December 30, 1837 (RG 75).

42. Treaty of New Echota, March 14, 1835 (RG 46).

43. Memorial of Pennsylvanians opposed to Indian removal, January 10, 1830 (RG 233).

44. Broadside of Orders #25 signed by General Scott, May 17, 1838 (RG 75).

45. Letter from Nathanial Smith to C. A. Harris with enclosures in Cherokee, March 15, 1838 (RG 75).

Slides on CD-ROM

A. Cherokee treaty map, Eastern lands, 1884 (RG 106).

B. Cherokee treaty map, Western lands, 1884 (RG 106).

C. Map of territories disputed between Georgia and the Cherokee, ca. 1830 (RG 75).

D. Map of the National Road, December 22, 1803 (RG 77).

E. Map produced by the Long Expedition, 1820-1821 (RG 77).

F. Snag boat design, ca. 1838 (RG 77).

G. Patent issued to Henry Shreve for snag boat, September 12, 1838 (RG 77).

H. Patent drawing of the cotton gin, 1794 (RG 241).

I. Erie Railroad map, 1832-1833 (RG 46).

J. Burr's *Postal Atlas*, 1839 (RG 28).

K. Minerals map, 1839-1841 (RG 46).

L. Map produced by the Pike Expedition, 1805-1806 (RG 77).

M. Map based on the Lewis and Clark Expedition, 1806 (RG 77).

N. Fort Dearborn groundplan and elevation, January 25, 1808 (RG 77).

O. Township plat, Alabama, Huntsville Meridian, Township 4 South, Range 5 East, 1822 (RG 49).

P. Proposed canal at Harper's Ferry, February 1803 (RG 79).

Q. *Buffalo Dance of the Mandans*, artwork by Karl Bodmer, 1833-1834 (RG 111).

R. *Osceola*, artwork by George Catlin, ca. 1837 (RG 111).

Exercise Summary Chart

EXERCISE	NUMBER OF DOCUMENTS	CONTENT	STUDENT ACTIVITIES	NUMBER OF CLASS PERIODS
Introductory Exercises	variable	Introduction to primary sources	Distinguishing between primary and secondary sources Analyzing written documents and maps Locating personal documents	variable
1. Western Expansion: An Overview Documents 1-45 Transcriptions of documents 17, 23, 35, 36, 39, 45 Slides A-R List of Documents Time line	all	Historian's methods Extent of federal government aid to western expansion	Working in groups Analyzing and categorizing a group of documents Making generalizations based on a group of documents Evaluating information under new circumstances	variable
2. The Role of the Federal Government Documents 1-45 Transcriptions of documents 17, 23, 35, 36, 39, 45 Slides A-R	all	Role of the federal government in western expansion Evaluating the role of individuals in westward migration	Analyzing in detail a single document Brainstorming stereotypes Using documents to evaluate validity of stereotypes Writing a position paper	variable
3. Government Motivations and the West: Louisiana, A Case Study Documents 5, 6, 7, 11, 14, 18, 19, 20-31 Transcription of document 23 Slides E, H, L, M, Q, R Worksheet 1	19	Motives behind the federal government support of western expansion Costs and benefits to the federal government of expansionism	Gathering information Analyzing and drawing conclusions from a group of documents Using creative writing skills to write an interior monologue	2
4. Formulating and Changing Government Policy: The Cherokee Nation, A Case Study Documents 32-45 Transcriptions of documents 35, 36, 39, 45 Slides A-C Written Document Analysis worksheet Worksheet 2	14	Formulating and changing policy towards the Cherokee Nation	Analyzing and drawing conclusions from a group of documents about the formulation of Indian policy Researching, writing, and presenting a dramatic production based on historical materials/events	3
5. Mythmaking and the West Document 2 Slide R	1	The growth of legends about historic events and people in the West	Formulating hypotheses about mythic and heroic figures Analyzing a portrait Analyzing a speech for stereotypes	2

EXERCISE	NUMBER OF DOCUMENTS	CONTENT	STUDENT ACTIVITIES	NUMBER OF CLASS PERIODS
6. The West of Opportunity Documents 1, 3-5, 8-13, 19, 26-28, 30, 34, 39 Transcription of document 39 Slides D, F, G, H, I, J, K Worksheets 3 and 4	17	Economic factors behind the settlement of the West Federal policy that encouraged economic expansion	Developing vocabulary of commercial terms Mapping activities Collecting and interpreting information from a group of documents Utilizing community resources	2-3
7. Western Waterways Documents 6, 7, 8, 17, 18, 23, 28, 42 Transcription of document 23 Slides E, F, G, L, P Worksheet 5	8	Role of waterways in the West	Translating a handwritten document Interpreting a chart Independently researching Working in groups Presenting oral reports	3-4
8. The Romantic Worldview and Exploration of the West Document 7 Slide E Written Document Analysis worksheet Map Analysis worksheet Worksheet 6	1	The Romantic approach to exploration The Yellowstone Expedition Deductive reasoning	Comparing and contrasting inductive and deductive reasoning Analyzing a document for Romantic viewpoints Evaluating contemporary methods to identify the type of reasoning used	1-2
9. The International West Documents 5, 12, 14, 15, 16, 20, 25, 26, 28, 29 Written Document Analysis worksheet Worksheet 7	10	International diplomacy in the West Ethnic diversity and communication in the West	Writing creative pieces Researching from community sources Analyzing and evaluating a document pertaining to one international incident	1-2
10. The Forgotten West Documents 5, 11, 22, 29, 31, 37, 38, 39 Transcription of document 39 Slide H Worksheet 8	8	Black American history in the West Religion in the history of the West Women in the West	Recognizing cause and effect in history Recognizing bias and point of view in primary sources Researching related topics	1

Introductory Exercises

These exercises introduce students to the general objectives of the unit. They focus students' attention on documents and their importance to historians, who interpret and record the past. We encourage you to use one or more of them as opening exercises for this unit.

Introduction to Documents

The Introduction to Documents worksheet is designed to increase students' awareness of documents in their environment and to make students more comfortable and sensitive to working with documents. It focuses on the availability of personal documents, the types of information found therein, and the informal creation and retention of documents in the students' lives. In section 1, students locate a personal document. In section 2, they present the document to the class, summarizing key information contained in the document. Finally, in section 3, the class considers possible reasons for the creation and retention of personal documents. This exercise is a basic introduction to personal documents that should precede study of more formal documents.

AVIS.   NOTICE.

La SOUSSIGNÉ Vendra à des conditions raisonnables une TERRE située fur le bayou La Fourche, de vingt arpens de face fur quarante de profondeur, fur la rive gauche de la rivière, à dix fept lieues du Miffiffipi, appartenant précédemment à M. Daniel Clark, & aujourd'hui à M. Wm. Brown, ci-devant Collecteur à la Nouvelle-Orléans. Il y a environ cent arpens défrichés fur cette habitation. Si elle n'eft pas vendue à l'amiable avant le fecond Lundi de Juillet prochain, elle fera alors expofée en Vente Publique à Donaldfonville, à un, deux, & trois ans de crédit, l'acheteur donnant une caution de toute fatisfaction pour le prix d'achat. Nlle.-Orléans, 18 Mai 1810.

P. Grymes,
Agent pour les Etats-Unis.

THE SUBSCRIBER will sell upon accommodating terms a TRACT of LAND fituated on the bayou La Fourche, of twenty arpents front, by forty in depth, on the left bank of the river, and seventeen leagues from the Miffiffipi, formerly the property of M. Daniel Clark, and now belonging to Wm. Brown late Collector at New Orleans. There are about one hundred arpents cleared on this plantation. If not fold by private contract before the fecond Monday in July next, it will then be exposed to Public Sale at Donaldsonville, on a credit of one, two and three years, the purchaser giving approved security for the purchase money. New Orleans, May 28th. 1810.

P. Grymes,
Agent for the United States.

The Historian's Tools

The Historian's Tools worksheet is designed to increase students' awareness of the process of analyzing historical information. It focuses on both the nature of the process of analyzing historical information and those factors that influence the historian's analysis of evidence. The worksheet includes specific questions on distinctions between primary and secondary sources, the reliability of those sources, and the influence of bias, point of view, and perspective on the historian's interpretation.

Students do not analyze documents to complete this worksheet as they do in other exercises in the unit. Class discussion, however, is essential to helping students understand the issues raised by the worksheet because there are many ways to answer the questions. In your discussion, stress the fact that reliability is affected by the events surrounding the creation of the document and the purposes for which the document is being evaluated. For this reason, it is essential to set documents in their historical context. Also, remind students that primary sources are not necessarily more reliable than well-researched secondary sources. You may wish to assign the worksheet as homework and discuss it with students in class.

Written Document Analysis

The Written Document Analysis worksheet helps students to analyze systematically any written document in this unit. In sections 1-5 of the worksheet, students locate basic details within the document. In section 6, students analyze the document more critically as they complete items A-E. There are many possible correct answers to section 6, A-E. We suggest you use one of documents 2, 5, 22, 39, 44, or 45 with this worksheet.

Map Analysis

The Map Analysis worksheet helps students to identify systematically the historical evidence within maps. It is designed to improve students' ability to use maps as historical documents. It can be used specifically with slides A, B, C, D, E, I, J, K, L, M, O, or P.

Introduction to Documents

Worksheet

1. This evening, with the help of a family member or an adult who is close to you, look through the souvenirs of your life that have been saved as you have grown. For example, these might include a photograph, a letter, a diary, a newspaper clipping, a birth certificate, a report card, or a library or social security card. Select one item to bring into class that you are willing to share with your classmates and teacher.

2. During your turn in class, present your document providing the following information:

   a. What type of document is this?

   b. What is the date of the document?

   c. Who created the document?

   d. How does the document relate to you?

3. Consider, for your document and the documents of your classmates, responses to the following questions:

   a. What does the existence of this document say about whoever created it?

   b. What does the existence of this document say about whoever saved it?

   c. What does the existence of this document say about American life in this era?

Designed and developed by the education staff of the National Archives and Records Administration, Washington, DC 20408.

The Historian's Tools

Worksheet

1. If you were writing a chapter in your textbook about westward expansion, list three things you would like to know about that subject.

   1. _____

   2. _____

   3. _____

2. Where might you look to find information about the three topics you listed in #1?

Topic	Source of Information
_____	_____
_____	_____
_____	_____

3. Historians classify sources of information as **PRIMARY** or **SECONDARY**. Primary sources are those created by people who actually saw or participated in an event and recorded that event or their reactions to it immediately after the event. Secondary sources are those created by someone either not present when that event occurred or removed from it by time. Classify the sources of information you listed in #2 as either primary or secondary by placing a **P** or **S** next to your answers in #2. Reconsider the sources you would use to find information about westward expansion; list three more here:

   1. _____

   2. _____

   3. _____

4. Some sources of historical information are viewed as more **RELIABLE** than others, though all of them may be useful. Factors such as bias, self-interest, distance, and faulty memory affect the reliability of a source. Below is a list of sources of information about Stephen Long's Yellowstone Expedition of 1819. Rate the reliability of each source on a numerical scale in which 1 is reliable and 5 very unreliable. Be able to support your ratings.

   A. John C. Calhoun's orders to Major Long in March
      1819 prior to the expedition's departure.   1   2   3   4   5

   B. Stephen Long's exploration notebook maintained
      during the expedition.   1   2   3   4   5

C. A newspaper article about the expedition written by a
reporter for the *Kentucky Gazette* in October 1819.   1   2   3   4   5

D. A printed map based on the sketches
made by Stephen Long's cartographer.   1   2   3   4   5

E. An account written by a historian based on an
interview with a member of the expedition in 1849.   1   2   3   4   5

F. A U.S. history high school textbook description
of the Long Yellowstone Expedition.   1   2   3   4   5

G. A description of Stephen Long's Yellowstone
Expedition in an encyclopedia.   1   2   3   4   5

5. What personal and social factors might influence historians as they write about people and
events of the past?

_____

_____

_____

6. What personal and social factors influence *you* as you read historical accounts of people
and events?

_____

_____

_____

Designed and developed by the education staff of the National Archives and Records Administration, Washington, DC 20408.

Written Document Analysis

Worksheet

1. Type of Document (Check one):

    ____ Newspaper   ____ Map   ____ Advertisement

    ____ Letter   ____ Telegram   ____ Congressional record

    ____ Patent   ____ Press release   ____ Census report

    ____ Memorandum   ____ Report   ____ Other

2. Unique Physical Qualities of the Document (check one or more):

    ____ Interesting letterhead   ____ Notations

    ____ Handwritten   ____ "RECEIVED" stamp

    ____ Typed   ____ Other

    ____ Seals

3. Date(s) of Document: _____

4. Author (or creator) of the Document: _____

   Position (Title): _____

5. For What Audience was the Document Written? _____

6. Document Information (There are many possible ways to answer A-E.)

   A. List three things the author said that you think are important:

      1. _____

      2. _____

      3. _____

   B. Why do you think this document was written?

   C. What evidence in the document helps you to know why it was written? Quote from the document.

   D. List two things the document tells you about life in the United States at the time it was written:

      1. _____

      2. _____

   E. Write a question to the author that is left unanswered by the document:

Designed and developed by the education staff of the National Archives and Records Administration, Washington, DC 20408.

Map Analysis

Worksheet

1. Type of Map (check one):

   _____ Raised relief map   _____ Topographic contour-line map
   _____ Political map   _____ Military map
   _____ Natural resource map   _____ Artifact map
   _____ Bird's-eye view map   _____ Pictograph
   _____ Satellite photograph/mosaic   _____ Other (_____)
   _____ Weather map

2. Physical Qualities of the Map (check one or more):

   _____ Compass   _____ Handwritten
   _____ Date   _____ Notations
   _____ Scale   _____ Name of mapmaker
   _____ Title   _____ Other (_____)
   _____ Legend (key)

3. Date of Map: _____

4. Creator of Map: _____

5. Where was the map produced? _____

6. Map Information

   A. List three things in this map that you think are important:

   1. _____
   2. _____
   3. _____

   B. Why do you think this map was drawn?

   _____
   _____

   C. What evidence in the map suggests why it was drawn?

   _____
   _____

   D. What information does the map add to the textbook's account of this event?

   _____
   _____

   E. Does the information in this map support or contradict information
   that you have read about this event? Explain.

   _____
   _____

   F. Write a question to the mapmaker that is left unanswered by this map.

   _____
   _____

Designed and developed by the education staff of the National Archives and Records Administration, Washington, DC 20408.

Exercise 1
Western Expansion: An Overview

Note to the Teacher:

The westward expansion of the United States fills the mind with images of Indians and teepees, trappers and pioneers, wagon trains and sod houses, and vast wilderness lands. These stirring elements are significant in the story of the growth of this nation.

A less familiar but equally significant aspect of this saga is chronicled at the National Archives. Notwithstanding the role of the rugged individual, millions of records show the contribution of the United States government to the great westward surge. This unit contains a representative sampling of records from Congress, the judiciary, and numerous executive departments, agencies, and offices. They document the intimate involvement of all branches of the federal government in each phase of western expansion. Government employees, both military and civilian, ranging from soldiers to surveyors and engineers to clerks, were vital players in the drama of the American west. The public servant may not seem a stirring figure until we recall that Lewis and Clark, Andrew Jackson, Sam Houston, and even Davy Crockett were federal Employees – bureaucrats – albeit flamboyant ones.

In addition to those employed by or for the government, the government then, as now, touched the lives of many citizens. A number of documents in this package are from men and women who called on or were called upon by the government in the midst of the first great westward movement. All of these documents remind us that the national migration was promoted and aided by the federal government, and that the rugged individual ordinarily was backed by the full faith and force of the national government.

In this exercise, students are introduced to documentation by the federal government. They are asked to assume the role of historians, suggesting ways of organizing a group of documents and considering how arrangement influences interpretation by historians. Because the documents in this unit are federal records, pupils will be asked, in particular, to focus on functions of the federal government that mandated activities that generated these records. Also, since the National Archives organizes and keeps its holdings according to originating agency, this exercise will help students understand how to do research in an archives.

Time: variable

Objectives:

- To survey the government's role in western expansion.

- To identify alternative ways of organizing information.

- To draw generalizations from a group of documents and evaluate their validity under new circumstances.

Materials Needed:

Documents 1-45
Slides A-R
List of Documents, p. 5
Time line, p. 64

Procedures:

1. Duplicate a class set of the List of Documents and five complete sets of documents. Distribute the List of Documents and then divide the class into five groups. Explain to the groups that each is responsible for arranging the documents; the method of organization is up to each group, but students are responsible for developing a rationale for arrangement that they can explain and arranging the documents according to that rationale. Students may not use the 1-45, A-R arrangement of the List of Documents. Ask students to suggest alternate possibilities (e.g., chronological, geographical, topical, manuscript v. print, etc.). Determine how quickly you wish to conduct the overview; it can take as little as a week or as long as a semester, depending on the objectives of the instructor and ability of the class. At each class meeting that you dedicate to this overview, distribute four to eight documents to each student group and allocate 5-10 minutes to show two to four slide documents to the class. At the time the activity culminates, each of the five groups should have a complete set of the 45 reproduced documents. After the students have received all of the documents, ask them to review their sets of documents and to formulate ideas about arrangement.

2. Begin the final class period of this activity by asking each group to report on its rationale of arrangement and the order of its set of documents.

3. Project a transparency of the time line. Ask students to consider the advantages and disadvantages of this type of organization. Then, ask students to consider arrangement of the documents according to the functions of the federal government. Using information gleaned from its survey of the documents, have the class brainstorm answers to the question: For what tasks was the federal government responsible during the expansion of the United States westward? Ask students to reorganize their set of documents according to that arrangement.

4. Discuss with the class how different arrangements altered its view of the documents. How might original arrangement of primary sources influence the way professional historians interpret history? Is arrangement of documents a necessary task of the historian?

5. Extended activity: Ask students to evaluate their list of the government's responsibilities for exploration and settlement of the west in light of modern space exploration. What similarities exist in the government's actions then and now? (e.g., military scientists such as Stephen Long have modern successors such as Alan Shepherd.) What differences exist? Is the government's traditional form of land colonization valid for space colonization?

Exercise 2
The Role of the Federal Government

Note to the Teacher:

From the cession of state-owned western lands in the 1780s to the Confederation, the national government has played a major role in the expansion of the United States. The federal government has performed a wide variety of essential tasks in extending and settling the frontier. It has acquired land through treaty cession, purchase, conquest, and litigation (**documents 20, 30, A, B, C**). Once land was obtained, explorers, scientists, and surveyors were sent forth to mark boundaries, measure and map the acquisition, and identify essential natural resources (**documents 1, 5, 6, 7, 12, 18, E, K, L, M, O**).

Once the public lands were identified and described, the government placed tracts up for sale, controlling the price, quantity available, and credit terms (**documents 1, 3, 4, 26, 27**). Territorial governments were quickly formed. Then, as population grew, states were admitted following the formula set down in the Northwest Ordinance of 1787 (**documents 2, 15, 24**). (A copy of the Northwest Ordinance is available in *The Constitution: Evolution of a Government.*) The government showed great concern in securing the safety of citizens from depredations by foreign nations, Indians, and criminals (**documents 16, 17, 23, 25, 28, 29, N**). At the same time, effort was expended to protect Indians from unscrupulous settlers and traders (**documents 10, 14, 19**) and to consolidate control over the Eastern tribes (**documents 32-45**).

With the growth of the nation, an acute need for improved transportation and communication arose. The federal government, through patents, public works programs, the postal service, and court decisions that encouraged dissemination of technology, fostered many improvements which bound the growing nation together (**documents 8, 9, 11, D, F, G, H, I, J, P**). Slavery, which had been prohibited by the Confederation in the old Northwest territories, was determined by territorial legislatures (**document 22**) until the enactment of the Missouri Compromise (**document 31**).

The cost of western expansion to the federal government was great, both in terms of cash spent on purchases and lives of U.S. troops lost in war (**document 21**). Indirect costs of funding and maintaining territorial and Indian affairs offices and the time and effort spent in administering the frontier were high. The documents in this collection confirm that territorial expansion was a top priority of the federal government from 1785 to 1842.

Time: variable

Objectives:

- To introduce original documents and document analysis.

- To recognize the efforts of the federal government in promoting western expansion.

Materials Needed:

Documents 1-45
Slides A-R

Procedures:

Some documents are very difficult to read and require close attention. Until the mid-19th century, handwriting and printing were much different in some ways from the way they appear today. The letter "S" creates problems for modern readers since a "long S" or "short S" could be used. Transcriptions for selected documents begin on page 56.

1. Distribute copies of document 2 to the students. Read the document aloud as the students follow. By following the teacher's oral reading, the students should become accustomed to reading a handwritten document. When they have completed the reading, ask them to summarize the meaning of each resolution in order. Ask a recorder to list these summaries for the class on the chalkboard.

2. Discuss the following questions with the students:

   a. What are the benefits of government over a state of nature, according to Governor St. Clair?

   b. What personal qualities must be present in a good public servant, according to St. Clair?

   c. According to St. Clair, what is the relationship between Congress and the territory? Between the states and the territory?

   d. What is the tone of St. Clair's inaugural address to the people of the territory?

   e. Through what means is a territory bound to the union, based on the evidence in this document?

   f. What is St. Clair's attitude towards wilderness land?

   g. What sort of relationship between settlers and Indians does St. Clair envision?

   h. Do you think St. Clair started his term of office well with the presentation of this address? Why or why not?

3. Ask each student to write and turn in a paragraph answering the question, "Based on his inaugural address, do you think St. Clair turned out to be a good territorial governor? Why or why not?" Afterwards, ask students to look up in their textbooks or a reference book the story of the remainder of Arthur St. Clair's public career to compare with their assessment of him.

4. Ask the whole class to brainstorm a list of stereotypical individuals associated with the western frontier, e.g., mountain man, pioneer, Indian fighter. Appoint a student to record these character types on the chalkboard. Divide the class, documents, and slides into five groups and distribute one-fifth of the documents and slides to each group. Set up an area where students can review the slides. Using the documents, ask each group to sort documents and identify government institutions that directly or indirectly stood behind the "rugged individual" on the frontier. Have each group share its findings by reporting to the other groups.

5. Based on their findings, ask students to write a position paper either defending or rejecting the premise that westward expansion was primarily the result of the effort of the individual.

Exercise 3
Government Motivations and the West: Louisiana, A Case Study

Note to the Teacher:

The federal government was motivated by political, military, economic, religious, and intellectual interests to promote the extension of the nation westward to the Mississippi and beyond. The vast majority of American citizens supported expansionist policies and elected representatives who would promote continued growth.

Following the Treaty of Paris in 1783, the unsettled state of the northern border with British Canada and tensions along the Mississippi boundary with Spain prompted the government to make a variety of treaties to ensure national security. Similarly, Indian treaties for land or alliance frequently had as their impulse military concerns.

Economic factors were also extremely important. The invention of the cotton gin and intensive cultivation of cotton wore out land, sending farmers westward in search of new soil. Western farmers and traders sending their products to market relied on Spain, and later, France, to maintain the neutrality of the Mississippi River. The vagaries of European politics made the right of deposit uncertain. Fortunes could be made in the fur trade, but trappers had to push ever farther into the interior as wildlife was overhunted. For most citizens, the American dream was land. The desire for land was, at its most base, pure greed and self-interest; at its noblest, land acquisition was essential to realize the Jeffersonian vision of a democracy of yeoman farmers. Regardless of motivation, it was common practice for settlers to jump federally established boundaries. Squatters gambled that the government would recognize their claims to their expanded and improved holdings by ratifying their actions at a future date. In doing so they alienated the Indians and jeopardized friendly relations between Indian and settler.

While the phrase "Manifest Destiny" had yet to be coined, there was a clear religious impulse to migration. Missionaries sought to convert Indians in remote areas to Christianity, proselytizing Catholic mission Indians, Spaniards, and Frenchmen on behalf of Protestantism. Evangelists sincerely believed they brought the blessings of eternal salvation, science, agriculture, and civilization to primitives living in a brutish state of nature while failing to recognize the problems they also created.

During the years from 1785 to 1842, the worldview of intellectuals changed from the selective, ordered vision of neoclassicism to the expansive, unstructured grasp of Romanticism. Scientists and artists were extraordinarily curious about a broad range of subjects, collecting vast amounts of information and adventuring widely to come to a more comprehensive understanding of the universe. This inquisitiveness contributed to the number of explorations undertaken and the breadth of the studies conducted.

Records of the Louisiana Territory (**documents 5, 6, 7, 11, 14, 18, 19, 20-31** and **slides E, H, L, M, Q, R**) help to illuminate some of the motives behind the government's actions as well as the costs and benefits to the nation of territorial expansion.

Time: 2 class periods

Objectives:

- To identify motives which prompted the federal government to support national expansion.

- To understand the costs and benefits to the federal government of westward expansion.

Materials Needed:

Documents 5, 6, 7, 11, 14, 18, 19, 20-31
Slides E, H, L, M, Q, R
Worksheet 1

Procedures:

1. Duplicate and distribute worksheet 1 to each student. You may wish to enlarge the worksheet to provide adequate space for the students' answers. Divide the class into five groups and distribute the set of Louisiana documents to each group. Ask students to review the documents and slides for evidence of the motives behind the expansion of the nation and to complete their worksheets recording this evidence. Remind students that a document can suggest more than one motive.

2. Discuss the following questions with the students:

   a. What groups of people (or individuals) were perceived by the creators of these documents as potential threats to the security of Louisiana and the United States and how so?

   b. Based on the information in these documents, what were the costs to the United States, monetary and otherwise, of acquiring the Louisiana Territory?

   c. Based on information in these documents, what were the benefits to the United States of acquiring the Louisiana Territory?

   d. What motives appear to be dominant in the purchase of Louisiana based on the evidence you have uncovered in these documents?

3. Ask students to assume the character of one of the following creators of a document and to write an interior monologue about his reasoning and emotions as he reflects upon the transfer of Louisiana from France to the United States:

   a. President Thomas Jefferson (document 18)

   b. James Monroe (document 20)

   c. Pierre Arceneau (document 26)

   d. Joseph St. Marie (document 28)

4. For further research, ask for volunteers to select from among the following literary works a title to read and to report on to the class:

   a. *The Man Without A Country*, by Edward E. Hale

   b. *Evangeline*, by Henry W. Longfellow

   c. *Burr*, by Gore Vidal

   d. *The Journals of Lewis and Clark*, edited by Bernard de Voto

   e. *Democracy in America*, by Alexis de Tocqueville

Exercise 3: Government Motivations and the West: Louisiana, A Case Study

Worksheet 1

Directions: Review the following documents and slides and state the evidence of motives behind the expansion of the United States. Not every document has every motivation but some have more than one.

#	POLITICAL	ECONOMIC	RELIGIOUS	MILITARY	INTELLECTUAL
5					
6					
7					
11					
14					
18					
19					
20					
21					
22					
23					
24					
25					
26					
27					
28					
29					
30					
31					
E					
H					
L					
M					
Q					
R					

Exercise 4
Formulating and Changing Government Policy: The Cherokee Nation, A Case Study

Note to the Teacher:

From its beginning the United States has grappled with formulating an Indian policy. Fundamental questions of land ownership, cultural integrity, and human rights framed the debate over this policy. By closely examining the earliest formulations of Indian policy, their impact on Indians, and the changes that were made during the early years of the republic, we can better understand the subsequent course of our history.

In the colonial period, Indian tribes were recognized as independent, sovereign nations and the land upon which they resided under Indian title. European states rather than companies or individuals had the primary option to acquire Indian lands by formal treaty with tribal government. This option was exercised in profitable ways. In the English colonies, the king conveyed his right to acquire Indian lands through his charter to the colonial governments. Thus, the colonies found it profitable to provoke Indian wars so as to impose peace treaties with harsh land penalties. Once a colony had the title to Indian lands, it would sell them to individuals or large land companies formed by speculators who could then raise the price and resell a tract piecemeal to small farmers at tremendous profit. The frontier figure loathed by Indians and colonial officials alike was the squatter. The former despised squatters because they encroached on Indian lands, the latter because squatters occupied lands without payment.

The American Revolution upset existing Indian policies and threw all Indian rights into confusion. Because most Eastern tribes had aligned themselves with the crown, they were generally regarded as conquered peoples, tenants at the will of the new nation. Yet, they had not been mentioned at all in the Treaty of Paris. Furthermore, under the Articles of Confederation, it was unclear whether Congress had the legal authority to extinguish native title to the land. Indeed, the ownership of the public domain was unresolved. Did the land belong to the United States or to the individual states? Could western settlers secede and assert their own rights to the land title? Adding to the confusion, the British, while ceding the old Northwest to the United States, had determined to make it into a buffer zone creating an Indian nation to contain the United States to the Atlantic coast, thereby protecting Canada. To that end, they delayed evacuation of Detroit and their other Northwest posts while channeling arms, aid, and propaganda to some tribes.

With the adoption of the United States Constitution, the vacuum in Indian policy was filled. The federal government was delegated full responsibility for Indian affairs. Officials at the highest administrative levels recognized the legitimacy of Indian rights and adopted a series of good-faith measures. Indian title to native lands was confirmed and sovereignty recognized in treaty after treaty. The United States conceded that it had merely replaced Great Britain as the agent with the primary option to treat for land and did not have the right to take land or property from Indians without their consent. Laws were enacted barring individuals from directly buying land from Indians; squatters were to be evicted. Trade with the Indians was regulated by license although licensees were still prohibited from selling alcohol to the Indians. The United States adopted other measures to encourage Indians to sell what it perceived as surplus land to the government. Reasoning that nomadic hunters required more land to sustain themselves than farmers, the government sponsored missionaries and Indian agents who were instructed to civilize the "savages" and teach them animal husbandry and agriculture. In April 1796, the first government trading houses were opened, prompted in part by the desire to encourage Indian dependence on domestic goods. Government Indian programs were underfunded and often at cross-

4

purposes with each other. For example, private traders continued to be licensed for Indian trade after 1796 although the government was supposed to have a trade monopoly with Indians. These programs were consistently undermined by frontiersmen who refused to recognize Indian possession of the land and disobeyed the government's unenforceable laws. In spite of these problems, government-directed acculturation contributed to internal changes in many tribes, particularly among the Five Civilized Tribes of what was then the Southwest.

Yet by 1825, after decades of acculturation and assimilation, of warfare, and of treaties promulgated by force, deceit, and occasionally even honor, the United States reversed its Indian policy saying that the Indians had resisted adaptation. The intensive settlement of the trans-Appalachian west by whites had precipitated a crisis. The government believed that the two cultures could not live in the same space harmoniously; therefore, the Indians had to go. In 1822 the government trading factories were closed on the pretext that they had failed to civilize the tribes. Shortly afterwards, citing the corruption of the noble Indians by white civilization, the government announced a stepped-up program of voluntary resettlement, its solution to this new "Indian problem."

Since colonial times, the government had sporadically purchased land, then transported the former owners westward. The remote lands of the west, seemingly barren and arid, appeared to be the ideal solution to the government's predicament of what to do with the Eastern Indians. As inducement to voluntary resettlement, the government provided reserved lands and annuities. The government had cleared the way for removal by treating with Western tribes and evicting white settlers in the territory to be designated for the Eastern tribes, which was west of the Mississippi River, south of the Platte River, and north of Texas. In exchange for eastern lands, tribes were assigned reservations in Indian territory which were guaranteed inviolable from white preemption or trespass. Forts Leavenworth, Gibson, and Towson were established to ensure the security of Indian lands. Rather than making a single, large cash payment for tribal lands, the federal government promised to provide to all tribe members an annuity of food, supplies, and petty cash. During the transitional period, the government licensed traders and pledged skilled workers and equipment to supply the tribes with necessary goods. Yet, in case after case, the government failed to meet these treaty obligations.

For the Indians, matters deteriorated rapidly. In decisions in 1831 and 1832, the Supreme Court ruled that the Indian nations were no longer sovereign foreign powers. While tribes were acknowledged to be distinct, self-governing entities, they were subject to the authority of the United States and therefore "domestic dependent" nations. Then, in 1833, President Andrew Jackson, impatient with voluntary resettlement, instituted involuntary removal with the acquiescence of Congress. Force was used to achieve compliance; soldiers escorted migrants west and fought those who remained behind.

By 1842, nearly 450 million acres of Indian land in the East had been acquired at the approximate cost of 10 cents an acre. It would be resold for $1.25 an acre. As early as 1789, Jedediah Morse had proclaimed, "The Mississippi was never designed as the western boundary of the American Empire." The 95th meridian was to prove as insubstantial a divide between Indian Territory and the United States as the invisible line it was.

The Cherokee Nation, by virtue of its superb documentation, affords the most complete case for study of all the Eastern tribes. Each phase of U.S. policy is illustrated in **documents 32-45** and **slides A-C**.

Time: 3 class periods

Objectives:

- To analyze the process by which government policy toward the Cherokee nation developed and changed.

- To examine the results of U.S. government policy towards the Cherokee nation.

- To research, script, and present a balanced, historically accurate dramatic production.

Materials Needed:

Documents 32-45
Slides A-C
Written Document Analysis worksheet, p. 14
Worksheet 2

Procedures:

1. Ask students to review what their textbook says about the federal government's Indian policy and, if necessary, supplement it with information from the preceeding Note to the Teacher.

2. Distribute a different document to 14 groups of 2 or 3 students and provide each student with a Written Document Analysis worksheet and worksheet 2. Each student should complete both worksheets. Ask each group to report to the entire class the background information about its document, a summary of the document's contents, and the group's estimation of which aspect of U.S. Indian policy this document illustrates.

3. Project slides A, B, and C for whole class discussion.

4. Ask for 10 volunteers to research, script, act, and, if possible, videotape a special half-hour edition of "Nightline" featuring the following characters involved in the Cherokee removal: President Andrew Jackson, Georgia Governor George R. Gilmer, Cherokee Chief John Ross, Chief Justice John Marshall, Missionary Samuel A. Worcester, Army Surgeon G. Townshend, General Winfield Scott, Pennsylvania Senator James Buchanan, a Cherokee immigrant, and a white squatter. Students should aim for a balanced, historically accurate production.

5. As a culminating activity, ask each student to write a paper analyzing the formulation of United States Indian policy from 1785 to 1842. In their papers the students should address the following questions:

    a. What was the substance of the debate?

    b. What was the socioeconomic context of the debate?

    c. How do advocates on each side of the debate perceive each other?

    d. How do the advocates on each side of the debate define the issues?

    e. How does the perception each side has of the other restrict each side's actions?

    f. What information was available to decision-makers upon which to formulate a policy?

    g. Were opportunities seized or lost during the time the debate occurred and policy formulated?

h. Who were the key individuals whose impact shaped policy, events, implementation and, ultimately, outcome of policy?

6. Extended activity: Mature students may wish to read these other accounts which touch upon the Indian diaspora. Some contain explicit material related either to ritual practice, medical practice, or warfare:

   Creek Mary's Blood, by Dee Brown

   Walk In My Soul, by Lucia Robson

   Magnificent Destiny, by Paul Wellman

   Disinherited, by Dale Van Every

Upon completion of their research, ask the students to write a journal or logbook as if written by one of the participants in the Cherokee removal.

In addition to the Cherokee removal, the Seminole Wars, where conventional military tactics of the United States Army failed to defeat a guerilla enemy in a subtropical environment, are well documented and of interest to students.

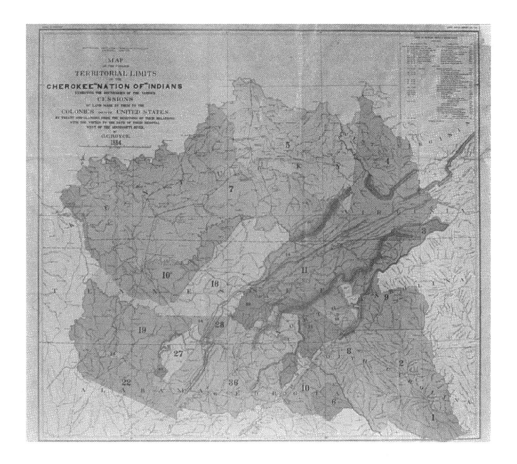

Exercise 4: Formulating and Changing Government Policy:
The Cherokee Nation, A Case Study
Worksheet 2

Directions: Use information from documents 32-45 and slides A-C to determine which aspect of Indian policy each illustrates.

POLICY	DOCUMENT #	EVIDENCE OF POLICY
Conquered peoples		
Sovereign nation		
Acculturation		
Voluntary removal		
Involuntary removal		

Exercise 5
Mythmaking and the West

Note to the Teacher:

In *The West of the Imagination*, William Goetzmann calls the story of the people of the West the great American tale of tribe. He asserts that this tale weaves together many strands of complex human experience into a single inspiring saga to sustain the people through time. He also indicates that new elements are continually being introduced to keep the tale relevant at all times. Against the forces of pluralism in American life, he asserts, this tale has a formidable power to unify.

Assuming that Goetzmann's observation is correct, it is profitable to follow his line of thought. Because much of the content of our literature, movies, television, and other popular entertainment is the myth of the West rather than documentary history, it is useful to look into the records of the period to identify the beginnings of myth. People of the late 18th and early 19th centuries seem to have been conscious of their participation in a great event in world history, the conquest of a continent. Many individuals kept diaries, wrote letters and accounts, or orally passed down the stories of their experiences. Explorers and scientists recorded the unfolding mystery of the continent in journals, charts, and maps (**documents 5, 6, 7; slides E, L, M**). Artists, mainly representational, attempted to convey both information and a sense of epic adventure in their works (**slides Q, R**). Government officials, too, seemed imbued with a sense of mission and history (**documents 2, 10, 18, 36**). These accounts are the raw material of the myth of the American West.

When the deeds of an historic figure are heroic, admirers begin to raise the figure above the level of mere mortal. Where they lack facts, mythmakers will invent miraculous powers and extraordinary adventures, then blend them with historic detail. As Joseph Campbell observed in *The Hero With a Thousand Faces*, "The hero died as a modern man; but as eternal man – perfected, unspecific, universal man – he has been reborn."

In studying the myth of the West, it is useful to focus on several traditional elements of mythology: the archetypal hero, the noble savage, the world beyond civilization, and the mythological journey. In addition to Goetzmann and Campbell, Carl Jung's *Man and His Symbols* is a useful reference for symbol analysis.

The archetypal hero is a pastoral adventurer, as are the first Western heroes: Daniel Boone, Davy Crockett, the fur trappers and mountain men such as Jim Bridger and Kit Carson, and Andrew Jackson, in his role as Indian-fighter (**document 36**). Folk songs, tall tales, and artwork by Alfred J. Miller, George Caleb Bingham, and, later, Thomas Hart Benton, capture the heroic figure in different media.

The American Indian was transmuted into the noble savage of the world beyond civilization, the man of nature who was master of the beasts, wise teacher and mediator between wilderness and white man. This element of the myth of the West was heavily embroidered upon by contemporary white observers. Even in government pronouncements and orders, the concern with uplifting the natives from savagery without corrupting their nobility is apparent. Government posts and reserved Indian lands were designed, in part, to prevent the debasing of the race (**documents 2, 10**). James Fenimore Cooper's early American Leatherstocking series did much to reinforce this typing of the American Indians.

The painters of the early West were particularly impressed by and sympathetic to the Indians. George Catlin, who painted the Seminole leader Osceola (**slide R**) passionately believed in the nobility of the American Indian. He saw as his vocation the collecting of a "literal and graphic delineation of the living manners, customs and characters of an interesting race of people who are rapidly passing away from the face of the earth." Catlin's sense of urgency was shared by Commissioner of Indian Affairs Thomas L. McKinney who encouraged both Catlin and Charles Bird King to record Indian life. McKinney gathered and displayed in his office paintings which formed the nucleus of the first Indian gallery in the United States. Karl Bodmer, a Swiss painter, traveled over much of the territory Catlin had visited, depicting similar subjects. His precise record of the Mandan tribe shortly before their decimation by smallpox in 1837 is of great ethnological value (**slide Q**). The combined power of his and Catlin's images, however, supplanted the Eastern forest tribes with the Plains Indians as the icon of all American Indians. Our vision of the noble savage is a mounted Indian on a pony, hunting buffalo with bow and arrow.

The uncharted continent became the sacred space, the world beyond civilization of mythology. Explorers venturing into the realm of the unknown assumed heroic stature, as they sought not merely wealth, but answers to life's mysteries. To early Spanish explorers, it was the logical setting for the Fountain of Youth, the Seven Cities of Cibola and fabled Quivira. European and, later, American explorers actively sought the Northwest Passage. Both British and Americans looked for descendants of a medieval Welsh prince, Madoc, among the tribes of the West. (George Catlin mistook a Mandan creation myth's reference to original ancestors arriving in a birchbark canoe as confirmation of this tale.) From de Crèvecoeur's *Letters from an American Farmer* to de Tocqueville's *Democracy in America*, from Lewis and Clark's journals to Richard Henry Dana's *Two Years Before the Mast*, the West was depicted as Eden before the fall. This reverence for what was incorrectly perceived as virgin wilderness shaped national attitudes, in the East as well as in the West, about idyllic nature. Nowhere has the world outside of civilization been more celebrated than in Henry David Thoreau's *Walden*.

Even the best efforts of explorers to demystify the West sometimes went astray, as when Stephen Long's notation of the existence of a Great Desert on his 1819 map (**slide E**) disseminated misinformation among a generation of Americans. Yet, accurate or not, the maps conveyed to all who looked upon them the vast dimension of the land, as awesome in that time as a star map is in ours (**slides L, M**).

The last mythic element is that of the journey. Mobility was noted early in the American experience by a critical Washington Irving in his *The Legend of Sleepy Hollow*. "Ghosts have scarcely time to turn themselves in their graves before their surviving friends have travelled away from the neighborhood." But what Irving viewed as the "shifting throng" has been transformed by artists such as Emmanuel Leutze into the heroic *Across the Continent, Westward the Course of Empire Takes its Way*, sometimes called *Westward Ho*. The Conestoga supplanted the conveyances of the waterways in paintings as the icon of mobility. And, finally, the Western experience assumes the rhythm of mythology as adventurers travel to the world outside their known world, endure hardships, are transfigured, and discover the panacea for all its ills of the old world.

Time: 2 class periods

Objectives:

- To study how legends grow up around historic events and figures.

- To analyze mythic elements in legends of the American West.

- To analyze a portrait.

Materials needed:

Document 2
Slide R

5 Procedures:

1. Introduce the topic of heroes with a class discussion.

   a. Ask students to brainstorm what they consider to be characteristics of heroic figures. Popular contemporary examples such as Luke Skywalker, Superman, or Indiana Jones are as useful as points of departure as more traditional figures such as Hercules, King Arthur, or Robin Hood.

   b. Pose the question to the students: Are historical heroes mythic heroes? Subjects upon which students could focus their discussion might include Cleopatra, Charlemagne, Elizabeth I, George Washington, Jim Bowie, Lawrence of Arabia, or Martin Luther King.

   c. Ask students for examples of tall tales that have been added to the facts of an historic figure's biography. (George Washington is a good example to start with.) How do they account for these additions?

2. Project slide R. Ask students to look at Catlin's portrait of Osceola and to consider the following points before deciding whether Catlin imbued Osceola with a heroic aura:

   a. What is the background in this picture? Does it draw attention from the subject or does it focus attention on the subject?

   b. What portions of the figure are included in this picture? What portions are excluded? What is the orientation of the figure? What features are deemphasized because of this composition? What features are emphasized because of this composition?

   c. How is the subject attired? What is the effect of the costume? What does it add to the portrait? Does it distract from the figure? Why do you think the painter chose to depict this costume?

   d. What is the expression on the subject's face? What attitude does the expression seem to convey? Why do you think the artist chose to depict the subject with this expression?

3. Duplicate and distribute copies of document 2 to each student. Direct students to focus their reading on pages 4-6 in the document.

   a. Underline the adjectives that St. Clair uses when he describes the land. What is the tone of his words? Does the Northwest Territory seem attractive, based on his description?

   b. Paying close attention to the words he uses to describe the Indians, what is his attitude towards them? Does he think they are capable of noble behavior?

   c. What evidence is there in his words that St. Clair is sensible of the historic nature of the work of the pioneers in subduing the land and evangelizing the Indians?

4. For further research: Either in cooperation with an American literature teacher or as part of your study of the American West, ask students to analyze the mythological elements of a variety of Western tales and stories and to share their findings in an oral report to the class. For example:

   a. The transformations of the archetypal hero from supernatural infant, to adventurer-warrior, to triumphant return, to sacrificial death could be followed by examining such figures as Davy Crockett, Daniel Boone, and Andrew Jackson.

b. The mythological adventure from the call to adventure, to crisis and transformation, to triumphant return could be applied to *Two Years Before the Mast* and an abridged version of the journals of Lewis and Clark.

c. The character attributes and development of the Indian as noble savage by James Fenimore Cooper could be traced through *The Last of the Mohicans* or another of Cooper's Leatherstocking tales. His treatment could be contrasted in more modern novels such as *Little Big Man*, *Light A Distant Fire* (a novel about Osceola), or *Creek Mary's Blood*.

d. Ask a motivated student to find evidence in Thoreau's words that Walden Pond is the unblemished Eden, the world outside of civilization, as depicted in *Walden*.

e. What dangers does mythologizing create? The typical absence of black Americans in the story of the West is doubly disturbing if it means they are not part of the American tale of tribe. Ask a student to analyze the problems presented by the myth of the West.

f. Mythmaking is alive and well in America. Ask two or more students to look into the following areas where history and myth are blended:

➤ Space, the new frontier

➤ Sports legends (e.g., Babe Ruth)

➤ Entertainers (e.g., Elvis Presley)

g. Ask the students to write a tall tale or folk story featuring their own lives.

Exercise 6
The West of Opportunity

Note to the Teacher:

he American ought therefore to love this country much better than that wherein either he or his forefathers were born. Here the rewards of his industry follow with equal steps the progress of his labour . . .

J. Hector St. John de Crèvecoeur
Letters From an American Farmer

From the first reports of the earliest explorers, the Western lands were depicted as bountiful, and settlers were encouraged to set forth in search of property and riches. The greatest lure of all was the land itself, but there were other enticements as well. Fortunes could be made from peltry (trade in furs and skins), minerals, trade and manufacture, and transportation.

For years the American dream was a family farm, derived from the Jeffersonian ideal of a nation of yeoman farmers. This hunger for farmland helped to propel the nation westward and to define public land policy as well. Under the Land Ordinance of 1785 (**document 1**) the government instituted direct sales to purchasers by the government, in part to combat swindlers. Because the vast majority of settlers paid their hard-earned money for property, the availability, price, down payment, and terms of payment were issues regularly debated in Congress (**document 4**). Once resolved they became policy (**document 3**) and were publicized (**document 5**). Title rights were confused by prior ownership by Indians (**document 39**), European powers (**document 26**), or other Americans (**document 27**). Squatters added another set of complications. Still, to the average American between 1785 and 1842, acquiring and cultivating land was the way to prosperity.

The lands of the Old Northwest were much preferred to those purchased in Louisiana Territory because they were closer to the settled East and because it was believed that land without trees was poor while humus-rich forestlands were fertile. Also, the lack of trees meant no wood for fuel or construction and suggested that the land was not well watered. Sod broke plows designed for looser soil and was mistakenly thought to be infertile. Farmers were far more interested in settling land in Spanish Florida, and the property of Eastern Indians in the Old Northwest and Old Southwest than in moving to Louisiana Territory. Thus, long after the boundaries of the United States leaped across the Mississippi, settlement lagged.

There was a dark underside to westward expansion. Much of America's gain came about because of the losses and exploitation suffered by Indians, Hispanics, and blacks. The average payment to Eastern Indians for over 440 million acres of land by the U.S. government was ten cents an acre. At an average sale price of $1.25 an acre, the government realized a profit of $500 million. At three cents an acre, Louisiana was an even greater windfall to the U.S. government; the native American received no money from the purchase and only nominal payment for lands transferred by treaty. Hispanics in the Floridas and French and Hispanics in Louisiana did marginally better, but were frequently embroiled in land title challenges (**document 26**). Availability of land coupled with the use of the cotton gin (**document 11** and **slide H**) enabled the extension of slave-based cotton cultivation throughout the old Southwest Territory and, according to the terms of the Missouri Compromise (**document 31**), into the southern portion of the Louisiana Purchase.

Peltry was a lure ever westwards, for while money could be made in the fur trade, over-trapping and the retreat of fur-bearing animals drew trappers deeper into the interior of the continent (**document 19**). The object of the first "fur rush" was the sea otter (**document 12**). When traders introduced sea otter pelts to Macao in 1779, traders of the Orient bid up the price to $80-$120 a skin. From 1790-1812, U.S. merchants exchanged trinkets with Northwest Indians and exported nearly 12,000 skins annually to China, reaping profits of 500 percent. Lewis and Clark had instructions to locate this valuable creature; they describe sea otters at length in the journal entry of February 23, 1806. Yet by 1830, this trade had virtually ended due to the rarity of the overhunted otters and sharp decreases in profits. The beaver replaced the sea otter as the most lucrative pelt in the trade and is the animal most closely associated with the mountain men. Still, prices crashed from $6 a pound in the fall of 1832 to $3.50 a pound a year later because of overtrapping and replacing beaver with nutria and silk by hat manufacturers. In 1834 the buffalo hide exceeded beaver pelts in value. Because buffalo skinning was so unpleasant, fur companies turned to the Indians to supply them with enough hides to meet demand and, ironically, for a short while trapping passed back to Native American control.

From the earliest days of exploration, fortunes were sought from minerals. While the great gold rushes were a thing of the future, the government carefully recorded finds of a more mundane character, from salt to lead (**slide K**), that were indispensible to the nation.

Free navigation of the Mississippi and the right to deposit goods in New Orleans before shipping to a final destination were economic necessities to traders of the tramontane West (**documents 28** and **30**). There was good money to be made as farmers, trappers, and tradesmen trafficked in farm produce, raw materials, and simple manufactures along the network of the western waterways. Trade between Americans along the river (**document 5**), with Indians (**documents 10** and **34**), and with the colonial powers of Spain, France, and England presaged American entry into global commerce. Jefferson had hoped that Lewis and Clark would find a river connection between the Missouri and Columbia rivers that would make passage to the Orient speedier. Although no such connector existed and U.S. ships continued to have to sail around Cape Horn Americans were active in the China trade from the 1780s onward. Additional wealth was generated by private companies and state governments by constructing internal improvements such as canals and roads (**documents 8** and **9; slides D** and **I**).

Robert Fulton's 1807 invention of the steamboat was highly significant, but its application would have been severely limited had not John Marshall and the Supreme Court ruled against monopoly in interstate steamboat operation in *Gibbons v. Ogden* in 1824 (**document 24**). In the wake of that decision, the federal government, empowered by the Constitution's commerce clause, increasingly exercised its authority by legislation and judicial decision over the whole range of the nation's economic life. Control was not universal; for example, enforcement of patent law was so lax that Eli Whitney saw few royalties from his cotton gin (**document 11**). Still, by expanding federal scope in the economy, the government succeeded in bringing opportunity to an even greater number of citizens such as pioneering western steamboat captain and snag boat inventor, Henry M. Shreve (**slides F** and **G**).

Of $1.25 an acre, the government realized a profit of $500 million. At three cents an acre, Louisiana was an even greater windfall to the U.S. government; the native American received no money from the purchase and only nominal payment for lands transferred by treaty. Hispanics in the Floridas and French and Hispanics in Louisiana did marginally better, but were frequently embroiled in land title challenges (**document 26**). Availability of land coupled with the use of the cotton gin (**document 11** and **slide H**) enabled the extension of slave

Time: 2 to 3 class periods

6

Objectives:

- To analyze documents to extract information on economic motivations behind the settlement of the West.

- To recognize how federal government policy opened many economic opportunities.

- To understand the importance of free navigation of the Mississippi River system to western settlers.

Materials Needed:

Documents 1, 3-5, 8-13, 19, 26-28, 30, 34, and 39
Slides D, F, G, H, I, J, and K
Worksheet 3
Worksheet 4
Outline map of the United States for student mapwork

Procedures:

1. Review with students the following vocabulary terms:

ell:	a measure of length, mainly for cloth, 45 inches
gorget:	a piece of armor covering the throat
league:	a measure of distance, 3 miles
livre:	French monetary unit equal to a pound of silver
peltry:	fur-bearing skins
pirogue:	a dugout canoe
relic:	an object associated with a saint which is looked upon with great respect
vermillion:	bright red or scarlet
worsted:	a woolen fabric made of smooth, hard-twisted yarn

   Ask students to write several sentences incorporating these archaic terms. (e.g., She traveled a league in the pirogue clad in her vermillion worsted cape, a silver gorget flashing at her neck.) Alternatively, have pupils create crossword puzzles or word scramble puzzles using these terms.

2. Duplicate and distribute to each student document 28 and worksheet 3 for students to complete. Tell students that they will see variant spellings for pirogue (peroque), relic (relique), vermillion (vermilion), Miro (Mero) and Arkansas (Arquancas). "Hkfs" is an abbreviation for handkerchiefs. Define pettianger as a small cargo boat. The Hutchins map referred to in Mr. St. Marie's account is the official survey of the western lands by Thomas Hutchins, Geographer to the United States. Discuss answers with the class.

3. Duplicate and distribute worksheet 4 and documents 11 and 13 to each student and project slide G to enable students to complete the worksheet. As a class, discuss how the documents show the efforts of the U.S. government to regulate the economy.

4. Assign one or two students to look at one of the following documents and slides: 1, 3, 4, 5, 8, 9, 10, 12, 19, 26, 27, 30, 34, 39, D, F, H, I, J, and K.

   Ask students to answer the following questions by citing evidence in the document: (If the document does not provide an answer, students should explain why it does not.)

   a. In what way or ways does this document indicate that wealth could be made by citizens?
   b. What evidence is there in this document that Americans were engaged in trade and with whom?
   c. What evidence does this document provide that federal government actions were helping citizens to take advantage of opportunities in the western lands?
   d. The exploitation of western resources had hidden costs and consequences. What evidence is there in these documents that human beings and the environment were both regarded as expendable? Where does this happen today?

   Discuss the answers in class and ask students to consider whether there is evidence that Americans today have begun to conserve and respect human and natural resources.

5. Extended activity: Ask a realtor knowledgeable about historic ownership in your locality, a title researcher with the county courthouse, or a person knowledgeable about the history of your locality to come to your class and talk to students about what were original land values, how a title is legally changed, and how current property values in your community compare to original land prices. If possible, ask the presenter to show a series of plats for the parcel of land on which your school is located from the time it originally was surveyed to the present.

6

Exercise 6: The West of Opportunity

Worksheet 3

Directions: Use information from document 28, an atlas, and your textbook to complete this worksheet and map.

PART A

1. What was the purpose of the voyage by Mr. St. Marie's employee, Mr. Swimmer, and the crew of the pettianger?

   _____

   _____

2. What reason was given by Mr. Valliere, the Spanish commandant, for seizing the pettianger?

   _____

   _____

3. What did Governor Mero [sic] threaten to do to Mr. St. Marie?

   _____

   _____

4. Why does Mr. St. Marie believe the Congress has reason to intervene in his case?

   _____

   _____

5. Why has Congress been slow to address this "grand national question?"

   _____

   _____

6. Look at the invoice Mr. St. Marie attaches to his plea itemizing his losses.
   a. What item is most numerous on this invoice?

   _____

   _____

   b. Name five or six major categories of goods from the invoice.

   _____

   _____

c. Are there any items that seem peculiar to be trading with the Indians? Explain.

_____

_____

d. Name three things you can tell about Indian trade from this invoice.

_____

_____

e. Name two things this document tells you about life in the United States at the time it was written.

_____

_____

PART B

1. Locate and mark on your map the following places:

   a. Vincennes, IN

   b. New Orleans, LA

   c. The intersection of 34° 40' N and the Mississippi River

2. Is there a modern location still called Chickasaw Lake in the area of 34° 40' N and the Mississippi River?

   _____

   _____

3. Shade in the area of the western territories claimed by Spain according to Commandant Valliere.

4. Use a different color to shade in the area of the western territories claimed by the United States in 1790 under the Treaty of Paris (1783).

5. Was the pettianger seized in a disputed area?

   _____

   _____

Exercise 6: The West of Opportunity

Worksheet 4

Directions: Use information from your textbook and from documents 11, 13, and slide G to complete the worksheet.

Gibbons v. Ogden

1. What type of writ is the Court of Chancery of the State of New York issuing in this case?

   _____

   _____

2. Whose actions is the writ intended to stop?

   _____

   _____

3. What must the people named cease doing?

   _____

   _____

4. Between what two states are the Mouse and the Bellona operating?

   _____

   _____

5. Did the Supreme Court uphold New York State's order? On what did the court base its opinion?

   _____

   _____

Patent of Henry M. Shreve

1. This is a form document which has blanks for providing specific details. Name four categories of information that were put into these blanks by patent office clerks.

   _____

   _____

2. Of what federal department was the Commissioner of Patents an employee?

   _____

   _____

3. What do you think the 29 stars over the patent building represent?

   _____

   _____

4. What two things did Henry Shreve have to do to get a patent? Once granted, how long was the patent valid?

_____

_____

5. Give a reason why a snag boat would be a useful invention to Americans of this time period.

_____

_____

Memorial of Eli Whitney

1. What, according to Whitney, were the reasons why a cotton gin was needed?

_____

_____

2. What had Congress done to encourage Whitney to apply his energies to inventing a cotton gin?

_____

_____

3. What does Whitney say was the impact of his invention on cotton cultivation?

_____

_____

4. What was the wording in the patent law that allowed widespread piracy of Whitney's invention to be permitted?

_____

_____

5. According to Whitney, the gin enabled one man to do the work of how many men?

_____

_____

6. How much time has passed on Whitney's patent?

_____

_____

7. According to his petition, has Whitney profited from his invention? Explain why or why not.

_____

_____

8. What relief does Whitney want Congress to provide him?

_____

_____

Exercise 7
Western Waterways

Note to the Teacher:

A dominant force shaping the exploration and settlement of the American West was the waterway. Pioneers and trappers followed stream-cut gaps through the Appalachians, then canoed down the tributaries of the Mississippi River system. Official government exploration focused on exploration of this vast water network. Instructions, such as those issued to Stephen Long (**document 7**), stressed collection of precise data about waterways. Zebulon Pike's notebook of his ascent of the Mississippi River (**document 6**) is a raw collection of observations; the result was a valuable map (**slide L**) for subsequent voyagers. The knowledge of rivers gained by explorers was stressed by Presidents, such as Jefferson (his own intellectual curiosity about natural history notwithstanding), in their annual reports to Congress, to show the wisdom of allocations for exploration (**document 18**). While the official government description of the land was by range, township, and section (**document 1**), the government nonetheless relied on description by river boundaries for areas not yet surveyed, as in article 3 of the Treaty of New Echota (**document 42**).

When one looks at patterns of settlement up to 1842, it is clear that population centers first grew along the rivers, then diffused into the interior along streams. Areas not served by waterways were bypassed by settlers, such as the plains erroneously labeled as desert by Stephen Long (**slide E**). The reason that water transportation was preferred was simple: it was faster and more economical. The fastest stage traveled at an estimated 6 mph while steamboats could average 12-15 mph carrying far larger loads.

Frederick Jackson Turner observed how fur trappers yielded to farmers, farmers to merchants. The prevailing boat types changed similarly as the West grew more settled. The canoes and skiffs of fur traders gave way to flatboats of all varieties used by settlers to move into the wilderness, then to send their produce to market. The 70-foot-long keelboat was the mainstay of river traffic; but, as trade intensified, larger flatboats, "broadhorn" barges and livestock "arks," joined the river traffic. The steamboat made commercial and passenger transport against the current practical at any time of the year. Where the steamboat stopped for wood and water, settlement thrived. Pittsburgh, PA, was the natural center for flatboat trade, Cairo, IL, a major junction for steamboats.

That is not to say that river travel was easy. Natural dangers such as heavy currents, strong winds, snags, and shifting sandbars took an appalling toll. The life expectancy of a steamboat before it snagged, blew up, caught fire, or vibrated apart was five years. Former fur trader Henry Shreve developed a practical, powerful, steam-operated snag boat (**slides F** and **G**) that helped make the western rivers safer. In spite of improvements that removed natural obstacles, rivermen and settlers were still plagued by foreign powers (**document 28**), Indians, and river pirates who seized goods and murdered crews (**document 17**). Perhaps the most notorious pirate was Jean Lafitte, who smuggled goods from Baratria Island through the bayous of the Mississippi River delta to the interior. Lafitte's pardon (**document 23**) for services rendered during the War of 1812 in no way reformed his character.

To eliminate the perils of river travel created by nature, people of the early republic turned to canals (**slide P**). Canals offered the possibility of moving settlers and manufactured goods westward and cereals and meats eastward both cheaply and safely (**document 8**). The years of the ascendancy of the canals were brief. In 1831 the Mohawk and Schenectady Railroad began operation. Although the Erie Railroad (**slide I**) followed waterways closely, subsequent railroads, freed by their tracks, would strike out cross-country with little attention to the great rivers.

The permeation of American culture by waterways is revealed by period folksongs (e.g., "Erie Canal," "Oh Shenandoah"), artwork (e.g., Thomas Cole, George Catlin, George Caleb Bingham), and tall tales (Mike Fink). Classic literary works would come from a later riverboatman, Mark Twain, whose stories are majestically dominated by the "Father of the Waters," the Mississippi River.

Time: 3 to 4 class periods

Objectives:

- To understand the dominance of waterways in early westward expansion.

- To translate a handwritten document.

- To interpret a chart.

Materials Needed:

Documents 6, 7, 8, 17, 18, 23, 28, 42
Slides E, F, G, L, P
Worksheet 5

Procedures:

You may wish to refer to ideas and activities in Exercise 5 and adapt them to the theme of western waterways.

1. Make a transparency of document 6 and project it. Explain to students that this is the rough journal of explorer Zebulon Pike containing his notes as he traveled up the Mississippi River northwards from St. Louis.

   a. Ask one student to serve as a recorder, transcribing Pike's headings as a list on the chalkboard. Ask the class to decipher the words. (The headings read: N; Shores–E, W; Rivers–Name, Width; Depth & etc.; Current; Course at its confluence; Islands–Length, Channel; Remarks on mines, quarries, traders, barrs [sic], creeks, shoals, & etc.)

   b. Ask students to hypothesize why Pike was gathering information under each of these headings. They should consider why the information might have been useful to the military as well as to settlers.

   c. As a class, brainstorm a list of obstacles occurring naturally on the river that might pose difficulties to riverboats in the year 1805.

2. Post document 8 and distribute worksheet 5 to each student. Over the successive five days allow 5-10 minutes a day, perhaps during roll call or announcements, for a fifth of your students at a time to review the document and complete the worksheet.

3. Divide the class into the following six groups:

   a. **Zebulon Pike Group:** Students in this group will study Zebulon Pike's life and explorations. In presenting their findings to the class they can use slide L for illustration as well as contemporary pictures of some of the locations Pike visited during his travels. They should trace onto a wall map of the United States the routes of Pike's major expeditions and use it in their presentation.

b. **Canal Group:** Ask students of this group to research American canals examining their development and extent, different ways in which they were financed (private versus public), and how a lock works, through either graphics or a model. One student might read Harriet Martineau on Erie Canal travel or other travel journals. Oral reports on student findings should be presented to the class.

c. **Waterways Music Group:** Ask the students of this group to compile a program of songs related to the waterways of the early republic. They should present some background information about the origin of each song, then present selections either taped from recordings or performed live.

d. **Mike Fink Group:** Ask students in this group to read document 17, then make a study of river piracy in the early republic and the means taken by authorities to combat the problem. If available, students may want to rent the Disney video, *Davy Crockett and the River Pirates,* and use their critique of it as a vehicle for presenting the information they have located. Students should also read Mike Fink tales and compile a brief biography of the historic figure. When presenting their findings to the class, the group members should contrast the legendary figure with this historic figure. The group might dramatize one or two incidents from the tall tales surrounding Mike Fink.

e. **Artists and Waterways Group:** Students should collect paintings by American artists of life on the waterways. Artists might include Thomas Cole, Karl Bodmer, George Catlin, George Caleb Bingham and others active before the Civil War. Students may use opaque projector, slides, or videotape for their classroom presentation. The group should give some biographical information about the artist and a title, date, and brief description of each painting.

f. **Biographies Group:** Andrew Jackson, Abraham Lincoln, and Mark Twain all traveled down the Mississippi River as young men. Ask students in this group to find out about the river experiences of these well-known figures in American history. Students should present their findings in an oral report. They may choose to present dramatic incidents in skit form.

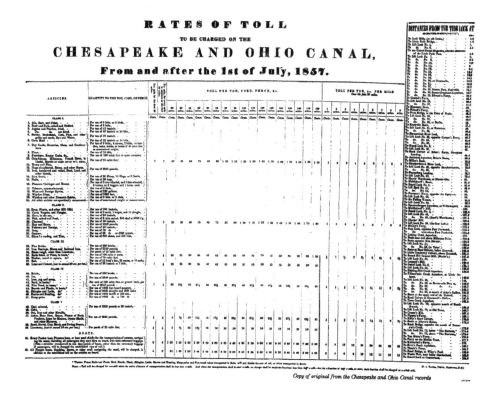

Copy of original from the Chesapeake and Ohio Canal records

Exercise 7: Western Waterways

Worksheet 5

Directions: Examine document 8 and a dictionary for information to complete this worksheet.

1. Check the article that was more expensive to transport 40 miles:
   - _____ whiskey   *or*   _____ corn on the ear
   - _____ furniture   *or*   _____ salted fish
   - _____ pleasure carriage *or*   _____ wagons
   - _____ fire bricks   *or*   _____ bricks
   - _____ charcoal   *or*   _____ coal

2. What is the distance from:

   a. Georgetown to Liftlock 33 opposite Harper's Ferry? _____

   b. Georgetown to Round Hill cement mill? _____

   c. Georgetown to Cumberland? _____

   d. Antietam aqueduct to Fort Frederick? _____

   e. Guardlock 5 to guardlock 4? _____

3. Define the following measurements:

   a. cord: _____

   b. perch: _____

   c. hogshead (hhd): _____

   d. bushel: _____

   e. bushel barrel: _____

4. Calculate the cost of transporting on the C & O Canal from Georgetown to Sharpsburg Landing one ton (total) of dry goods, groceries, and crockery.

   _____

5. What traffic does the toll rate structure seem to encourage? What traffic does the toll rate structure seem to discourage? Provide evidence to support your answer.

   _____

   _____

Exercise 8
The Romantic Worldview and Exploration of the West

Note to the Teacher:

One of the characteristics of 19th-century Romantic thinking was a strong sense of nationalism. The nationalistic urge soon to be named Manifest Destiny was at the root of government-sponsored expeditions from Lewis and Clark onward. Exploration was a matter of national pride as well as security. Only by sending expeditions into western lands could the United States consolidate its control over those areas and defend them. In *Army Exploration in the American West: 1803-1863*, historian William Goetzmann suggested that the Corps of Topographical Engineers embodied "a general spirit of Romanticism that governed its purpose and prescribed its methods."

In greater detail, Goetzmann demonstrated how the Romantic worldview shaped what information army explorers would collect. Rejecting the tight constraints of neoclassicism, the Romantics looked at the world around them cosmically. They believed that the universe was ordered, but that sublime infinity defied reduction into mathematical formulae. Exploration and scientific research was pursued as a means to collect data towards a unified theory of the universe.

The means scientists of the Romantic era employed to accomplish this end was inductive reasoning – moving from particular data to general conclusions – as opposed to the deductive approach – moving from the general theory to a specific case – favored by neoclassicists. Secretary of War John C. Calhoun's instructions to Maj. Stephen Long (**document 7**) are a good example of the Romantic exhortation to pursue the widest range of experiences possible. Long and other government explorers were instructed to observe, record, and collect all data whether significant or minor; to attend to the exotic, rare, and remote; and to collect information with an open mind rather than by a preconceived plan.

In the Romantic worldview, there was no dichotomy between art and science. As both explored nature free from restrictive neoclassical forms, a kinship formed. Artists were brought on many expeditions to provide a visual record. Their point of view was seen as fully compatible with that of topographical engineers. The final report filed by military engineers such as Maj. Stephen Long, or later, by Lt. John C. Fremont, reads more like Romantic or transcendentalist literature than modern scientific study.

The American West was a region studied with rare intensity and purpose. A Romantic worldview, combined with the participants' sense of history and their patriotic concern for national security, ensured that unprecedented amounts of scientific information would be collected before the approach of the white man's civilization irrevocably altered wilderness habitat and aboriginal society.

The following procedures are designed to help students understand a point of view quite different from the modern way of thinking.

Time: 1 to 2 class periods

Objectives:

- To introduce students to the Romantic approach to science and exploration in the early 19th century.

- To contrast deductive reasoning with inductive reasoning.

Materials Needed:

Document 7
Slide E
Written Document Analysis worksheet, p. 14
Map Analysis worksheet, p. 15
Worksheet 6

Procedures:

1. Duplicate and distribute document 7 and the Written Document Analysis worksheet to each student to read and complete. Review the answers as a class. Project slide E and ask students to complete the Map Analysis worksheet. Ask students to evaluate the accuracy of Long's notation of "Great Desert" on the high plains.

2. Define inductive reasoning and deductive reasoning and give an example to help students differentiate between the two. Ask students to consider a mechanical problem. If the faucet is leaking, how would an inductive plumber approach the problem? How would a deductive plumber approach the problem? Ask students to consider a problem they have recently solved from locating a lost piece of clothing or being locked out of their home to fixing a broken boom box, and to decide whether they did so inductively or deductively. Discuss whether the scientific method used in their science classes is inductive or deductive. Distribute worksheet 6 and direct students to complete the assignment. Discuss their answers in class and ask students whether document 7 exemplifies inductive or deductive methodology.

3. Extended activities:

    a. Give students an assignment to write instructions for an astronaut conducting research on the space shuttle from the point of view of an expedition commander who wants his crew to use the inductive approach.

    b. Ask your more motivated students to read Thomas Jefferson's *Notes on the State of Virginia* and instructions to Captain Meriwether Lewis from 1803 and then write a report evaluating whether, in his approach to science, Jefferson was a neoclassicist or a Romantic. The selections can be found in various collected works of Jefferson including *The Portable Thomas Jefferson*, a paperback edited by Merrill D. Peterson.

    c. Ask a motivated reader to research Long's expedition and, if possible, to locate a copy of his final report to Calhoun. The student should present an oral report to the class recounting the story of Long's Yellowstone Expedition, the conclusions he reached in his report, and the impact of misinformation in his map, then report on subsequent western settlement.

    d. Work cooperatively with a science teacher in your school to identify a laboratory exercise that lends itself to the inductive approach or to design one that can be used with the students. Help to prepare, set up, run, and evaluate reports of students in this inductive exercise. Afterwards, ask students to comment on their reactions to the activity, giving the advantages and disadvantages of the inductive approach.

Exercise 8: The Romantic Worldview
and Exploration of the West

Worksheet 6

Directions: Examine document 7 for information to answer the following questions:

1. What is the primary object of this survey? _____

   _____

2. Review the expedition orders and identify the scientific discipline for which the following members of the party were responsible:

   Dr. Baldwin _____

   Mr. Say _____

   Mr. Jesup _____

   Mr. Peale _____

3. Which member of the expedition appears to have had responsibility for collecting information about cultural anthropology? _____

   Which member of the expedition appears to have had responsibility for collecting information about paleontology? _____

4. For what reason is Mr. Seymour accompanying the expedition?

   _____

   _____

5. All the topics of study of this expedition were believed by Long, his party and the Secretary of War, John C. Calhoun, to have bearing on national security. Explain for two scientific disciplines (for example, botany or zoology) how they related to the well-being of the nation.

   _____

   _____

6. Find examples of the Romantic approach to science in this document and quote at least one supporting passage that illustrates:

   a. How everything from the important to the trivial was collected.

   _____

   _____

b. How the rare, unusual, or the remote attracted particular attention.

_____

_____

c. How scientists were expected to collect information with an open mind.

_____

_____

d. How art was seen as compatible with science.

_____

_____

7. What was to happen at the conclusion of the expedition to the notes collected by the members of the party?

_____

_____

8. Mr. Seymour produced 150 pictures on the expedition, only 8 of which appeared in the final report. One view entitled "James Peak in the Rain" shows vegetation and a rainstorm over Pike's Peak. It was not included in Long's published report which classified the high plains prairie a "Great Desert."

a. Why do you suppose this view was omitted?

_____

_____

b. What do you think Long's negative report about the high plains did to would-be settlers?

_____

_____

Exercise 9
The International West

Note to the Teacher:

One of the premises of Manifest Destiny was that there were vast, uncontrolled spaces in the West into which, inexorably, American pioneers would settle and over which U.S. sovereignty would extend. It was a hopelessly false premise because the fledgling United States shared the North American continent uneasily with powerful Indian tribes and confederations in addition to the international superpowers of the late 18th and early 19th centuries: Great Britain, France, Spain, and Russia. Much of western history is diplomatic history concerning trade arrangements, boundary disputes, negotiations, transfers of territory, separatist intrigue, and avoidance of war.

Following the Treaty of Paris of 1783, the United States expected Great Britain to evacuate military posts in the Northwest Territories. Instead, Great Britain continued to occupy them and regarrisoned Fort Miami. To constrict further U.S. expansion, the British worked to form an Indian buffer state between the United States, Canada, and the far west. Toward this end, the Governor General of Canada sent military supplies and promises of active British support to Indian chiefs of the Old Northwest. British failure to assist the confederation headed by Little Turtle of the Miami and a warrior shortage resulting from a 1781 smallpox epidemic led to an Indian rout following the battle of Fallen Timbers in 1794 and extinction of Indian claims to many northwestern lands under the 1795 Treaty of Greenville. Tecumseh and his brother, Tenskwatawa (the Prophet), attempted to forge a new Indian alliance to overturn the treaty and to sweep the Americans from Indian lands. Following the defeat of the Prophet's forces at Tippecanoe, **(document 16)**, Tecumseh allied himself with the British. The U.S. government, for its part, was anxious to form its own Indian alliance against the British **(document 15)**. Following the British loss of Fort Detroit, and its defeats on the Great Lakes and at the Battle of the Thames, where Tecumseh died, remaining tribal leaders in the Great Lakes region yielded to control by the U.S. government. Since the Treaty of Ghent ended the War of 1812, Anglo-American disputes have been resolved by treaty and negotiated agreements.

"There is on the globe one single spot, the possessor of which is our natural and habitual enemy. It is New Orleans . . . ," wrote Thomas Jefferson in 1803. Because nearly half of American products were transported down the Mississippi to New Orleans, the young United States was at the mercy of Spain, which alternated between loose and tight control **(document 28)** of the port in an effort to enforce its claims to disputed portions of the Old Southwest and to seize control of the trans-Appalachian United States. From the first year of the republic, the United States sought to purchase New Orleans, first to control the valuable outlet and secondly to calm western agitators who threatened to forcibly seize the city and either establish a new western republic or embroil the United States in a war with Spain.

The secret transfer of Spanish "Luisiana" to France placed the United States and the French Republic on a similar collision course. It also drew the British into the controversy. Jefferson instantly pledged to form an alliance with the detested British; Napoleon feared that the British fleet would seize New Orleans. In need of money for his planned European campaigns, Napoleon authorized the sale of his indefensible New World realm of Louisiana to the United States.

Many Louisianans were shocked by the rapid transfer of sovereignty from Spain to France, then to the United States. While the French promised to provide documentation of their title to the land in the purchase agreement **(document 20)**, titles remained confused for years **(document 26)**. Spain did not accept the validity of the treaty and intrigued over the next decade with malcontent Louisianans (**document 29**) and, later, Aaron Burr (**document 14**) to detach Louisiana from the United States. Spain sent an expeditionary force into Louisiana which clashed with U.S. troops under General Wilkinson (**document 25**). War was narrowly averted.

In spite of U.S. efforts to purchase the Floridas at the time of the Louisiana Purchase, Spain retained title and control over them until 1819. The Adams-Onis treaty (**document 5**) resolved territorial disputes between the United States and Spain by ceding the Floridas to the United States, defining the southern border of the Louisiana Purchase shared with Spain's dominions, and deeding to the United States Spanish claims (**document 12**) in Oregon.

Competition between Russia, Spain, Great Britain, and the United States for control of the fur trade in the Pacific Northwest resulted in periodic seizure of ships and cargoes by one country or the other. In 1821, the Czar claimed territory as far south as 51° N, slightly north of the modern U.S.-Canada border. The Monroe Doctrine was issued, in part as a response to the Russian move. Russia continued to be a significant force in the Pacific territories through the time of the Alaskan Purchase in 1867.

In addition to the lands acquired from foreign powers, another legacy of the international West is its people. These western lands were far from uninhabited. With the accession of new territories into the republic, Hispanics, Creoles, Russians, French Canadians, and a myriad of other ethnic groups were absorbed into the population of the United States. Thus, as early as 1819, the population of the United States had ceased to be primarily Anglo-Saxon and had taken on the ethnic pluralism characteristic of the nation ever since.

Time: 1 to 2 class periods

Objectives:

- To trace the role of international diplomacy in the acquisition of western lands by the United States.

- To examine international disputes related to the western frontier and the means by which they were resolved.

- To identify problems of communication and assimilation for non-English-speaking peoples of the West.

Materials Needed:

Documents 5, 12, 14, 15, 16, 20, 25, 26, 28, and 29
Written Document Analysis worksheet, p. 14
Worksheet 7

Procedures:

1. Divide the class into pairs of students. Duplicate and distribute to each pair a copy of the Written Document Analysis worksheet and document 25. When the students have completed the assignment, discuss their answers aloud in class. In addition, pose to the students the following questions:

a. Were the United States and Spain at war at this time?

b. What has caused the hostility between Spain and the United States, according to this document?

c. Where was the engagement expected to take place?

d. What is General Wilkinson's estimation of the Spanish force's abilities?

e. What behavior does General Wilkinson expect from his troops?

2. Post documents 5, 12, 15, 20, 25, 26, 28, and 29 on the bulletin board. Distribute worksheet 7 to each student to complete over the course of the next week or two, providing 5 to 10 minutes daily when students may review the contents of the documents.

3. Ask students to write a pair of diary entries from the point of view of native Louisianans in 1802 and in 1806. Students may assume the identity of people mentioned in or alluded to in the documents such as Pierre Arceneau, Landau (a Creole), Julia Bryan (Landau's sister-in-law), or Friar Antonio de Sedela (priest of Cathedral of St. Louis in New Orleans).

4. Extended activities: In addition to the variety of European languages spoken in the West there were some 250 separate Indian languages with numerous dialects spoken by tribes across the continent. Communication, particularly for trade, was a problem. Individuals and groups were often bilingual and trilingual. Nonetheless, sign language became the common denominator of communications between these many disparate linguistic groups. The thirty tribes of the Plains culture developed the best known of the sign languages. While each tribe had its own spoken tongue, and some, such as the Lakota, had written languages, signing was important as an aid to trade.

a. Ask two or three students to research Plains Indian sign language, to make a poster illustrating gestures and their meanings and to demonstrate Plains sign language using the vehicle of a skit or, perhaps, a song. Encourage them to locate samples of written Plains language and include those words along with the signs. Following this presentation, ask the rest of the class to consider examples of sign language that we still use. Symbolic language such as "stop," "hush," and "I don't know" should be considered as well as American Standard Signing used by the hearing-impaired. Students should identify how these are similar to and different from Plains Indian sign language.

b. Ask several students to look at the influence of French-Americans and Hispanic-Americans on life in the United States, first for the time period between 1785 and 1842 and then for today. They should consider the social, cultural, religious, and political impact of these groups, then present their findings in an oral report. Encourage the group to use visuals and recorded material to illustrate its talk.

Exercise 9: The International West

Worksheet 7

Directions: Examine documents 5, 12, 15, 20, 25, 26, 28, and 29 to complete this worksheet.

DOCUMENT #	DESCRIPTION OF DOCUMENT	FOREIGN POWER(S) MENTIONED IN THE DOCUMENT
5		
12		
15		
20		
25		
26		
28		
29		

Exercise 10

The Forgotten West

Note to the Teacher:

Conventional histories of the American West have neglected the contributions of women and blacks to western expansion. These minorities are particularly elusive during the early stages of westward expansion, in part because their numbers were less significant than they would become after the Civil War. An additional problem is the scarcity of written accounts by blacks and women. Those who did participate in the great migration often were not literate; many stories were simply never recorded. Those who were literate, who kept government records, discounted women and blacks. For example, the 1790 census lists the names only of male heads of households. Women, children, and slaves were indicated simply by number. Also, although some Indian tribes accorded their women leadership roles, U.S. government officials typically refused to deal with any but male chiefs. Thus, the "Beloved Women" of the Cherokee influenced negotiations with the United States, but federal records are silent about their role. The primary sources available are typically located in state and local historical societies and museums. Diaries and journals, captivity accounts of white women seized by Indians, and artifacts of women and blacks help to restore this forgotten part of western history.

Elements of black history have survived in federal documents. The expansion by the United States into the Old Southwest was transformed by the impact of the cotton gin invented by Eli Whitney in 1793 (**slide H**). [To access a lesson plan and documents related to Whitney's cotton gin patent, go to **http://www.nara.gov/education/cc/whitney.html.**] Whitney exaggerated only slightly when he claimed, "it is an invention which enables one man to perform in a given time that which would require a thousand men without it and in the same time . . ." (**Document 11**). Green seed cotton was so difficult to clean by hand that only a pound a day could be processed. In contrast, the hand-powered gin cleaned 50 pounds per day, and water powered gins over 500. "The means furnished by this discovery of cleaning that species of cotton, were at once so cheap and expeditious, and the prospect of advantage so alluring that it suddenly became the general crop of the country," Whitney concludes.

With the increase in cotton cultivation came a rising demand for labor, a need that was met by expanding the use of slave labor. Thus, slavery became inseparable from cotton. As cotton depleted the soil, planters pushed westward in search of fresh lands, bringing with them involuntary migrants, their slaves. It is sometimes forgotten that the western experience was as much a black experience as a white one.

It is significant to note, however, that the black frontier experience is not entirely synonymous with slavery. Free blacks constituted 13.5 percent of the population of the County of Orleans in 1806. They were a well-educated, politically active group that represented an economic power in Spanish "Luisiana." Under the Spanish they maintained a military organization, a privilege that was withdrawn by the United States' territorial government. This and other disabilities placed on their race prompted some free blacks to look to Spain for remedy. Governor Claiborne feared not simply a slave revolt, but a revolt led by the free blacks, enlisting the support of slaves (49 percent of the population), Indian nations, and Spanish regular troops (**document 29**). With Toussaint L'Ouverture's recent success in Haiti the possibility seemed all too likely, although it never materialized.

When Louisiana was being organized as a territory, abolitionists again sought to prevent the extension of slavery in western lands. But an amendment to ban slavery in the Louisiana Territory, as in the Northwest Territory in 1787, failed to pass Congress (**document 22**).

The classified ads of an 1819 *Kentucky Gazette* offer brief glimpses into the lives of black westerners (**document 5**). A want notice for a black woman to serve as a domestic might have been directed at a slave owner willing to rent out a slave or at a free black woman. Certainly the sales notice for a slave and the reward announcement for runaways (headed to the Northwest) illustrate the spread of the "peculiar institution" into the trans-Appalachian West. Local historical societies possess letters, diaries, and artifacts which fill in with personal details the triumphs and tragedies of blacks in the West.

The federal government's records, at their best, preserve the nation's struggle with the transcendent issue of slavery or freedom. In 1819 the question erupted in Congress when the territory of Missouri petitioned for admission as a slave state. The House passed an abolition amendment; the Senate defeated it. This sectional stalemate threatened the young union. Largely due to Henry Clay's efforts, both houses of Congress agreed to a compromise in 1820 (**document 31**), which delayed civil war for another generation. But, as if gifted with prophecy, Thomas Jefferson cautioned "All, I fear, do not see the speck on our horizon which is to burst on us as a tornado, sooner or later."

One other element of western history that is often neglected is the role of religion. **Document 38**, a report of the Protestant Episcopal Mission at Green Bay, reveals the active part played by organized religion in educating and training Indians. Many religious sects sent missionaries west to convert the Indians to Christianity. While missionaries were not tolerant of the religions of Native Americans, they were often sympathetic to the rights of Indians in other matters, including land rights. The Samuel Worcester who figured in litigation with Georgia (**documents 37** and **39**) was a Protestant minister who championed Cherokee rights. As white settlement increased, other religious personnel went along to minister to the pioneers' spiritual needs. The frontier church was often the social, cultural, and educational center of a new settlement, as well as its religious center.

Time: 1 class period

Objectives:

- To identify the roles played by blacks in the history of the American West.

- To recognize cause and effect in relationship to the cotton gin and subsequent American history.

- To examine the growth of slavery as a sectional issue.

- To recognize the contribution of religion to the history of the American West.

Materials Needed:

Documents 5, 11, 22, 29, 31, 37, 38, 39
Slide H
Worksheet 8

Procedures:

Note that the language in these documents may include offensive racial stereotyping and that it is essential to set these documents in their historical context.

1. Duplicate and distribute document 29 and worksheet 8. Answer any vocabulary questions the students may have. When students have completed the worksheets, go over their answers as a class.

2. Divide the class into groups of four and provide each group with the set of documents 5, 11, 22, 29, and 31. Each group should review the documents and its textbooks and consult further references, if necessary, to compile a time line of significant events in black history in the United States between 1787 and 1820.

3. After students have completed the assignment, you may wish to examine the variety of descriptions used by 19th century whites to note racial distinctions in these documents. Ask the class to consider what such minute distinction of race revealed about American attitudes towards race at that time.

4. Duplicate and distribute document 38 to each student and discuss in class the following questions:

   a. Compare and contrast the subjects taught in the mission school in 1833 with those that are taught in school today.

   b. Compare and contrast the physical facility of the mission school with that of your school.

   c. Compare and contrast the ethnic composition of the student body at the mission school with that of your school.

   d. What vocational education is offered at the school? How important is vocational education in the overall curriculum, based on Mr. Boyd's comments? How do you account for it? What subjects may be dropped from the curriculum? Why are they more expendable?

   e. How do the activities for boys differ from those of girls? Account for the differences.

   f. What accomplishments of the school seem to be most important to the government official, Mr. Boyd? Why might this be so? What accomplishments of the school would be most important to the Protestant Episcopal Church and why? What accomplishment of the school would be the most valuable to the tribes and why?

5. Extended activities:

   a. Ask students to research and prepare a paper about the role of blacks in the American West. They may wish to focus on biographical studies of black explorers such as:

   Jean Baptiste Pointe du Sable (founder of Chicago)

   York (William Clark's slave, who accompanied the Lewis and Clark expedition)

   James P. Beckwourth (mountain man)

   b. Ask for volunteers to trace the history of their religious denomination during the period 1800-1850 or a denomination in which they might be interested.

Exercise 10: The Forgotten West

Worksheet 8

Directions: Read document 29 to answer the questions on this worksheet.

1. Who is Stephen? _____

_____

2. What preparations has Stephen observed that suggest a rebellion is about to break out?

_____

_____

3. What signal is to be given to start the massacre? _____

_____

4. What groups are expected to assist the rebels? _____

_____

5. What do slaves hope to gain from this rebellion? _____

_____

6. What do the Spanish stand to gain from this rebellion? _____

_____

7. What do the Indians stand to gain from this rebellion? _____

_____

8. What advice does Stephen give the Americans to ensure their safety? ____

_____

_____

9. Who has received Stephen's deposition? _____

_____

10. Why do you think he is passing this on to the Secretary of State in Washington, DC?

_____

_____

Transcription of Document 17

New York July 24th 1790

Sir

    I left Muskingum the 2nd instant; nothing new in that quarter Sence Mr. Morgan came on, except, that a number of Horses have been stolen & one man killed at Belleville (a Virginia Settlement about three miles below the Great Hockhocking) which appears to be a mischief altogether unprovoked. Also about the 20th of last month a woman was taken neer the mouth of Buffaloe Creek, and was afterward murdered, but this business was prefaced by the white people stealing a number of Horses from the the Indians & refusing to deliver them up when demanded.

    The Muskingum Settlements have lost many Horses, the last fall & this Sumer, Some Stollen by white people but more by the Indians, and their is Sufficient evidence that Some of the Dellawares and Wyndots who attended the Treaty at Fort Harmar, as well as the Shawonies have been concerned in the thieft – Their is also good reason to believe that Several belonging to the Dellaware & Wyndot Nations, have been concerned in Murdering the people and plundering the boats, going down the Ohio; the last Winter and Spring & it is likewise Said that a number of white men were among that gang of robbers.

    It seems that they are possessed of Some boats or other Craft on the Sioto, in which they Issue out of that River into the Ohio, and haveing obtained their booty retire again with Saifty –; would not a small detachment of Troops stationed at the mouth of the Sioto in great measure, if not wholly, put a Stop to this kind of business, and at the Same time give confidence to the people in the new Settlements on the Ohio, which are commenceing betwen the Sioto and the Great Kenhawa–

    By letters received at Muskingum, from Mr. Secretary Sargent, and also from Major Doughty information I learnt that Governor St. Clair was Still in the Illinois Country & would not probably return to Muskingum till October, & that M'sieus. Syms & Turner left the Miamis in the month of May to attend the Governor – Under these circumstances I conceived it best to to return imedately for my family.

    I leve thir on Monday morning, Shall be in town again the first or 2d week in September on my way to the Western world –

I have the honour to be Sir with every
posable Sentement of the most perfect
esteem your Excellencys most
obedient Humble
Servent,
Rufus Putnam,
Judge of the Western Ty.

The President

Transcription of Document 23

New Orleans 10th February 1815

Sir,

In the letter of the Attorney General of the United States of the 10th of December, addressed to you in relation to the pirates or smugglers of Barrataria, and which you did me the honour to hand to me for perusal, it is remarked, I am directed by him "the President" to say to you, that a discrimination between the cases proper, and improper, for lenity may be made, by the District Attorney with your approbation. The course that it was deemed necessary to pursue with regard to the discription of persons here allu.....[lost]... invasion of this State; the promise of pardon or intercession for Pardon that was then held out to them, and their subsequent good conduct, during a period of difficulty and danger, are circumstances well known to you, and which, if known to the Government, would doubtless increase the disposition to lenity that is manifested by the letter already referred to. Under the impression of this belief, and as you have suggested to me, in conversation, the propriety of entering nolle prosequi in the cases of all these offenders, I think it proper to hand to you the names of those against whom prosecutions have been commenced at presentments found, with an indication of the offences alledged against each: and I have to request the favour of you to signify your "approbation" of my entering a nolle prosequi in each cause, or to make ...[lost]... the cases proper & improper, to lenity," agreeably to the course pointed out by the Attorney General, under the direction of the President.

I have the honour to be
Sir very Respectfully
Yr obedient Serv't
John Dick
attorney of the U.S. for
the Louisiana District

His Excellency
Governor Claiborne

Enumberation of prosecutions commenced in the District Court of the United States for the Louisiana district against persons committed from Barataria, & c

1. *The U. States vs.*
   Johannes & Peter Lafitte
   Piracy–The first, as principal; the Second as accessory before the fact

2. *The U. States vs. Jarry, alias Jauretty, and Peter Lafitte*
   Piracy–The first principal; the Second as accessory before the fact

3. *The U. S. vs. Joachim Santos*
   Piracy

4. *The U. States vs. Manuel Joachim*
   Piracy

5. *The U. States vs.*
   Juan Juanilles alias Sapia
   Piracy

6. *The U. States vs. Bernard Lafon*
   Piracy

7. *The U. States vs. Jacque Cannon*
   Piracy

8. *The U. States vs. Rene Roland*
   Piracy

9. *The U. States vs. Dominique, alias Frederick Youx*
   Piracy

10. *The U. States vs. Alexr. St. Elmo*
    Piracy

11. *The U. States vs. Severne Courtou*
    Piracy

12. *The U. States vs. John Rudolph*
    Piracy

13. *The U. States vs. Alexr. Bonneval*
    Piracy

14. *The U. States vs. Antoine Laserone alias (lost) Patte Grasse*
    Accessory to piracy and illegally fitting out

15. *The U. States vs. J. J. Contras*
    Fitting out, within the waters of the U.S. with intent to cruize and commit hostilities against States with whom the U.S. were at peace

16. *The U. States vs. Wm. Fleming*
    Illegally fitting out

17. (lost) *vs. Henry St. Geore*
    For operating & arming, without the limits of the U.S. with intent to cruize & commit hostilities upon the subjects and property of Princes & States, with whom the U.S. were then at peace, with a view to Share in the profit thereof.

Transcription of Document 35

Washington City March 5th 1819

Father,

The delegation of your red children the Cherokees has heard your talk with attention and satisfaction. The hearts of their people were burthened with grief and oppression when they left the Nation – You can justly imagine what was and ought to have been the feelings of the delegation on that occasion – but now the scene we hope will be changed and that the burthen will be lightened and their hearts relieved from that grief and oppression, by the illuminations of justice and humanity which have been produced by the magnanimous hands of the Government. We have long since been induced to believe that civilized life was preferable to that of the hunters – but circumstances arising from the situation of our people, require time to make the change – the Cherokees do not depend on hunting for a livelihood, and they are fully sensible that game cannot always exist – experience has clearly demonstrated this matter to them had they been insensible of that fact – they would not have objected to follow those of their fellow countrymen who have separated themselves from the soil of their nativity and emigrated to the West – the establishment of schools in our Nation has been productive of the greatest good, there are now two missionary establishments in our nation, one at Spring place under the patronage of the Moravian society and the other at Brainerd on Chickamaugah, under that of the American Board of Foreign Missions – and they are both in a flattering and progressive situation – the numerous public roads leading through our nation in various directions, have also been a great cause of stimulating the Cherokees to the industrious pursuits of agriculture and husbandry – the habitations of the Cherokees are also progressing in comfort – many of their improvements and farms are extensive, and their circumstances in relation to domesticated property, such as horses, cattle, hogs, sheep, &c are sufficiently abundant to produce comfort. This we have communicated for your more comprehensive knowledge of our true situations – As the Chief Magistrate of this extensive Republic and as the Father and protector of the American Aborigines, we feel ourselves bound to make known to you our sentiments and actual situations with frankness. We have now surrendered to the United States a large portion of our country for the benifit of those of our Countrymen who have emigrated to the Arkansas – And we hope that the Government will now strictly protect us from the intrusions of her bad citizens and not solicit us for more land – As we positively believe that the comfort and convenience of our nation requires us to retain our present limits.

Father, there is one great existing cause which has hitherto placed our nation under a peculiar disadvantage and inconvenience and incurred much unnecessary trouble and expence to the United States, to which we beg leave to call your attention. When treaties for lands have been contemplated to be held with us, by the consent of the Government, our National Council have been summoned together on the spur of the occasion, without any previous knowledge of the object. had we refused to attend the call, we would have been represented as obstinate and unfriendly. This we believe has operated as an evil, and hope you will view it as an object worthy to be remedied by the friendly interposition of your Fatherly hand. May the Great Spirit keep the chains of friendship between the United States and the Red children of America, in perpetual brightness – And that the conditions of the American Aborigines be made prosperous and happy, under the fostering hands of the Government of this great republic – And that your life may be preserved many years in peace, prosperity and happiness are the sincere wishes of your Cherokee Children.

Ch. Nicks	his
Jno. Ross	Cabbin X Smith
Lewis Ross	mark
James Brown	Sleeping X Rabbit
John Martin	Small Wood X mark
Geo. Lowry	Cherokee X

To His Excellency
    James Monroe
        President of the U. States

Transcription of Document 36

Novr. 18th 1830

Dr Sir

In reply to your note of this morning enclosing the letter from the Gov. of Georgia I have to observe that I can see no good to be Derived to the State of Georgia, or the United States, by the enrolling plan but an accumulation of expense to the Government & a constant drain to our Treasury – Suppose 1000 enrolled for emigration, this Does not lessen the claims of the Cherokees, or a tribe, to the territory now claimed by them within Georgia, and from the temper that has lately appeared amonghst them to emigrate, it is evident to my mind, that they Chiefs must shortly propose a treaty under which the whole will emigrate, that do not intend to remain as citizens. – but if the enrolling system is commenced, it will have the effect to lissen the ardor that now begins to shew itself for emigrating to the west - This ardor ought to be increased & delay will have this effect until the hoping spirit of the Indians will compel their chiefs to send Deputies duly authorized to treat for the whole country - Therefore you will answer the Govr of Georgia that this enrolling scheme ought to be postponed for the present until the course the Legislature of Congress may take on this subject is jointly designated and until it is seen what effect the late spirit for emigration, by many of them, may produce upon the whole nation.

I have no doubt but the common Indian seeing that their chiefs have become wealthy by the course pursued by them whilst the common Indians have been reduced to beggary, will soon burst their bonds of slavery & compel their chiefs to propose terms for their removal. For the present the enrolling scheme ought to be postponed.

Yrs.
Andrew Jackson

The Honble
J. H. Eaton
Sec. of War

Transcription of Document 39

Copy

Executive Department
Milledgeville April 20, 1831

Sir,

I am desirous of receiving from you such information in answer to the following inquiries as your official station may enable you to obtain.

What effect has the late decision of the Supreme Court of the U. States in dismissing this Bill of Injuction against Georgia had upon the Cherokees.

Are their Chiefs disposed to make a Treaty, if so what means will be most efficient to secure the result?

If their Chiefs are not so disposed, is the temper of the middle and lower Classes different? – Could they be induced to have a general meeting of the whole Tribe without the concurrence of their Chiefs.

If a Treaty cannot be made with the whole Tribe thro their Chiefs or the body of the People would these who reside in Georgia be disposed immediately to sell the Lands within its limits either by Treaty or by the Government agreeing to pay each Individual the value for his improvements?

How can the Opinions and wishes and designee of the Chiefs and the People upon that subject be most Certainly ascertained.

What Whitemen residing among the Indians or elsewhere can with the greatest probability of success be imployed to explain to them the policy of the General Government in desiring their removal to the Arkansas and the rights of the State which induced the extension of its Jurisdiction over them and to convince them of the great advantage they will derive from an immediate removal?

Are there any Individuals so situated that they could be employed for this object without exciting the Suspicions of the Indians that they were the agents of the Government. Are there any of the half breeds who could be trusted with such an employment?

What portion of the Indians will probably remain in this State if a Treaty should be formed and Individuals allowed to take reservations?

Are the Indians now prepared for the appointment of Commissioners to Treat with them or would further delay more certainly accomplish the object?

You are also requested to communicate to me whatever information you may have of the Conduct of the Missionary Worcestor and Thompson or either of them in opposing the removal of the Indians to the West of the Mississippi – creating opposition to the Laws of Georgia or inducing the Indians to persist in their attempt to establish an Independent Government – What has been their conduct since their discharge? – What is the name of the White Man whose appointment you recommend should Worcestor be removed from the Post Office at Echota?

Should Mr. Byhan cease to be Post Master at Spring Place, can any respectable Whiteman be found to succeede him?

Very Respectfully
Yours,
George R. Gilmer

Col John W. A. Sanford
Commander of the Guard

Transcription of Document 45

Cherokee Agency East
March 15, 1838

Hon. C. A. Harris
Com. Ind. Affairs

Sir

In order that you may know what measures are resorted to here to prevent emigration, I have the honor to enclose herewith a translated copy of a letter written in Cherokee and purporting to be from White Path to Thomas Manning a near neighbour of Mr. Jno. Ross. White Path is a very old man and can neither read nor write Cherokee. This is another plan invented by the Delegation at Washington to keep the Indians here, and having been copied and sent through the Nation by runners to Leading men in all the towns who called meetings and read it it has had considerable effect in stopping emigration.

This with no doubt numbers of other measures that are practised accounts for the delay and disappointment to which I am Subjected in getting these miserable and deluded people started for their Country west.

I am extremely mortified at not being able to do more towards their removal on account of such heavy and daily expenses that are incurred. But I assure you their delay here is caused by only a few of their leading men, who are now misleading their people with their eyes open.

Very Respectfully,
Yr. Mo. Obt. Serv.
Nathanial Smith
Supt. Ch. Removal

(Enclosed translation)

Washington City
Jany. 27, 1838

Sir

I write these lines in order to let you hear of your delegation at Washington. We are all well, also the delegation that was sent to the Seminoles is in good health. We are all together at one place. We bear news of this kind, that you are informed that we cannot do any thing nor make any alterations whatever, but we do not think it the case ourselves. We are here with some encouragement. You are told these things at home in order to dishearten you, but it will not do to believe such news as that, for if we believe we cannot do any thing we will let you know for we will not be silent. It is done in order to outwit you, and get you to acknowledge the Treaty. They know that we have the Question before the Senate that is the reason they are so uneasy and work so hard against us. Their proceedings will be done away, and that makes them restless, and that is the reason you hear so many false reports. But the answer will not be hard to make them – just tell them you have sent on a delegation, and you are waiting for them to come home and tell you the Secretary of War and the man he appointed to have an interview with us, did disappoint us. They did it for one reason, it was for this – they want to get something to help them on with some news they send to dishearten you. They know very well that the President alone could not break the Treaty that was made by Jackson or by his order. That is the way the President got his seat and he is at this time afraid to interfere with Jackson proceedings. That was the reason why he wanted us to lay the case before the Senate, then if the Senate will say that the treaty was made by unauthorized power, that would give the President a chance to make a new treaty, for we have already given them evidence that there was a fraud put on the Nation, and we have laid in our Memorial before the Senate, and it is not long before they will let it be known. We have given up all our papers to the person who will present them, and we are in great hopes that there will be some alteration in that which they strive so ha·d for us to acknowledge that is one of the most hurtful thing to us, but just bear it the time will not be long before you can hear how it was determined. They tell you they will drive you off by force, it is very doubtful about us being drove. No more. When you receive this show and let the people of Ollijay hear of it.

(Signed) White Path

Time Line

1783	October 15	Committee report on Indian affairs (**Document 32**)
1785	**May 20**	Land Ordinance of 1785 (**Document 1**)
1786	**December 18**	Address from Confederated Tribes to Confederation Congress (**Document 33**) Letter from Joseph Barrett to Capt. John Kendrick (**Document 12**)
1787		
1788	**July 9**	St. Clair Inaugural Address (**Document 2**)
1789		
1790	**July 24**	Letter from Judge Rufus Putnam to President Washington (**Document 17**)
	July 29	Letter from Joseph St. Marie to Territorial Secretary Sargent (**Document 28**)
1791		
1792		
1793		
1794		Patent drawing of the cotton gin (**Slide H**)
1795		
1796		
1797		
1798		
1799		
1800		
1801		
1802	**July 28**	Letter from H. Dearborn to Thomas Peterkin (**Document 10**)
1803	**February**	Map of proposed canal at Harper's Ferry (**Slide P**)
	April 30	Louisiana Purchase treaty (**Document 20**)
	July 29	Letter from Secretary of State Madison to Robert Livingston and James Monroe (**Document 30**)
	December 22	Map of the National Road (**Slide D**)
	December 30	Proposed amendment to prohibit slavery in Louisiana Territory (**Document 22**)
1804	**January 16**	Authorization from President Thomas Jefferson to Secretary of the Treasury Gallatin to pay for the Louisiana Purchase (**Document 21**)
1805	**July 26**	Proclamation on territorial elections (**Document 24**)
1806	**January 24**	Letter from Governor Claiborne to Secretary of State (**Document 29**)
	February 19	Message from Jefferson about exploration (**Document 18**)
	October 28	Wilkinson's General Orders (**Document 25**) Zebulon Pike's exploration notebook (**Document 6**) Lewis and Clark map (**Slide M**) Pike manuscript map of the Mississippi River (**Slide L**)
1807	**January 25**	Letter from John Chisholm to Colonel Meigs (**Document 14**)
1808	**January 25**	Fort Dearborn ground plan and elevation (**Slide N**)

1809		
1810	January 10	Petition regarding public land (**Document 4**)
	May 28	Land Sale Notice (**Document 27**)
1811	July 10	Choctaw factory daybook (**Document 34**)
	December 27	Land certificate (**Document 3**)
1812	February 18	Letter from Thomas Forsyth to Governor Howard (**Document 16**)
	April 16	Memorial of Eli Whitney to renew cotton gin patent (**Document 11**).
1813		
1814	June 11	Letter from the War Department to territorial governors (**Document 15**)
1815	February 10	Letter from District Attorney John Dick to Governor Claiborne (**Document 23**)
1816		
1817		
1818	July 30	Packing list for pelts (**Document 19**)
	October 21	Injunction against Thomas Gibbons (**Document 13**)
1819	March 5	Letter from Cherokee Chiefs to President James Monroe (**Document 35**)
	March 30	Exploration instructions to Stephen Long (**Document 7**)
	October 8	*Kentucky Gazette* (**Document 5**)
1820	March 8	Missouri Compromise (**Document 31**)
		Map by Stephen Long (**Slide E**)
1821		
1822	January 23	Act laying out roads (**Document 9**)
		Alabama Township plat (**Slide O**)
1823		
1824		
1825		
1826		
1827		
1828		
1829		
1830	January 10	Memorial of Pennsylvanians opposing Indian removal (**Document 43**)
	November 18	Letter from President Andrew Jackson to Secretary of War Eaton (**Document 36**)
		Map of territories disputed between Georgia and the Cherokee Nation (**Slide C**)
1831	January 10	Private Land Claim of Pierre Arceneau (**Document 26**)
	April 20	Letter from Governor Gilmer to Colonel Sanford (**Document 39**)
1832	January	Court order in *Worcester v. Georgia* (**Document 37**)
	March 31	Enrolled Cherokee immigrant (**Document 40**)
1833	September 30	Statement of Protestant Episcopal Mission at Green Bay (**Document 38**)
		Map of proposed Erie railroad (**Slide l**)
1834		Artwork by Karl Bodmer of the buffalo dance of the Mandans (**Slide Q**)
1835	March 14	Treaty of New Echota (**Document 42**)
1836		

1837	**December 30**	Cherokee mortality schedule **(Document 41)**
		Artwork by George Catlin of Osceola, the Seminole leader **(Slide R)**
1838	**March 15**	Letter from Nathaniel Smith to C. A. Harris with Cherokee letter enclosure **(Document 45)**
	May 17	Orders #25 signed by Winfield Scott **(Document 44)**
	September 12	Patent for snag boat **(Slide G)**
		Snag boat design **(Slide F)**
1839		Burr's Postal Atlas, Sheet 1 **(Slide J)**
1840		Minerals map of Iowa **(Slide K)**
1841		
1842		
1857	**July 1**	C & O Canal toll rates **(Document 8)**
1884		Cherokee treaty map, Eastern Lands **(Slide A)**
		Cherokee treaty map, Western Lands **(Slide B)**

Bibliography

Nonfiction

Abernethy, Thomas. *The Burr Conspiracy*. Gloucester, MA: P. Smith, 1968.

Bailey, Thomas. *A Diplomatic History of the American People*. Englewood Cliffs, NJ: Prentice-Hall, Inc., 1980.

Bannon, John F. *The Spanish Borderlands Frontier: 1513-1821*. New York: Holt, Rinehart, and Winston, 1971.

Billington, Ray. *The Far Western Frontier: 1830-1860*. Albuquerque: University of New Mexico Press, 1995.

Bird, Harrison. *War for the West: 1790-1813*. New York: Oxford University Press, 1971.

Boorstin, Daniel J. *The Americans: The Colonial Experiment*. New York: Random House, 1958.

Buchanan, John. *Jackson's Way: Andrew Jackson and the People of the Western Waters*. New York: J. Wiley, 2001.

Campbell, Joseph. *The Hero with a Thousand Faces*. New York: MJF Books, 1996.

Cayton, Andrew R. L. and Fredrika J. Teute, eds. *Contact Points: American Frontiers from the Mohawk Valley to the Mississippi, 1750-1830*. Chapel Hill: University of North Carolina Press, 1998.

Crockett, David. *A Narrative of the Life of David Crockett of the State of Tennessee Written by Himself*. Ed. by Joseph Arpad. Bedford, MA: Applewood Books, 1993.

Dana, Richard. *Two Years Before the Mast*. New York: Signet Classic, 2000.

Davidson, Marshall. *The American Heritage History of the Artists' America*. New York: American Heritage, 1973.

Debo, Angie. *A History of the Indians of the United States*. Norman: University of Oklahoma Press, 1970.

De Conde, Alexander. *This Affair of Louisiana*. New York: Charles Scribner and Son, 1976.

De Crèvecoeur, J. Hector St. John. *Letters from an American Farmer*. New York: Oxford University Press, 1997.

De Tocqueville, Alexis. *Democracy in America*. Chicago: University of Chicago Press, 2000.

De Voto, Bernard. *Across the Wide Missouri*. Boston: Houghton Mifflin, 1987.

_____. *The Course of Empire*. Norwalk, CT.: Easton Press, 1988.

_____. *The Journals of Lewis and Clark*. Boston: Houghton Mifflin Co., 1997.

Furnas, J. C. *The Americans: A Social History of the United States 1587-1914*. New York: G. P. Putnam's Sons, 1969.

Goetzmann, William. *Army Exploration in the American West: 1803-1863*. Lincoln: University of Nebraska Press, 1979.

_____. *Exploration and Empire, The Explorer and the Scientists in the Winning of the American West*. New York: Norton, 1978.

_____. *New Lands, New Men: America and the Second Great Age of Discovery*. New York: Viking, 1986.

_____. *The West of the Imagination*. New York: W. W. Norton & Company, 1986.

Hartley, William and Hartley, Ellen. *Osceola: The Unconquered Indian*. New York: Hawthorn Books, 1973.

Horsman, Reginald. *Expansion and American Indian Policy: 1783-1815*. Norman: University of Oklahoma Press, 1992.

_____. *The Frontier in the Formative Years, 1783-1815*. New York: Holt, Rinehart and Winston, 1970.

_____. *Race and Manifest Destiny: The Origins of American Racial Anglo-Saxonism*. Cambridge, MA: Harvard University Press, 1981.

Hunter, Louis. *Steamboats on the Western Rivers*. New York: Dover Publications, 1993.

Jehlen, Myra. *American Incarnation: The Individual, the Nation, and the Continent*. Cambridge, MA: Harvard University Press, 1986.

Katz, William. *The Black West*. Trenton, NJ: Africa World Press, 1992.

Lavender, David. *The American Heritage History of the West*. New York: American Heritage, 1965.

Lofaro, Michael, ed. *Davy Crockett: The Man, the Legend, the Legacy, 1786-1976*. Knoxville: University of Tennessee Press, 1985.

Marquis, James. *The Raven: A Biography of Sam Houston*. Norwalk, CT: Easton Press, 1988.

Merk, Frederick. *History of the Westward Movement*. New York: Knopf, 1978.

Nichols, Roger, and Halley, Patrick. *Stephen Long and American Frontier Exploration*. Norman: University of Oklahoma Press, 1995.

Peterson, Merrill, ed. *The Portable Thomas Jefferson*. New York: Penguin Books, 1977.

Phillips, Paul. *The Fur Trade*. Norman: University of Oklahoma Press, 1961.

Prucha, Francis P. *American Indian Policy in the Formative Years*. Cambridge: Harvard University Press, 1962.

Remini, Robert V. *Andrew Jackson and the Course of American Empire*. New York: Harper & Row, 1977.

Sandburg, Carl. *Abraham Lincoln: The Prairie Years*. Norwalk, CT: Easton Press, 1984.

Schwartz, Seymour, and Ehrenburg, Ralph. *The Mapping of America*. New York: H. N. Abrams, 1980.

Stephanson, Anders. *Manifest Destiny: American Expansionism and the Empire of Right*. New York: Hill and Wang, 1995.

Stuart, Reginald C. *United States Expansionism and British North America, 1775-1871*. Chapel Hill: University of North Carolina Press, 1988.

Thoreau, Henry. *Walden*. New York, NY: Penguin Books, 1983.

Tucker, Glenn. *Tecumseh: Vision of Glory*. New York: Russell & Russell, 1973.

Turner, Frederick Jackson. *Frontier in American History*. New York: Dover Publications, 1996.

Van Every, Dale. *Disinherited: The Lost Birthright of the American Indian*. New York: Morrow, 1966.

Weeks, William Earl. *Building the Continental Empire: American Expansion from the Revolution to the Civil War*. Chicago, IL: Ivan R. Dee, 1996.

Weinberg, Albert Katz. *Manifest Destiny: A Study of Nationalist Expansionism in American History*. New York: AMS Press, 1979.

Fiction

Brown, Dee. *Creek Mary's Blood*. New York: Holt, Rinehart, and Winston, 1980.

Clemens, Samuel. *Life on the Mississippi*. New York: Oxford Unviversity Press, 1996.

Cooper, James Fenimore. *The Last of the Mohicans*. New York: Scribners, 1986.

Dick, Everett. *Tales of the Frontier*. Lincoln: University of Nebraska Press, 1963.

Irving, Washington. *Astoria*. New York: KPI, 1987.

_____. *The Legend of Sleepy Hollow*. New York: Dover Publications, 1995.

Robson, Lucia. *Walk in My Soul*. New York: Ballantine, 1985.

_____. *Light a Distant Fire*. New York: Ballantine Books, 1988.

Stone, Irving. *The President's Lady*. Nashville, TN: Rutledge Hill Press, 1996.

Vidal, Gore. *Burr*. New York: Modern Library, 1998.

The United States Expands West: 1785-1842
Archival Citations of Documents

1. Land Ordinance of 1785, May 20, 1785; (HR9A-C4.1); 9th Congress; Records of the U.S. House of Representatives, Record Group 233; National Archives Building, Washington, DC.

2. Address by Governor Arthur St. Clair at his inauguration, July 9, 1788; Territorial Papers-Northwest Territory; Vol. 1, July 13, 1787-Aug. 1, 1791, p. 67; General Records of the Department of State, Record Group 59; National Archives at College Park, College Park, MD.

3. Land certificate, December 27, 1811; Land Entry Files, Marietta, OH; Credit Prior Final Certificate; CPFC1-52; Records of the Bureau of Land Management, Record Group 49; National Archives Building, Washington, DC.

4. Petition of Ohioans regarding land sale policy, January 10, 1810; (HR 11A-F8.2); 11th Congress; Records of the U.S. House of Representatives, Record Group 233; National Archives Building, Washington, DC.

5. *Kentucky Gazette*, October 8, 1819; Letters Received by the Secretary of War; Unregistered Series, 1789-1861; (National Archives Microfilm Publication M222, roll 21; 1819-1829, A-M); J-1819; Records of the Office of the Secretary of War, Record Group 107; National Archives Building, Washington, DC.

6. Traverse table; Lt. Zebulon Pike's Notebooks of Maps, Traverse, Tables, and Meteorological Observations, 1805-1807; (National Archives Microfilm Publication T36, roll 1); Records of the Adjutant General's office, 1780's–1917, Records Group 94; National Archives Building, Washington, DC.

7. Instructions from John C. Calhoun to Major Stephen Long, March 30, 1819; Letters Received by the Secretary of War L-R; Registered Series, 1801-1870; (National Archives Microfilm Publication M221, roll 82); Records of the Office of the Secretary of War, Record Group 107; National Archives Building, Washington, DC.

8. Chart of Chesapeake and Ohio Canal toll rates, July 1, 1857; *Toll Book*, 1855-80; Records Concerning Traffic on the Canal; Records of the Chesapeake and Ohio Canal Co.; Records of the National Park Service, Record Group 79; National Archives at College Park, College Park, MD.

9. Act authorizing road construction, January 23, 1822; Act, Cumberland Road (HR 16A-D24.1); 16th Congress; Records of the U.S. House of Representatives, Record Group 233; National Archives Building, Washington, DC.

10. Letter from H. Dearborn to Thomas Peterkin, July 28, 1802; Received Secretary of War; Letters Sent, 1800-1824; Vol. A, pp. 251-252; Records of the Bureau of Indian Affairs, Record Group 75; National Archives Building, Washington, DC.

11. Memorial of Eli Whitney, April 16, 1812; (HR 12A-F11.2); 12th Congress; Records of the U.S. House of Representatives, Record Group 233; National Archives Building, Washington, DC.

12. Letter from Joseph Barrett to Captain John Kendrick, ca. 1786-1787; Territorial Papers-Oregon; Vol. 1, 1792-1858, pp.1-2; General Records of the Department of State, Record Group 59; National Archives at College Park, College Park, MD.

13. Injunction in *Gibbons v. Ogden*, October 21, 1818; Case #1148; (9 Wheaton 1); Records of the Supreme Court of the United States, Record Group 267; National Archives Building, Washington, DC.

14. Letter from John Chisholm to Colonel Meigs, January 25, 1807; Letters Received by the Office of the Secretary of War Related to Indian Affairs, 1824-1881; (National Archives Microfilm Publication M271, roll 10); Records of the Bureau of Indian Affairs, Record Group 75; National Archives Building, Washington, DC.

15. Letter from the War Department to various territorial governors, June 11, 1814; Letters Sent by Secretary of War Related to Indian Affairs, 1800-1824; (National Archives Microfilm Publication M15, roll 3, pp. 170-171); Records of the Bureau of Indian Affairs, Record Group 75; National Archives Building, Washington, DC.

16. Letter from Thomas Forsyth to Governor Howard, February 18, 1812; Committee on the Judiciary; Resolution of the Legislature of Missouri Territory (HR14A-F6.1); 14th Congress; Records of the U.S. House of Representatives, Record Group 233; National Archives Building, Washington, DC.

17. Letter from Judge Rufus Putnam to President George Washington, July 24, 1790; Territorial Papers-Northwest Territory; Vol. II, p. 38; General Records of the Department of State, Record Group 59; National Archives at College Park, College Park, MD.

18. Message from President Thomas Jefferson to Congress; Annual Message, February 19, 1806; Jefferson on Lewis and Clark (SEN9-AE2); 9th Congress; Records of the U.S. Senate, Record Group 46; National Archives Building, Washington, DC.

19. Packing list for pelts, July 30, 1818; Special Files of Office of Indian Affairs, 1824-1881; (National Archives Microfilm Publication M574, roll 2; File 14, 0286); Records of the Bureau of Indian Affairs, Record Group 75; National Archives Building, Washington, DC.

20. The Louisiana Purchase, April 30, 1803; Treaty Series 86; Documents Having General Legal Effects; General Records of the U.S. Government, Record Group 11; National Archives at College Park, College Park, MD.

21. Authorization from President Thomas Jefferson to Secretary of the Treasury Gallatin, January 16, 1804; Treasury Department Papers Relating to the Louisiana Purchase; (National Archives Microfilm Publication T712 (10-51-6), pp. 31-32); General Records of the Department of the Treasury, Record Group 56; National Archives at College Park, College Park, MD.

22. Proposed amendment to Louisiana territorial organization to restrict slavery, December 30, 1803; LA Territory Bill (SEN8A-B1); 8th Congress; Records of the U.S. Senate, Record Group 46; National Archives Building, Washington, DC.

23. Letter from Louisiana District Attorney John Dick to Governor Claiborne about Jean Lafitte, February 10, 1815; Attorney General's Papers; Letters Received, LA 1815-1860; File 1; General Records of the Department of Justice, Record Group 60; National Archives at College Park, College Park, MD.

24. Proclamation about territorial elections, July 26, 1805; State Department Territorial Papers, Orleans, 1764-1813; (National Archives Microfilm Publication T260, roll, 7); General Records of the Department of State, Record Group 59; National Archives at College Park, College Park, MD.

25. General Orders from General Wilkinson's letterbook, October 28, 1806; General James Wilkinson's Order Book, Dec. 31, 1796-Mar. 8, 1808 (National Archives Microfilm Publication M654, roll 3, pp. 634-637); Records of the Adjutant General's Office, 1780's-1917, Record Group 94; National Archives Building, Washington, DC.

26. Private Land Claim, January 10, 1831; Louisiana Private Land Claims; Case File #94; Pierre Arceneau; Records of the Bureau of Land Management, Record Group 49; National Archives Building, Washington, DC.

27. Land sale notice, May 28, 1810; Bilingual Land Sale Notice; May 28, 1810; Box 37; Records of the Solicitor of the Treasury, Record Group 206; National Archives at College Park, College Park, MD.

28. Letter from Joseph St. Marie to Territorial Secretary Sargent, July 29, 1790; Territorial Papers of Northwest Territory; Vol. II, pp. 66-73; General Records of the Department of State, Record Group 59; National Archives at College Park, College Park, MD.

29. Letter from Governor Claiborne to Secretary of State Madison, January 24, 1806; State Department Territorial Papers, Orleans, 1764-1813; (National Archives Microfilm Publication T260, roll 7 or 8, pp. 32-34); General Records of the Department of State, Records Group 59; National Archives at College Park, College Park, MD.

30. Letter from Secretary of State Madison to Robert Livingston and James Monroe, July 29, 1803; Diplomatic Instructions of the Department of State, 1801-1906; (National Archives Microfilm Publication M77, roll 1, pp. 142-144); General Records of the Department of State, Records Group 59; National Archives at College Park, College Park, MD.

31. The Missouri Compromise, March 6, 1820; Enrolled Acts of Congress (Public Laws), 16th Congress, sess.1; General Records of the U.S. Government, Record Group 11; National Archives at College Park, College Park, MD.

32. Committee draft report on Indian affairs, October15, 1783; Papers of the Continental Congress, 1774-1789; (National Archives Microfilm Publication M247, Roll 37); Records of the Continental and Confederation Congresses and the Constitutional Convention, Record Group 360; National Archives Building, Washington, DC.

33. Address from Confederated Tribes to the Confederation Congress, December 18, 1786; (SEN1B-C1); 1st Congress; Records of the U.S. Senate, Record Group 46; National Archives Building, Washington, DC.

34. Choctaw factory daybook, July 10, 1811; Office of Indian Trade; Choctaw factory daybook, 1808-18; Records of the Bureau of Indian Affairs, Record Group 75; National Archives Building, Washington, DC.

35. Letter from chiefs of the Cherokee Nation to President James Monroe, March 5, 1819; Letters Received by Office of Secretary of War; Related to Indian Affairs, 1800-1823; (National Archives Microfilm Publication M271, roll 2, frames 1123-1125); Records of the Bureau of Indian Affairs, Record Group 75; National Archives Building, Washington, DC.

36. Letter from President Andrew Jackson to Secretary of War Eaton, November 18, 1830; Letters Received by the Office of Indian Affairs, 1824-1881 (National Archives Microfilm Publication M234, roll 113, frames 0131-0132); Records of the Bureau of Indian Affairs, Record Group 75; National Archives Building, Washington, DC.

37. Court order in *Worcester v. Georgia*, January 1832; 6 Pet 515, #1706; Records of the Supreme Court of the United States, Record Group 267; National Archives Building, Washington, DC.

38. Statement of the Protestant Episcopal Mission at Green Bay, September 30, 1833; Special Files of Office of Indian Affairs, 1807-1904 (National Archives Microfilm Publication; M574, roll 7, file 65, frame 0730); Records of the Bureau of Indian Affairs, Record Group 75; National Archives Building, Washington, DC.

39. Letter from Governor Gilmer to Colonel Sanford, April 20, 1831; Letters Received by Office of Indian Affairs, 1824-1881 (National Archives Microfilm Publication M234, roll 113, frames 0217-0219); Records of the Bureau of Indian Affairs, Record Group 75; National Archives Building, Washington, DC.

40. Enrolled Cherokee immigrants, March 31, 1832; Letters Received by Office of Indian Affairs, 1824-1881 (National Archives Microfilm Publication M234, roll 113); Records of the Bureau of Indian Affairs, Record Group 75; National Archives Building, Washington, DC.

41. Cherokee mortality schedule, December 30, 1837; Letters Received by Office of Indian Affairs, 1824-1881 (National Archives Microfilm Publication M234, roll 115, frame 1094); Records of the Bureau of Indian Affairs, Record Group 75; National Archives Building, Washington, DC.

42. Treaty of New Echota, March 14, 1835; Treaty, Cherokee Removal (SEN 24B-C4); 24th Congress; Records of the U.S. Senate, Record Group 46; National Archives Building, Washington, DC.

43. Memorial of Pennsylvanians opposed to Indian removal, January 10, 1830; Folder 4, Petition, Indian Removal (HR21A-68.2); 21st Congress; Records of the U.S. House of Representatives, Record Group 233; National Archives Building, Washington, DC.

44. Broadside of Orders #25 signed by General Scott, May 17, 1838; Letters Received by Office of Indian Affairs, 1824-1881 (National Microfilm Publication M234, roll 115, frame 0433); Records of the Bureau of Indian Affairs, Record Group 75; National Archives Building, Washington, DC.

45. Letter from Nathanial Smith to C.A. Harris with enclosures in Cherokee, March 15, 1838; Letters Received by Office of Indian Affairs, 1824-1881; (National Archives Microfilm Publication M234, roll 115, frames 0400-404); Records of the Bureau of Indian Affairs, Record Group 75; National Archives Building, Washington, DC.

46. Cherokee treaty map, Eastern lands, 1884; SF 106; Fifth Annual Report, Pl. VIII; Records of the Smithsonian Institution, Record Group 106; National Archives at College Park, College Park, MD.

47. Cherokee treaty map, Western lands, 1884; SF 106; Fifth Annual Report, Pl. IX; Records of the Smithsonian Institution, Record Group 106; National Archives at College Park, College Park, MD.

48. Map of territories disputed between Georgia and the Cherokee, ca. 1830; Central Map File 144; Close-up of Georgia/Cherokee disputed territories; Records of the Bureau of Indian Affairs, Record Group 75; National Archives at College Park, College Park, MD.

49. Map of the National Road, December 22, 1803; Road, Published Maps; Roads 354; Records of the Office of the Chief of Engineers, Record Group 77; National Archives at College Park, College Park, MD.

50. Map produced by the Long Expedition, 1820-1821; U.S. 62, File #107; Records of the Office of the Chief of Engineers, Record Group 77; National Archives at College Park, College Park, MD.

51. Snag boat design, ca. 1838; Civil Works Map; CONS 121; Records of the Office of the Chief of Engineers, Record Group 77; National Archives at College Park, College Park, MD.

52. Patent issued to Henry Shreve for snag boat, September 12, 1838; Civil Works Map File; CONS 121; Shreve's snag boat patent; Records of the Office of the Chief of Engineers, Record Group 77; National Archives at College Park, College Park, MD.

53. Patent drawing of the cotton gin, 1794; 72-x; Patent drawing of Cotton Gin; Records of the Patent and Trademark Office, Record Group 241; National Archives at College Park, College Park, MD.

54. Erie Railroad map, 1832-1833; Erie Railroad Map; U.S. Internal Improvements, Experimental Survey Manuscript, PT maps, #100; Records of the U.S. Senate, Record Group 46; National Archives Building, Washington, DC.

55. Burr's *Postal Atlas*, 1839; Sheet 1; United States, p. # 3 of 4, (Northwest quadrant map); Records of the Post Office Department, Record Group 28; National Archives Building, Washington, DC.

56. Minerals map, 1839-1841; Minerals Map #1, #2; MS Maps; 26th Congress; Records of the U.S. Senate, Record Group 46; National Archives Building, Washington, DC.

57. Map produced by the Pike Expedition, 1805-1806; M34, 4 large pieces; Special File #7; Records of the Office of the Chief of Engineers, Record Group 77; National Archives at College Park, College Park, MD.

58. Map based on the Lewis and Clark Expedition, 1806; AMA 21; Lewis and Clark Map; Records of the Office of the Chief of Engineers, Record Group 77; National Archives at College Park, College Park, MD.

59. Fort Dearborn groundplan and elevation, January 25, 1808; Fort Dearborn groundplan; Dr. 130, sheet 3; Records of the Office of the Chief of Engineers, Record Group 77; National Archives at College Park, College Park, MD.

60. Township plat, Alabama, Huntsville Meridian, Township 4 South, Range 5 East, 1822; T45, R5E, Huntsville Meridian; Records of the Bureau of Land Management, Record Group 49; National Archives at College Park, College Park, MD.

61. Proposed canal at Harper's Ferry, February 1803; C & O Canal #2; Records of the National Park Service, Record Group 79; National Archives at College Park, College Park, MD.

62. Painting No. 111-SC-92847; "Buffalo Dance of the Mandans," artwork by Karl Bodmer, 1833-34; Records of the Office of the Chief Signal Officer, 1833-1834; Record Group 111; National Archives at College Park, College Park, MD.

63. Painting No. 111-SC-93123; "Osceola," ca. 1837, artwork by George Catlin; Records of the Office of the Chief Signal Officer, Record Group 111; National Archives at College Park, College Park, MD.

About the National Archives:
A Word to Educators

The National Archives and Records Administration (NARA) is responsible for the preservation and use of the permanently valuable records of the federal government. These materials provide evidence of the activities of the government from 1774 to the present in the form of written and printed documents, maps and posters, sound recordings, photographs, films, computer tapes, and other media. These rich archival sources are useful to everyone: federal officials seeking information on past government activities, citizens needing data for use in legal matters, historians, social scientists and public policy planners, environmentalists, historic preservationists, medical researchers, architects and engineers, novelists and playwrights, journalists researching stories, students preparing papers, and persons tracing their ancestry or satisfying their curiosity about particular historical events. These records are useful to you as educators either in preparing your own instructional materials or pursuing your own research.

The National Archives records are organized by the governmental body that created them rather than under a library's subject/author/title categories. There is no Dewey decimal or Library of Congress designation; each departmental bureau or collection of agency's records is assigned a record group number. In lieu of a card catalog, inventories and other finding aids assist the researcher in locating material in records not originally created for research purposes, often consisting of thousands of cubic feet of documentation.

The National Archives is a public institution whose records and research facilities nationwide are open to anyone 14 years of age and over. These facilities are found in the Washington, DC, metropolitan area, in the 11 Presidential libraries, the Nixon Presidential Materials Project, and in 16 regional archives across the nation. Whether you are pursuing broad historical questions or are interested in the history of your family, admittance to the research room at each location requires only that you fill out a simple form stating your name, address, and research interest. A staff member then issues an identification card, which is good for two years.

If you come to do research, you will be offered an initial interview with a reference archivist. You will also be able to talk with archivists who have custody of the records. If you have a clear definition of your questions and have prepared in advance by reading as many of the secondary sources as possible, you will find that these interviews can be very helpful in guiding you to the research material you need.

The best printed source of information about the overall holdings of the National Archives is the *Guide to the National Archives of the United States* (issued in 1974, reprinted in 1988), which is available in university libraries and many public libraries and online at **www.nara.gov**. The *Guide* describes in very general terms the records in the National Archives, gives the background and history of each agency represented by those records, and provides useful information about access to the records. To accommodate users outside of Washington, DC, the regional archives hold microfilm copies of much that is found in Washington. In addition, the regional archives contain records created by field offices of the federal government, including district and federal appellate court records, records of the Bureau of Indian Affairs, National Park Service, Bureau of Land Management, Forest Service, Bureau of the Census, and others. These records are particularly useful for local and regional history studies and in linking local with national historical events.

For more information about the National Archives and its educational and cultural programs, visit NARA's Web site at **www.nara.gov**.

Presidential Libraries

Herbert Hoover Library
210 Parkside Drive
West Branch, IA 52358-0488
319-643-5301

Franklin D. Roosevelt Library
511 Albany Post Road
Hyde Park, NY 12538-1999
914-229-8114

Harry S. Truman Library
500 West U.S. Highway 24
Independence, MO 64050-1798
816-833-1400

Dwight D. Eisenhower Library
200 Southeast Fourth Street
Abilene, KS 67410-2900
785-263-4751

John Fitzgerald Kennedy Library
Columbia Point
Boston, MA 02125-3398
617-929-4500

Lyndon Baines Johnson Library
2313 Red River Street
Austin, TX 78705-5702
512-916-5137

Gerald R. Ford Library
1000 Beal Avenue
Ann Arbor, MI 48109-2114
734-741-2218

Jimmy Carter Library
441 Freedom Parkway
Atlanta, GA 30307-1498
404-331-3942

Ronald Reagan Library
40 Presidential Drive
Simi Valley, CA 93065-0600
805-522-8444/800-410-8354

George Bush Library
1000 George Bush Drive
P.O. Box 10410
College Station, TX 77842-0410
409-260-9552

Clinton Presidential Materials Project
1000 LaHarpe Boulevard
Little Rock, AR 72201
501-254-6866

National Archives Regional Archives

NARA-Northeast Region
380 Trapelo Road
Waltham, MA 02452-6399
781-647-8104

NARA-Northeast Region
10 Conte Drive
Pittsfield, MA 01201-8230
413-445-6885

NARA-Northeast Region
201 Varick Street, 12th Floor
New York, NY 10014-4811
212-337-1300

NARA-Mid Atlantic Region
900 Market Street
Philadelphia, PA 19107-4292
215-597-3000

NARA-Mid Atlantic Region
14700 Townsend Road
Philadelphia, PA 19154-1096
215-671-9027

NARA-Southeast Region
1557 St. Joseph Avenue
East Point, GA 30344-2593
404-763-7474

NARA-Great Lakes Region
7358 South Pulaski Road
Chicago, IL 60629-5898
773-581-7816

NARA-Great Lakes Region
3150 Springboro Road
Dayton, OH 45439-1883
937-225-2852

NARA-Central Plains Region
2312 East Bannister Road
Kansas City, MO 64131-3011
816-926-6272

NARA-Central Plains Region
200 Space Center Drive
Lee's Summit, MO 64064-1182
816-478-7079

NARA-Southwest Region
501 West Felix Street
P.O. Box 6216
Fort Worth, TX 76115-0216
817-334-5525

NARA-Rocky Mountain Region
Denver Federal Center, Building 48
P.O. Box 25307
Denver, CO 80225-0307
303-236-0804

NARA-Pacific Region
24000 Avila Road
P.O. Box 6719
Laguna Niguel, CA 92607-6719
949-360-2641

NARA-Pacific Region
1000 Commodore Drive
San Bruno, CA 94066-2350
650-876-9009

NARA-Pacific Alaska Region
6125 Sand Point Way, NE
Seattle, WA 98115-7999
206-526-6507

NARA-Pacific Alaska Region
654 West Third Avenue
Anchorage, AK 99501-2145
907-271-2443

Reproductions of Documents

Reproductions of the oversized print documents included in these units are available in their original size by special order from Graphic Visions.

MAY 20, 1785.

An ORDINANCE for afcertaining the Mode of difpofing of LANDS in the WESTERN TERRITORY.

BE IT ORDAINED BY THE UNITED STATES IN CONGRESS ASSEMBLED, That the territory ceded by individual ftates, to the United States, which has been purchafed of the Indian inhabitants, fhall be difpofed of in the following manner.——

A furveyor from each ftate fhall be appointed by Congrefs or a Committee of the States, who fhall take an oath for the faithful difcharge of his duty, before the geographer of the United States, who is hereby empowered and directed to adminifter the fame; and the like oath fhall be adminiftered to each chain carrier, by the furveyor under whom he acts.

The geographer, under whofe direction the furveyors fhall act, fhall occafionally form fuch regulations for their conduct, as he fhall deem neceffary; and fhall have authority to fufpend them for mifconduct in office, and fhall make report of the fame to Congrefs or to the Committee of the States; and he fhall make report in cafe of ficknefs, death, or refignation of any furveyor.

The furveyors, as they are refpectively qualified, fhall proceed to divide the faid territory into townfhips of fix miles fquare, by lines running due north and fouth, and others croffing thefe at right angles, as near as may be, unlefs where the boundaries of the late Indian purchafes may render the fame impracticable, and then they fhall depart from this rule no farther than fuch particular circumftances may require. And each furveyor fhall be allowed and paid at the rate of two dollars for every mile in length he fhall run, including the wages of chain carriers, markers, and every other expence attending the fame.

The firft line running north and fouth as aforefaid, fhall begin on the river Ohio, at a point that fhall be found to be due north from the weftern termination of a line which has been run as the fouthern boundary of the ftate of Pennfylvania: and the firft line running eaft and weft, fhall begin at the fame point, and fhall extend throughout the whole territory; provided that nothing herein fhall be conftrued, as fixing the weftern boundary of the ftate of Pennfylvania. The geographer fhall defignate the townfhips or fractional parts of townfhips, by numbers progreffively from fouth to north; always beginning each range with No. 1; and the ranges fhall be diftinguifhed by their progreffive numbers to the weftward. The firft range extending from the Ohio to the lake Erie, being marked No. 1. The geographer fhall perfonally attend to the running of the firft eaft and weft line; and fhall take the latitude of the extremes of the firft north and fouth line, and of the mouths of the principal rivers.

The lines fhall be meafured with a chain; fhall be plainly marked by chaps on the trees, and exactly defcribed on a plat; whereon fhall be noted by the furveyor, at their proper diftances, all mines, falt fprings, falt licks and mill feats, that fhall come to his knowledge; and all water-courfes, mountains and other remarkable and permanent things over or near which fuch lines fhall pafs, and alfo the quality of the lands.

The plats of the townfhips refpectively, fhall be marked by fubdivifions into lots of one mile fquare, or 640 acres, in the fame direction as the external lines, and numbered from 1 to 36; always beginning the fucceeding range of the lots with the number next to that with which the preceding one concluded: And where from the caufes before mentioned, only a fractional part of a townfhip fhall be furveyed, the lots protracted thereon, fhall bear the fame numbers as if the townfhip had been entire. And the furveyors in running the external lines of the townfhips, fhall at the interval of every mile, mark corners for the lots which are adjacent, always defignating the fame in a different manner from thofe of the townfhips.

The geographer and furveyors, fhall pay the utmoft attention to the variation of the magnetic needle; and fhall run and note all lines by the true meridian, certifying with every plat what was the variation at the times of running the lines thereon noted.

As foon as feven ranges of townfhips, and fractional parts of townfhips, in the direction from fouth to north, fhall have been furveyed, the geographer fhall tranfmit plats thereof to the board of treafury, who fhall record the fame with the report, in well bound books to be kept for that purpofe. And the geographer fhall make fimilar returns from time to time of every feven ranges as they may be furveyed. The fecretary at war fhall have recourfe thereto, and fhall take by lot therefrom, a number of townfhips and fractional parts of townfhips, as well from thofe to be fold entire, as from thofe to be fold in lots, as will be equal to one feventh part of the whole of fuch feven ranges, as nearly as may be, for the ufe of the late continental army; and he fhall make a fimilar draught from time to time, until a fufficient quantity is drawn to fatisfy the fame, to be applied in manner hereinafter directed. The board of treafury fhall from time to time, caufe the remaining numbers, as well thofe to be fold entire, as thofe to be fold in lots, to be drawn for, in the name of the thirteen ftates refpectively, according to the quotas in the laft preceding requifition on all the ftates: provided that in cafe more land than its proportion is allotted for fale in any ftate at any diftribution, a deduction be made therefor at the next.

The board of treafury fhall tranfmit a copy of the original plats, previoufly noting thereon, the townfhips and fractional parts of townfhips, which fhall have fallen to the feveral ftates by the diftribution aforefaid, to the commiffioners of the loan-office of the feveral ftates, who, after giving notice of not lefs than two nor more than fix months, by caufing advertifements to be pofted up at the court-houfes or other noted places in every county, and to be inferted in one newfpaper publifhed in the ftates of their refidence refpectively, fhall proceed to fell the townfhips or fractional parts of townfhips, at public vendue, in the following manner, viz. The townfhip or fractional part of a townfhip No. 1, in the firft range, fhall be fold entire; and No. 2, in the fame range, by lots; and thus in alternate order through the whole of the firft range. The townfhip or fractional part of a townfhip No. 1, in the fecond range, fhall be fold by lots; and No. 2 in the fame range, entire; and fo in alternate order through the whole of the fecond range; and the third range fhall be fold in the fame manner as the firft, and the fourth in the fame manner as the fecond, and thus alternately throughout all the ranges: provided that none of the lands within the faid territory, be fold under the price of one dollar the acre, to be paid in fpecie or loan-office certificates, reduced to fpecie value by the fcale of depreciation, or certificates of liquidated debts of the United States, including intereft, befides the expence of the furvey and other charges thereon, which are hereby rated at thirty-fix dollars the townfhip, in fpecie or certificates as aforefaid, and fo in the fame proportion for a fractional part of a townfhip or of a lot, to be paid at the time of fales, on failure of which payment, the faid lands fhall again be offered for fale.

There fhall be referved for the United States out of every townfhip, the four lots, being numbered 8, 11, 26, 29, and out of every fractional part of a townfhip, fo many lots of the fame numbers as fhall be found thereon, for future fale. There fhall be referved the lot No. 16, of every townfhip, for the maintainance of public fchools within the faid townfhip; alfo one third part of all gold, filver, lead and copper mines, to be fold, or otherwife difpofed of, as Congrefs fhall hereafter direct.

When any townfhip or fractional part of a townfhip fhall have been fold as aforefaid, and the money or certificates received therefor, the loan officer fhall deliver a deed in the following terms.

The UNITED STATES of AMERICA, to all to whom thefe prefents fhall come greeting.

Know ye, that for the confideration of   dollars, we have granted, and hereby do grant and confirm unto   the townfhip [or fractional part of the townfhip, as the cafe may be] numbered   in the   range, excepting therefrom, and referving one third part of all gold, filver, lead and copper mines within the fame; and the lots No. 8, 11, 26, and 29, for future fale or difpofition; and the lot No. 16, for the maintainance of public fchools. To have to the faid   his heirs and affigns forever; (or if more than one purchafer, to the faid   and their heirs and affigns forever as tenants in common.) In witnefs whereof, A. B. commiffioner of the loan-office in the ftate of hath, in conformity to the ordinance paffed by the United States in Congrefs affembled, the   day of   in the year of our Lord   , hereunto fet his hand, and affixed his feal, this   day of in the year of our Lord   and of the independence of the United States of America

And when any townfhip or fractional part of a townfhip fhall be fold by lots as aforefaid, the commiffioner of the loan-office fhall deliver a deed therefor in the following form.

The UNITED STATES of AMERICA, to all to whom thefe prefents fhall come greeting.

Know ye, That for the confideration of   dollars, we have granted, and hereby do grant and confirm unto   the lot (or lots as the cafe may be) numbered   in the townfhip (or fractional part of the townfhip, as the cafe may be) numbered   in the range,   excepting and referving one third part of all gold, filver, lead and copper mines within the fame, for future fale or difpofition. To have to the faid   his heirs and affigns forever; (or if more than one purchafer, to the faid   their heirs and affigns forever as tenants in common.) In witnefs whereof, A. B. commiffioner of the loan-office in the ftate of   hath, in conformity to the ordinance paffed by the United States in Congrefs affembled, the   day of   in the year of our Lord   , hereunto fet his hand, and affixed his feal, this   day of   in the year of our Lord   and of the independence of the United States of America

Which deeds fhall be recorded in proper books, by the commiffioners of the loan-office, and fhall be certified to have been recorded, previous to their being delivered to the purchafer, and fhall be good and valid to convey the lands in the fame defcribed.

The commiffioners of the loan-offices refpectively, fhall tranfmit to the board of treafury every three months, an account of the townfhips, fractional parts of townfhips, and lots committed to their charge; fpecifying therein the names of the perfons to whom fold; and the fums of money or certificates received for the fame. And fhall caufe all certificates by them received, to be ftruck through with a circular punch; and they fhall be duly charged in the books of the treafury, with the amount of the monies or certificates, diftinguifhing the fame, by them received as aforefaid.

If any townfhip or fractional part of a townfhip or lot, remains unfold for eighteen months, after the plat fhall have been received by the commiffioners of the loan office, the fame fhall be returned to the board of treafury, and fhall be fold in fuch manner as Congrefs may hereafter direct.

And whereas Congrefs by their refolutions of September 16th and 18th, in the year 1776, and the 12th of Auguft 1780, ftipulated grants of land to certain officers and foldiers of the late continental army, and by the refolution of 22d September 1780, ftipulated grants of land to certain officers in the hofpital department of the late continental army; for complying therefore with fuch engagements, Be it ordained, That the fecretary at war, from the returns in his office, or fuch other fufficient evidence as the nature of the cafe may admit, determine who are the objects of the above refolutions and engagements, and the quantity of land to which such persons or their representatives are respectively entitled, and cause the townships or fractional parts of townships herein before reserved for the use of the late continental army, to be drawn for in such manner as he shall deem expedient, to answer the purpose of an impartial distribution. He shall from time to time transmit certificates, to the commissioners of the loan offices of the different states, to the lines of which the military claimants have respectively belonged, specifying the name and rank of the party, the terms of his engagement, and time of his service, and the division, brigade, regiment or company to which he belonged, the quantity of land he is entitled to, and the township or fractional part of a township and range out of which his portion is to be taken.

The commissioners of the loan offices shall execute deeds for such undivided proportions in manner and form herein before mentioned, varying only in such a degree as to make the same conformable to the certificate from the secretary at war.

Where any military claimants of bounty in lands shall not have belonged to the line of any particular state, similar certificates shall be sent to the board of treasury, who shall execute deeds to the parties for the same.

The secretary at war, from the proper returns, shall transmit to the board of treasury, a certificate, specifying the name and rank of the several claimants of the hospital department of the late continental army, together with the quantity of land each claimant is entitled to, and the township or fractional part of a township and range out of which his portion is to be taken; and thereupon the board of treasury shall proceed to execute deeds to such claimants.

The board of treasury, and the commissioners of the loan-offices in the states, shall within eighteen months, return receipts to the secretary at war, for all deeds which have been delivered, as also all the original deeds which remain in their hands for want of applicants, having been first recorded; which deeds so returned, shall be preserved in the office, until the parties or their representatives require the same.

And be it further ordained, That three townships adjacent to lake Erie, be reserved to be hereafter disposed of by Congress, for the use of the officers, men, and others, refugees from Canada, and the refugees from Nova-Scotia, who are or may be entitled to grants of land under resolutions of Congress now existing, or which may hereafter be made respecting them, and for such other purposes as Congress may hereafter direct.

And be it further ordained, That the towns of Gnadenhutten, Schoenbrun and Salem, on the Muskingum, and so much of the lands adjoining to the said towns, with the buildings and improvements thereon, shall be reserved for the sole use of the Christian Indians, who were formerly settled there, or the remains of that society, as may, in the judgment of the geographer, be sufficient for them to cultivate.

Saving and reserving always, to all officers and soldiers entitled to lands on the northwest side of the Ohio, by donation or bounty from the commonwealth of Virginia, and to all persons claiming under them, all rights to which they are so entitled, under the deed of cession executed by the delegates for the state of Virginia, on the first day of March, 1784, and the act of Congress, accepting the same; and to the end that the said rights may be fully and effectually secured, according to the true intent and meaning of the said deed of cession and act aforesaid: Be it ordained, that no part of the land included between the rivers called little Miami and Scioto, on the northwest side of the river Ohio, be sold, or in any manner alienated, until there shall first have been laid off and appropriated for the said officers and soldiers, and persons claiming under them, the lands they are entitled to, agreeably to the said deed of cession and act of Congress accepting the same.

DONE *by the* UNITED STATES *in* CONGRESS ASSEMBLED, *the Twentieth Day of May, in the Year of our Lord One Thousand Seven Hundred and Eighty-five, and of our Sovereignty and Independence the Ninth.*

RICHARD HENRY LEE, P.

of the Proceedings of His Excellency Arthur St Clair
Governour & Commander in Chief of the Territory
the United States North west of the River Ohio.

―――――――

On Wednesday the 9th of July 1788 His Excellency arrived
at ~~the Muskingum~~, & on the 15th was published the Ordi
:nance of the honourable Congress for the Government
of the Territory — the Commissions of the Governour,
the honourable Judges Samuel Holden Parsons, James
Mitchell Varnum, and the Secretary: — after
which His Excellency addressed the People assembled
at _Marietta_; as follows.—

From the Ordinance for the Establishment of civil
Government in this Quarter, that has been just now
read, you have a Proof Gentlemen of the Attention
of Congress to the Welfare of the Citizens of the United
States how remote soever their Situation may be.

A good Government well administered is the first of
Blessings to a People — every thing desirable in Life is
thereby secured to them, & from the Operation of who=
:lesome & equal Laws, the Passions of Men are restrained
within due Bounds & their Actions receive a proper
direction; the Virtues are cultivated, & the beautiful
Fabric of civilized Life is reared & brought to Perfection.

The Executive Part of the Administration of this Gov=
:ernment has been entrusted to me, & I am truly sen:
:sible of the Importance of the Trust, & how much de:
:pends upon the due Execution of it — to you Gentlemen
over whom it is to be immediately exercised! to your
Posterity! perhaps to the whole Community of Ame
:rica!— Would to God I were more equal to the Discharge
of it! but my best Endeavours shall not be wanting to
fulfil the Desire & the Expectations of Congress, that you
may find yourselves happy under it; which is the su:
:rest Way for me, at once, to meet their Approbation, &
to render it honourable to myself: Nor, when I reflect

Document 2a. Address by Governor Arthur St. Clair at his inauguration, July 9, 1788. [National Archives] upon the Characters of the Men under whose immediate Influence & Example this particular Settlement, which will probably give a Tone to all that may succeed it, will be formed, have I much Reason to fear a Disappointment—Men who duly weigh the Importance to Society of a strict Attention to the Duties of Religion & Morality; in whose Bosoms the Love of Liberty & of Order is a masterly Passion;—who respect the Rights of Mankind & have sacrificed much to support them, & who are no Strangers to the Decencies & to the Elegancies of Life. I esteem it also a singular Happiness, to you and to me that the Gentlemen appointed to the judicial Department are of such distinguished Characters & so well known to you—on one Side the Respect which is due to their Stations is secured; whilst on the other it will be yielded with the most perfect good Will.

You will observe Gentlemen, that the System which has been formed for this Country, & is now to take Effect, is temporary only—suited to your Infant Situation, & to continue no longer than that State of Infancy shall last: during that Period the Judges, with my Assistance are to select from the Codes of the Mother States such Laws as may be thought proper for you. This is a very important Part of our Duty, & will be attended to with the greatest Care—But Congress have not wholly intrusted this great Business to our Prudence or Discretion;—& here again you have a fresh Proof of their Paternal Attention.—We are bound to report to them all Laws which shall be introduced, & they have reserved to themselves the Power of annulling them—So that if any Law not proper in itself, or not suited to your Circumstances, either from our not seeing the whole Extent of its Opera: tion, or any other Circumstance should be imposed it will be immediately repealed. But with all the Care & Attention to your Interest & Happiness that can be taken, you have many Difficulties to struggle with—The subduing a new Country, notwithstanding its natural Advantages, is alone an arduous Task;—a Task

Document 2b. Address by Governor Arthur St. Clair at his inauguration, July 9, 1788. [National Archives]

however that Patience & Perseverance will surmount, & these Virtues so necessary in every Situation, but peculiarly so in yours, you must resolve to exercise—neither in the reducing a Country from a State of Nature to a State of Civilization so irksome as it may appear from a slight or superficial View — even very sensible Pleasures attend it;— the gradual Progress of Impro:—:vement fills the Mind with delectable Ideas — Vast forests converted into arable Fields, & Cities rising in Places which were lately the Habitation of wild Beasts give Pleasure something like that atten:—:dant on Creation, if we can form an Idea of it—The Imagination is ravished, & a Taste communi:—:cated of even the Joy of God to see a happy World."—

The Advantages however are not merely ima:—:ginary — situated as you are in the most tem:—:perate Climate, favour'd with the most fer:—:tile Soil, surrounded by the noblest & most beautiful Rivers, every Portion of Labour will meet its due Reward: But you have upon your Frontiers numbers of savage and, too often, hostile Nations — against them it is necessary that you should be guarded, & the Measures that may be thought proper for that End, tho' they may a little interrupt your usual Pursuits, I am certain, will be cheerfully submitted to.— One Mode however I will at this Time venture to recommend, which as it is in every Point of View the easiest & most eligible, so I am persuaded it will be attended with much Success — Endeavour to cultivate a good Understan:—:ding with the Natives, without much Familiarity; Treat them on all Occasions with Kindness & the strictest Regard to Justice; Run not into their Cus:—:toms & Habits, which is but too frequent with those who settle near them, but Endeavour to induce them to adopt yours; Prevent, by every Means, that dreadful Reproach, perhaps too justly brought by them against all the People they have been yet acquainted with, That, professing the most holy & benevolent Religion

they are uninfluenced by its Dictates & regardless of its
Precepts — Such a Conduct will produce on their Parts
the utmost Confidence — they will soon become sen-
:sible of the superior Advantages of a State of Civilizat:
:ion — They will gradually lose their present Manners,
& a Way be opened for introducing amongst them the
Gospel of Peace, & you be the happy Instruments in
the Hand of Providence of bringing forward that Time
which will surely arrive, when all the Nations of the
Earth shall become the Kingdom of JESUS CHRIST.

The present Situation of the Country calls for Atten-
:tion in various Places, & will necessarily induce
frequent Absence both of the Judges & myself, from this
delightful Spot, but at all Times & Places as it is my
indispensable Duty, so it is very much my Desire to do
every Thing within the Compass of my Power for the
Peace, good Order & perfect Establishment of the
Settlement — & as I look, for, not only, a cheerful
Acquiescence in, & Submission to, necessary Measures
but a cordial Cooperation, so I flatter myself my
well meant Endeavours will be accepted in the
Spirit in which they are rendered, & our Satisfaction
will be mutual and complete.

Copy of a Letter to the Judges
upon the Subject of a Militia Law.

Fort Harmar July the 18th, 1788

Gentlemen

I have looked over the proposed Law
for establishing the Militia, & I have some Objections
to it in its present Form, which I shall take the
Liberty to detail. — In the Title Page is ought it
not to be styled the Militia Law of the United
States — if these Words "United States" were expunged
the Title would be well enough. — The enacting

No. 86

LAND-OFFICE at Marietta
Decem 27th 1811

It is hereby certified,

That pursuant to an act of Congress, passed on the 10th day of May, 1800, entitled " An act to amend the act, entitled " An act providing for the sale of the lands of the United States, in the territory north-west of the Ohio, and above the mouth of Kentucky river," *Thomas Dickinson* of Ohio County Virginia on the *fifteenth* day of *December 1804* purchased of the Register of the Land-office at *Marietta* the lot or section numbered *Twenty Seven* in the township No. *one* in the *fifth* range of the *Marietta* district, containing *four hundred and three* acres, and *four hundred th.* at the rate of *two* dollars and _____ cents per acre, for which *full* section account therefor being finally settled and closed in the books of this office, as will appear by the following statement thereof, viz.

the said *Thomas Dickinson* has made full payment, his

DEBIT.

	$
(1804)	
Decr 15 To amount of purchase money	806 08
(1809)	
Nov 9 To Interest on 3 & 4 Instalt }	120 91
(1810)	
Decr 15 To Ditto on 362,95 the bal 79	
(1811)	
To Interest for one year	24 75
Decr 15 To Ditto on ___ Due }	12 03
purchase money ___	960 80

CREDIT.

	$
(1805)	
Novr 8 By amount of 1st Instalment	204 52
(1806)	
Decemr By amount of 2d Ditto	204 52
(1809)	
Nov 9 By cash paid this Day	161 00
Dec 15 By cash &c	183 24
(1811)	
Dec 15 By cash in full	213 55
Doll	960 80

Now THEREFORE, BE IT KNOWN, That on presentation of this certificate to the Secretary of the Treasury,

shall be entitled to receive a patent for the lot or section

above described.

Joseph Wood
REGISTER OF THE LAND-OFFICE.

To the Honorable the Senate and House of Representatives of the United States of America, in Congress assembled.

THE Subscribers, inhabitants of the state of Ohio, by their Petition, respectfully pray—That your honorable bodies will be pleased to extend the law of Congress passed the second day of March, 1809, entitled " An act to extend the time of making payment for the public lands of the United States, so as to relievet he purchasers of the public lands in a similar mannier as in the years 1805, and 1806." The same embarrassments, and from the same reasons ; the same scarcity of circulating medium, and from the same causes, operate to distress your petitioners, as was set forth by many of us in our humble petition to your honorable bodies at your last annual session. Your petitioners find the means of payment suspended in a greater degree, than was felt last year ; little emigration ; no market for our surplus produce, and forbidding prospects of collecting our money from those that purchased our real or personal property in states from whence we emigrated, in time to make our payments to the United States, as stipulated by the laws of Congress now in force.

Your petitioners also further pray, that your honorable bodies will be pleased to grant a pre-emption to the original purchaser, or his or their assignee or assignees, who was legally entitled to the survey so forfeited, had he or they made the payments agreeably to the laws now in force. This humane, and to us, beneficial regulation, will prevent the greedy speculators from depriving us of the comforts of our labor and honest industry, and often save us and our helpless families from total ruin. Many of your petitioners have made large improvements on our lands, under a full conviction that we should be per-

fectly able to complete our payments, agreeably to the laws of the United States—But the possibility of a failure in payment, from the causes before adverted to, has brought amongst us a number of land speculators, men who live on the sweat from other men's brows, who generally place themselves in the most considerable towns in the state, and particularly in those towns where the land-offices are fixed—At the public sales for the non-payment of lands, (which happens three times in every year, i. e. at every court of common pleas) these adventurers closely attend the sales, frequently to the number of twenty or thirty, and sometimes to the exclusion of the ignorant farmer from the office ; and immediately on the reversion of the lands to the United States, apply in a body, and often obtain the very lands which we have toiled and labored on for years, and thereby made the wilderness a smiling paradise—From this property we are immediately dispossessed, and by such persons, and by such means ; or we must comply with their terms, which generally is, to give our bonds to the fortunate speculator for a considerable sum, sometimes more than the original price of the land, and also take the future payments to the United States on ourselves—The payment of these obligations, disenables us to comply with the future payments to the United States ; and only procrastinates the day of poverty and distress a few years longer.—Much more could be detailed on this, to us, important subject ; but we forbear—believing and depending in the wisdom and justice of Congress to grant us such relief, as in their superior wisdom may seem meet.—And your petitioners, as in duty bound, will ever pray.

Samuel Bunn

John Cutright first

Abner Espey

Benjamin Ross

John P. Ross

John Montgomery

James Morrison

Thomas Esey

James Morison

William

Joseph Minks

William Montgomery

Hughs M

Kennedy

John Russell

Moses M. Earl

Joseph Lockard

Daniel

Abraham Doll

Jas M. Kinney

William Pyle

Edward Salts

Lawson Linton

Linton

20 petitioners

Document 4. Petition of Ohioans regarding land sale policy, January 10, 1810. [National Archives]

Kentucky Gazette.

"True to his charge—he comes, the Herald of a noisy world : News from all nations hurab'ring at his back."

NEW SERIES—NO. 41. VOL. V.]   LEXINGTON, K. FRIDAY, OCTOBER 8, 1819.   [VOL. XXXIII.

TERMS OF THE

Kentucky Gazette,

PUBLISHED EVERY FRIDAY MORNING,

By Norvell & Cavins.

☞ The price to Subscribers, is, THREE DOLLARS per annum, PAID IN ADVANCE, or FOUR DOLLARS at the end of the year.

☞ The terms of ADVERTISING in this paper, are, FIFTY CENTS for the first insertion of every 15 lines or under, and TWENTY-FIVE CENTS for each continuance; longer advertisements in the same proportion.

☞ All advertisements not paid for in advance, must be paid for when ordered to be discontinued.

☞ All communications addressed to the editors must be post paid.

NEW GOODS.

GEORGE TROTTER & SON,

In addition to their former Importation last month, have received a further supply of the most

ELEGANT AND FASHIONABLE

GOODS,

For the Spring and Summer,

That the Philadelphia Market affords : which, having been purchased upon the most moderate terms, they are determined to sell extremely low for CASH IN HAND.

PART OF THE ASSORTMENT CONSISTS OF THE FOLLOWING ARTICLES, VIZ.

DAMASK and plain Canton and Ceurban Crapes, black, blue, crimson, pink, yellow, orange, black, drab and brown.

Canton Crape Shawls, and Scarfs of same colours

Thread and Silk Laces, Edgings & Insertings

Parasols and Umbrellas

Straw Bonnets and suitable Trimmings

Plain and figured Moll Mull and Jacconett Muslins 4-4 and 6-4 wide

Fine wide Muslins, white and pink stripe

Florence, Lutestring & Levantine Silks, black and changeable colours

Yellow and blue Nankeens

Blue and striped Cotton Cassimeres

Irish, Scotch and Russia sheetings

German and Irish Linens

Steam Loom and New England Shirtings

Bed Tickings of every price and qual'ty

Cloths and Cassimeres, well assorted

Blue, mixt and brown Cassinetts

Ladies' black and coloured Morocco Shoes & Booteos, plain and figured, with and without heels

Low priced Hats

Elegant and common Knives and Forks

Plaid, striped and chambray Cottons

6-4 and 4-4 Linen and Cotton Checks

Liverpool China and common Ware, completely assorted

Flowered Paper by the piece, and in setts for rooms

And every other article in their line of business.

Lexington, June 21, 1819—29tf

Shreve and Combs,

HAVE JUST RECEIVED,

And are now opening for Sale,

ONE CASE of elegant double barreled FOWLING PIECES, London make, with scroll guards, double rollers, rain pan locks, break offs, silver escutcheons, platina holes, gold bands, &c.

ONE CASE single barreled do. with spider sights, &c. &c.

One Cask of Hardware,

CONSISTING

Freight standing Vices, assorted

Brass bushed Coffee Mills

Black Pump Hammers

Saddler's Hammers

Brass battery Kettles, wired and bailed

10 inch Patent Brick Trowels, riveted

Bright Thumb Latches and Iron Squares

Iron and Brass headed Shovel and Tongs

Patent Box Coffee Mills

Steel Yards, from 50 to 250lbs.

Patent Beams

Strong Ward plate Stock Locks

Fancy plate   do.   do.

6 bored Curry Combs

Iron Sash Pullies

Japan'd Norfolk Thumb Latches

Do. Chest Handles

4, 5, 6 inch closet Locks, complete

6, 7, 8, 9 do. Knob Locks, do.

Fine Fancy bitted Pad, double bolted Pad, Cupboard and Chest Locks

4 keyed Till and Trunk Locks

Brass Bag Locks

Bright Hand Vices

Sadler's Punches, assorted

Shoe Pincheers and Screws, assorted

Joint Compasses and Ship Augurs

Chest Hinges

Short handled Frying Pans, assorted

ALLO FOR SALE,

Superior Domestic COTTONS,

Manufactured at Providence, (R. I.)

CONSISTING OF

GINGHAMS,

STRIPES,

PLAIDS,

CHAMBRAYS,

CHECKS, and

TICKING.

All which will be sold low for cash.

SHREVE & COMBS,

Auc'rs. & Com. Merchants.

August 19.—33tf

NOTICE.

THE subscriber contemplates going to the eastward in a few days, and requests those indebted to him, either by bond, note or book account, to come forward and settle their respective dues, as no further indulgence can be given by their obedient servant,

ROBERT J. GATEWOOD.

Lexington, Sept. 3, 1819.—36tf

Cash in Hand

Will be given for 2 NEGRO BOYS and 1 GIRL of an unexceptionable character.

Enquire of the Printers.

June, 34, 1819—22tf

NEW GOODS.

Thompson & January,

HAVE just received and are now opening, at their store on Main-street, formerly occupied by TANDY & ALLEN, a general assortment, suitable for the present and coming season, consisting of

Black Canton Crapes

Fancy coloured ditto

Thread Laces and Lace Veils

Merino Shawls

Lace Pellerines and Handkerchiefs

Best doubled Levantines

— Sundones and Florences

— Bumbazines and Bombaretts

Plain and figured Ribbons, assorted

Plain and figured Jacconet, Book, Mull and Leno Muslin

4-4 and 6-4 Cambric, assorted

Do   do Ginghams, assorted

White and coloured Cotton Socks, ass'd

Black and white Silk Stockings and Socks

Ditto and coloured worsted   ditto

Corded Velvet and Velveteens

London superfine Cloths and Cassimeres

Blue, mixed and brown Cassinetts

Striped and white Jeans

Superfine white and printed Marsailles, with a variety of Silk & other Vestings

Steam Loom and Cambric Shirtings

Irish Linens and Long Lawns

Linen and Cotton Checks

Light and dark Calicoes

Furniture and Cambric Dimities

Black and Fancy Silk Handkerchiefs

Company and Flag Bandanas

Buckskin, Beaver, Kid and Silk Gloves

Linen Cambric and Cambric Handk'fs

Domestic Cottons and Checks

Do   Stripes and Chambrays

Do   Shirtings and Sheetings

Plain and Furniture Checks

A large quantity of excellent Tow Linen

Also, a General assortment of

GROCERIES,

Real French Brandy

Do   Madeira Wine

Very old Jamaica Spirits

Old Whiskey

Loaf and Lump Sugar

Spices and Dye-stuffs in great variety

Together with a large quantity of

Liverpool and Queensware.

All of which they will sell very low for Cash.

They have also on Commission, Bakewell, Page & Bakewell's

Common, Engraved and Cut Glassware, by the Box, at Pittsburgh prices.

Likewise a large assortment open for the accommodation of private families, with Black Porter and Claret Bottles.

Hamilton's best Maccoboy Snuff, and Real Spanish Segars, at reduced prices.

Lexington, July 9, 1819—29t

Dancing Academy.

JOHN DARRAC,

(Professor of Dancing,)

RESPECTFULLY informs his friends and the public generally, that he

Dancing School,

Will open on Friday the 20th instant, in the elegant room formerly of the Kentucky Hotel, which he is now preparing for that purpose, next door to Maj. Morrison's house.

Persons desirous of being instructed, are solicited to make immediate application to J. DARRAC, at the above place, or at Mr. Wickliffe's Inn.

Days of tuition, Friday and Saturday, every week. Number of lessons per quarter, thirty two.

☞Terms as heretofore.

A night School will also be opened for gentlemen, as soon as a sufficient number is made up.

32tf   August 13, 1819.

Asa Blanchard,

REPAIRS WATCHES and CLOCKS of every description in the best manner. He keeps constantly on hand, a large assortment of the best

Silver Ware, Watches & Jewelry, Steel Chains & Keys, Patent Time Pieces,

Also, Masonic Breastpins,

Made neatly strongest and neatest manner. All of which will be sold as low as any in the state, of the same quality. Opposite the Ky. Branch Bank of Lexington.

September 9.—37tf

AUCTION NOTICE.

Charles Edwards,

INFORMS his friends and the public, that he will attend to Sales at Auction, of his own account, } of Real and Personal Estates, Merchandise, Bank Stock, &c. and solicits a share of public patronage, which by his attention to the interests of his employers he will endeavor to merit. Apply to him at the Store of Messrs. Shreve & Combs, where all orders will meet prompt attention.

CHARLES EDWARDS, Auc.

September 14.—38tm

OHIO MONEY

RECEIVED FOR SALT.

WM. SNELLING will receive the following Bank Notes for SALT :

Lancaster, Ohio,

Marietta, Do.

Columbus, do.

Bank of Cincinnati,

The two Banks of Steubenville,

Old Bank of Chillicothe,

Western Reserve,

North Western Bank of Virginia,

The Bank of the Valley of Winchester,

And both the old Bank of Kentucky and United States will not be refused.

A constant supply will be kept on hand and sold at the lowest rate, wholesale and retail, corner of Main-Cross street.

Be also sells for Sale,

A Dearborn Wagon & Handsome Gig

With harness complete—Likewise

ONE HANDSOME GIG HORSE

Lexington, August 19, 1812—34-8t

Replevin Bonds,

FOR SALE AT THIS OFFICE.

To the Public.

THE Trustees of the Transylvania University, in communicating to the public that the ensuing session will commence on Wednesday the 29th of this month, have the satisfaction to state that, during the past year, the most gratifying progress have been afforded of the improved condition of the institution. The number of students greatly exceeded that of any prior year since the establishment of the University, and their progress in education, as evinced at the late commencement, was highly creditable to their diligence and to the ability of their instructors. They are so happy results of the just confidence of the community in the present, professors and tutors, and of the system of regulations prepared, with great care, for the government of the College, after consulting the experience of the most highly reputed seminaries in the United States. It was not to be anticipated that this system, in all its parts would command unanimous approbation, and accordingly one or two of its provisions have been the subject of some animadversion. It has been objected, that the vacation is too long, and that it would be better to divide it between different parts of the year. The entire period of vacation is less in this college than in any other whose bye-laws the Trustees have had an opportunity of examining. It was considered preferable to assign the whole of it in the warm months of the summer and September, when a certain degree of relaxation is necessary, than to appropriate any portion of it to the winter, the most favorable season for intense study. Nor will the time be lost by the industrious student, who will employ it in a review of his past studies, in preparation for the future, in acquiring ornamental accomplishments. The practice varies, in this respect, in other colleges, according to the peculiar condition of the society where they happen to be situate. In William and Mary the vacation, much longer than it is here, is altogether in the summer and early part of the fall. The trustees, in all the regulations which they have adopted, having had the object constantly in view of rendering the University useful and respectable, will not fail to change this or any other regulation which shall be found incompatible with that object, or contrary to the wishes of the public, whose convenience they will be always anxious to consult and promote. They have afforded a revision of the disposition by requiring the requisition, upon evidence entering in advanced classes, to pay the tuition fees incident to the previous classes.

They will require the performance of divine Service at least once every Sabbath in the chapel of the University, but also leave the subject of some observations. It is in the following terms: "It shall be the duty of the President, whilst in office, and of the Professors, to perform divine service, on every Sabbath, at least once, in the Chapel of the University, to such officers and students as may choose to attend: and it is particularly enjoined upon the students to attend public worship somewhere on the Sabbath." It will be seen that it is permanent, exclusively applicable to no existing incumbent, and entirely optional on the part of those who may attend the service. A similar regulation exists in most, if not in every other well reputed college in the U. States, with this important difference, that in there it is compulsory. Independent of the leaning thought proper that the students should participate in divine service some where on the Sabbath, it was thought that the greater number, if not all of the bye-laws of public worship for the year. As the students, many of whom live in common, detached from the families of the place, could not of right attend at these places, without incurring expense not to be reasonable. And it is particularly desirable to secure them some certain place in which they might go without the danger of intrusion. The duty to perform the service, which is enjoined by the rule is, considered by the faculty as onerous, and from a wish to be economical. Nothing was farther from the intention of the trustees than to propagate, by means of this regulation, the peculiar tenets of any sect, and nothing they believe is further from the fact than any new or extraordinary doctrines have been advanced under its operation. Both the Board of Trustees and the Faculty, comprising within their respective bodies, persons attached to various denominations of religion, would feel it just as difficult to agree among themselves, as the great mass of the community do, in any particular sectarian principles. The trustees feel it a solemn and primary duty to preserve the institution open alike to all denominations. It is the common property of the public. It ought not to be devoted to the interests of any one sect exclusively. And there would not fail promptly to interpose their authority to repress every attempt, if any should be made, to render it subservient to the particular views of any sect.

Several departments of instructions will be well filled during the approaching session, which were unoccupied during the last. The terms of tuition remain the same as last year, and the price of Board in Commons will not exceed one hund'ed and seventeen dollars for the college year.

Notwithstanding the very extraordinary pressure of the times, there is reason to believe that the number of students will be greater than during the last year. As far as depends upon the Board, no exertion shall be spared in the performance of the duty of the most rigid economy which that pressure imposes, and they earnestly invite the co-operation of parents and guardians. They recommend as prompt an attendance of students at the beginning of the session as practicable, as well for their own comfort as on account of the advantage of early classification.

By order of the Board of Trustees,

ROBERT WICKLIFFE, Chairman.

Lexington, Ky. Sept. 13, 1819

Land and Mills For Sale.

THE SUBSCRIBER HAS FOR SALE ABOUT

40 Acres of Land,

With a Merchant Mill, Saw Mill, and Distillery,

ON Jessamine creek, about 4 miles from Nicholasville, and 5 from Shaker Ferry, which they will sell on reasonable terms.

2,000 dollars required to be paid in hand, the balance on terms to suit the purchaser. For further particulars, apply to either of the subscribers, living on the premises.

JACOB HOOVER,

ANDREW DILLMAN,

HENRY BRUNER.

Sept. 13, 1819.—20*3t

COTTON YARNS.

THE SUBSCRIBER HAVING PURCHASED OF CHARLES WILKINS, ESQ. THE

Manufacturing Establishment.

(late the Property of Mr. Lewis Sanders,)

IN the neighborhood of Lexington, and having, at considerable expense, repaired the Machinery &c. announce to the public, that they are ready to supply orders with COTTON YARNS of superior quality, and of any number.

☞ Persons wishing to purchase Yarns, will find it for their interest to call on us and examine for themselves, as we will sell those purchased to the eastward, or those purchased here to the eastward, before confidently expect the patronage of Western Merchants.

JOHN POSTLETHWAIT,

JOHN BRAND,

ELISHA WINFIELD,

JOSIAH TILFORD.

Postlethwait, Brand & Co.

COTTON YARNS, COTTON Factory, Sept. 30, 1819.

OUR YARNS are deposited at the Stores of WINFIELD, and TILFORD, TROTTER in Lexington, and for sale at reduced prices. Orders being left will be promptly attended to.

For the benefit of the Public Advertiser, Louisville, the Whig, Nashville, Republican Advocate, &c. La Enquirer, St. Louis Gazette, Missouri Enquirer, Knoxville, Ten., Missouri Nashville, will please insert the above 4 months, and forward their accounts to Postlethwait, Brand & Co.   40-2m

WOOL.

WANTED, a quantity of clean washed and sorted WOOL. Apply at the Fayette Manufactory.

POSTLETHWAIT, BRAND & Co.

N. B. 1819—40tf

Grand Lodge of Kentucky.

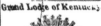

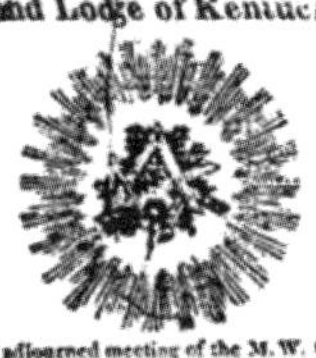

AN adjourned meeting of the M. W. Grand Lodge will be held at the MASONIC HALL in the town of Lexington, on the 3d Monday in NOVEMBER, at 10 o'clock, in the morning.

THOMAS T. BARR, G. Sec'y.

Lexington, Sept. 30. A. L. 5819, A. D. 1819—40

Mr. Schader,

INSTRUCTOR OF DANCING,

INTENDS opening a School for the purpose of instructing Masters and Misses at the above art, in the most fashionable style, at MR. GIBON'S HALL. A subscription paper will be left at Mr. Hunt's Lottery Office, and Mr. Giron's Store. As soon as a sufficient number is obtained, Mr. S. will commence

EVENING SCHOOL,

Mr. S. will give Lessons to young gentlemen who are desirous of acquiring the above art—Cotillion parties and private instruction respectfully attended to. Mr. S. has some very fashionable Cotillion, and superior music.

N. B. Terms of Tuition may be known by applying at the above places. For character reference to the Rev. Mr. Holley, and Mr J. C.

Sept. 17, 1819—38 4t

Notice.

MR. ROCHE will give private instruction at his Rooms in the University, to such young Gentlemen as may apply, at Twenty Dollars for three months. Any pupil continuing longer than a week, shall be liable to pay for three months tuition.

Sept. 3, 1819—39tf

New Thread Laces.

JUST RECEIVED and for sale, a superb assortment of THREAD LACES and EDGINGS, at very reduced prices.

Also, a few Pieces of Elegant

Damask Canton Crapes,

ASSORTED COLORS. Apply to

ARCAMBAL & NOUVEL.

Lexington, Sept. 3, 1819—37-4t

DR. SOMERBY,

Surgeon Dentist,

RESPECTFULLY tenders his professional services to the ladies and gentlemen of Lexington and its vicinity. His practice embraces, and he operates for every disease incident to the teeth and gums, removes the tartar, cleans, separates and polishes the teeth without injuring the enamel. He extracts foreign and decayed teeth, roots and stumps, with the utmost care and case—plugs and mends teeth with gold or foil, and renders them as lasting and useful as second teeth. He inserts natural and artificial teeth, from one to a full set, in the neatest and most durable manner, regulates children's teeth, and will give the best advice upon teeth in all cases.

His room is on Main street, for the house occupied by Mrs. Robert, opposite the Court-house.

Lexington, Sept. 14—38 tf

For Sale or to Hire,

A NEGRO MAN,

WHO has been used to driving a team and working on a farm for several years but has recently been employed as a waiter in a Tavern. His character for industry, sobriety and honesty, is indisputable, and the owner's reason for selling him is on account of his leaving the state, and the man having a wife and family, from whom he does not wish to part. A long credit will be given.

Apply at this Office.

August 5, 1819—32-tf

Domestic.

PITTSBURG, SEPT. 3.

Messrs. Scull & Neville,

I have just received a letter from my friend Mr. Richard Flower of the English settlement, Illinois. As its contents may be interesting to some of those emigrants who are seeking a residence in the western country, by publishing the following extract you will much oblige

A SUBSCRIBER.

Mr. Illinois, (near Albion) July 1.

"Dear Sir—I know your family takes a sufficient interest in our concerns to be pleased to hear, that we have arrived here in safety, and that nearly a month's residence promises the pleasing assurance of health, which we have enjoyed most perfectly since we came in, and all in the settlement are enjoying the same blessing. Our farming promises well. Our herd of cattle (now upwards of two hundred, and which will soon be increased to three or four hundred) bids fair to be profitable—my own and my son's haystacks will at least contain one hundred tons, gathered at less expense than in England, and which we shall dispose of to others and consume in fattening cattle in the winter. The gardens are very luxuriant, and afford us abundance of vegetables.

"You will have heard it repeated, that our water is scarce and not good; and this is in some degree true; for the creek being dry we have been driven to the necessity of drawing water for our cattle to the very deep and the work of well-digging has not succeeded in the same proportion as the increase of the inhabitants and cattle. Last week a spring of most delightful water was found at 26 feet, and the inconvenience will be obviated in a little time.

"It remains to be seen, whether now we have our house built, sickness will attend us in the Autumn. I hope and trust it will not. The country is delightful, and although the thermometer has one day risen to 90 degrees, yet the average has been about 80 in the night 75, with almost unani uted refreshing breezes. Personal interest apart, it is my decided opinion that for health, profit and pleasure there is no part of America where you could live more comfortably.

Your sincere friend,

RICHARD FLOWER."

From the Peters-burg Intelligencer.

MAIL ROBBERY,

Mr. Shore, Post Master, has ascertained that his mail to Philadelphia, of the 16th ult. never reached that place. It contained a large sum of money, it is apprehended, from the size of the portfolio.

Mr. Shore has accidentally called in some of our respectable merchants, who large sums were to be remitted. On the night of the 16th ult. Mr. Lewis Mabry, of the house of Starke and Mabry, was requested to attend ; who, with his own hand, subscribed the package, containing many letters ; among these one from Salisbury, N. C. addressed to Mr. James Patton, Philadelphia, supposed to contain money, and which we are advised did contain the first halves of $2300. The mail portmanteau was delivered to the driver in the presence of Mr. Mabry.

The two other halves, we are informed, Mr. Patton received some days subsequent to the 16th ult.

We infer that this money is in possession of the persons who have been apprehended in Richmond, for attempting to pass checks, &c. which were transmitted in letters from Petersburg and Richmond, on the 16th ult.

A letter from Jefferson county, New York, of the 8th inst. says, Joseph Bonaparte, Ex-King of Spain, is now here. He has purchased of M. Le Ray Chaumont, a tract of one hundred and fifty thousand acres of land, and is about to make improvements upon it.—Reff.

Gen. Thomas Cadwallader, of Philadelphia, and Gen. Boyd, lately of the army, arrived at Boston on Monday last in the ship London Packet, Tracy, from London.

BONAPARTE.

The London Courier of the 9th of August, states that the purser of the company's ship Phoenix, had landed at South Hampton on the preceding Thursday, with despatches from Bengal and St. Helena. Bonaparte's new mansion was in a state of great forwardness, but he takes no notice of it ; that he continues inflexible in his determination not to admit visitors, and it is a long time since he has been seen by the inhabitants. The Phoenix left St. Helena, the 7th of June.

South America.

The Bombay Gazette has the following paragraph respecting America :

"We think it not improbable that the whole of North America will ultimately be subject to the dominion of the United States. They have already extended their settlements almost across the continent to the western sea, and their ships visit their colonies in that quarter by the Pacific. By the expulsion of the Spaniards from the Floridas and on the eastern coast, the spirit of independence will gain ground among all those who were formerly subject to their power in that neighborhood, on the Spanish Main, the shores of the Gulf of Mexico, and the Isthmus of Darien. It will be impossible, if the ardor of the patriots continues to keep pace with their successes, that Spain should be able to keep possession of her ports on the eastern coast, or in the Pacific, namely Acapulco, Valparaiso, and Lima, accessible only by doubling Cape Horn, if the Patriots interrupt their access by land. Assailed thus by the Americans on the North, and the Patriots on the South, but little hope seems to remain for the duration of the Spanish power in that quarter ; and if it has here long a subject of our wish to see so fine a portion of the globe in the hands of so unfetter a government, and the progress of knowledge, mutual intercourse, and the best interest of humanity retarded by the galling fetters of tyranny, bigotry and sloth, it will be a triumph not only for liberty, but for philosophy also, to hail the emancipation of the millions that have so long bent their necks in darkness to this heavy yoke." Such is the language of philanthropy among enlightened Englishmen, which they contemplate the best hopes of the human race.—S. Reg.

FROM TEXAS.

On the 19th inst. the detachment under the command of Gen. Long, met a Spanish woman 40 miles west of Nacogdoches, by the name of Maria El Garma Freminia. She was found in a state of starvation, and comparatively naked.— She states that she left Labadie a few weeks ago in company with two men, both soldiers in the service of the king of Spain, and not knowing the road, they wandered about in the woods for many days in search of provision, but without finding any. One of the men turned off by himself to look for water, but he never returned to them, and they suppose he must have died. The other man and this woman journeyed on but a short distance when he died for want of provisions, and her being too weak to aid in the service, and plentiful subsistence is before them.

HERALD OFFICE,

Norfolk, September 17.

We are indebted to Mr. Wm. G. Lyford, keeper of the Steam Boat Hotel Reading Room, for the following extract of a letter from his attentive and intelligent correspondent at Bermuda, and also for the subsequent selections from West India papers of late dates, received by him per the same vessel.

"BERMUDA, AUG. 30.

"I have just received a letter from a respectable merchant in Trinidad, informing me that Barcelona, on the Spanish Main, has been captured by Col. Inglis, (or English) with about 1000 British troops, and Col. Usher, with 400 Germans and 400 Creole troops ;—and that a fleet under Brion had captured about 20 vessels of different descriptions, belonging to the royalists, some of which were armed. The Nymphe, the largest vessel, escaped by fast sailing, and got into Cumana, which place is besieged by the Independent squadron and the army which took Barcelona. All the women belonging to the Independent army were in a transport which fell into the possession of the royalists. Barcelona and Cumana are the only towns of much importance, in point of size and population, between Angostura and Caraccas. Angostura is the head quarters of the Independents, and Caraccas that of Morillo, the Royalist chief. The taking of Caraccas is the great object to which the Independents aspire ; and to that end it is necessary for Barcelona and Cumana to be secured by Barcelona and their own forces first, that they need not have an enemy in their rear as well as in their front."

Kentucky Gazette.

THREE DOLLARS PER ANNUM—IN ADVANCE.

LEXINGTON::::FRIDAY, OCTOBER 8.

THE LEGISLATURE.

The proverbial obstinacy of the acting governing, it appears by the last Argus, has so far yielded, as to consent to convene the legislature at an earlier period than usual, if a majority of the members elect will signify their wish for such a step. We hope the members will, with avidity, avail themselves of this *kind concession of his excellency*, and thus contribute to consummate the views of those who have successfully suggested the course to him. It is, perhaps, the last good intention that will ever flow from the mind of the acting governor towards his country, and 'twere pity, in a ten fold degree, it should be lost. We devoutly hope the legislature will be assembled; because much is to be expected from them in alleviating the distresses of the state. There are many who differ with us on this subject; but engage them in argument, they adopt the convenient Socratic mode of reasoning, and never advance any idea or fact, except evidence of the ease with which *deep* and *profound* political wisdom can be affected. All the causes of pressure, they flippantly say, are to be traced to Europe. No blame whatever can be attached to the American community. Our country is incapable of bringing misery upon itself. Well, we heartily wish these were the facts.—But we must beg pardon of our readers, for not being able to view the reasons of our present miserable condition, on so extensive a scale, as entirely to exclude America from participation in fault.

We are inclined to believe much might be done at home. Our political economy can be greatly aided by legislative means. The people can be protected from the griping oppression of the rich and callous *nabob*, who is constantly seeking to know where he can perfect the most agonizing ruin. There are men of this description—and in Kentucky too—who have filled their coffers by the most unwarrantable speculations:—and each additional hundred dollars acquired and hoarded up, have operated, in a certain degree, to deaden those sensibilities, kindnesses and charities of human nature, which the supreme ruler of the universe originally implanted in their bosoms. Individuals apart, the wretched state of our banking system—bottomed, as it is, upon the ignoble design of practising fraud and corruption, requires some interposing hand. The national councils should be foremost to correct great evils. But if they are timid and backward, the people and the states must interfere and become their own physicians. Protection can be given to the citizens of each state by the enactment of proper laws, with proper remedies and restrictions. A course of this kind would encourage a retrenchment of expenses—would open our eyes to the extravagant indulgence in foreign luxuries, which has hitherto marked our character—and would inspire us with a pride for the products of our own manufactories.

Besides these considerations, there is nothing to be lost by a convention of the legislature in November. It is a pleasant season—and by commencing the session thus early, the recess at Christmas, which nearly always takes place, would be suspended.

KENTUCKY AND TENNESSEE LINE.

The legislature of Tennessee is now in session at Murfreesboro; and, as many had anticipated, the boundary line between this state and that, was among the first subjects introduced into that body; & appears, as it often before has done, to excite considerable warmth among the members. A Mr Jetton commenced the business, by introducing the following motion:

"Resolved, that the governor be and he is hereby requested to lay before this house, any communications he may have received from the Governor of Kentucky, respecting the boundary of the two states. since the last session of the legislature."

Which was very tamely opposed—when

Mr. GRUNDY rose, and continued—"That all the information which could be "gathered on this subject, ought to be "put into their possession with as *little* "*delay as possible*. Correct informa"tion, (said he) as to the limits of the "state, was indispensable to the forma"tion of the country acquired, into dis"tricts. The state of Kentucky, he was "induced to believe, was acting, at this "time, in running the line between the "states. If the country in dispute was "fairly and honestly ours, he was deci"dedly of opinion *we ought to maintain* "*our title to it—for which purpose, pos*"*session was necessary. If future inves*"*tigation shewed that the claims of this* "*state were well founded, he apprehend*"*ed, the regaining possession of the dis*"*puted territory, if parted with, would* "*be attended with much more difficulty* "*than was generally expected.*"

Mr. Grundy was followed by Mr. Mitchell, who, with more temper, observed, that he "hoped the house would "act on so important a subject, as the "dispute between this state and Ken"tucky, with the *most dispassionate* "*coolness; that their deliberations would* "*be as calm as the high merits of the* "*question required. He apprehended* "*that a great deal too much warmth had* "*already been elicited. He well remem*"*bered that during a former session,* "*he had witnessed, and was sorry to ob*"*serve it, that members of the best in*"*formation the state afforded—men who* "*on all other occasions, he had noticed* "*as being cool and deliberate, had on* "*this subject evinced a degree of anima*"*tion, which to him had proved alarm*"*ing, as having a tendency to endanger* "*the peace of the two states.*"

Upon the suggestion of a Mr. Miller, that the governor had already promised to make some communication on this subject, the mover, with apparent reluctance, suffered his motion to lay on the table for the present, and so it rested at the date of our last advices from Tennessee.

From all that can be gathered, from the past conduct and present temper of the legislature of Tennessee, it appears that she intends to obtain from Kentucky, all the territory which she can;—and as our state is immensely interested in the result of the contest which exists with Tennessee, we propose, for the information of the public, to take hereafter, a brief view of the origin, rise, and present state of the controversy.

ARKANSAS.

We received this week, from the new territory of Arkansas, an account of the proceedings of the citizens of the town and neighborhood, held on the Fourth of July last, together with the toasts drank on the occasion. It is so late now, that their publication would scarcely be gratifying. Their preparations were very considerable, expecting to meet, on that day, the executive and judicial officers of the new government. Among the rest of the toasts, we feel happy in seeing our CLAY, our JOHNSON, and the South American patriots, noticed.

MISSOURI EXPEDITION.

We copy from a Philadelphia paper into the Gazette of to-day, some very judicious remarks concerning the Yellow Stone expedition. Many of the eastern prints notice this splendid undertaking in a style and manner which its importance requires. To those who only take a superficial glance at the subject, it seems extraordinary expense bestowed by government without any defined object. We think, however, it may be safely affirmed, that there are but few great movements of government, which will turn out of more importance to the nation. The protection of our great western waters from the invasion of British trading companies—and British traders—and the establishment of an immense line of fortifications, which it is presumed will be done, reaching from the Missouri to some point on the upper Mississippi, by which the extensive country, yet to be settled west of the latter river, will be secured from the cruelties of savage incursion, are objects worthy of the "youthful," but emphatically "matured" secretary of war:—and we greatly rejoice that Kentucky has it in her power to boast of some of the prominent agents who are carrying the views of the government into execution.

We believe that most of the outcries against the Yellow Stone expedition, which are occasionally found in some of the western newspapers, and sometimes to be heard in street conversations, are predicated upon political animosity to our patriotic JOHNSONS, and a deep rooted envy of their high standing with the American government. If such be the motives, we can only express our regret at the frailty of human nature. It would not have been expected by the host of western soldiers who witnessed, on the 5th of October, 1813, the valorous achievements of two JOHNSONS of the Thames, that in 1819, any number of individuals would be found in the very same country which they shed their blood to protect, ready to do them all the pecuniary, moral and political harm, which slander can inflict, or prejudice impose.

Extract of a letter from a gentleman in a neighboring town, to Richd. Bache.

"My attention has been attracted to a late article in the papers, in which the progress of the steam boat [illegible] is noticed; and I perceive she [illegible] Franklin, Missouri, on the [illegible]

"This magnificent undertaking [illegible] government is rendered, [illegible] the adoption of [illegible] Perhaps [illegible] ance is better suited [illegible] of the world than another, [illegible] the vast, and, I had like to have said, interminable water-courses of the western division of our country. "The current's thwarting course" ceases to be any barrier to the progress of this description of vessels; and 'tis *there* the currents flow; and 'tis there human labor, and sweat and toil, must have been expended for ages, had not this unrivalled design been perfected, and by the movements of its own interior, suspended all this toil, and bid the laboring boatman look on and admire this victory over the force of current, and his own freedom from the labors of conquering it.

"The certainty, as well as celerity of steam boat navigation; the cheaper rates of transportation which it secures; the satisfaction and comfort of passengers, all unite to make it an object which must continue to rise in importance, in the estimation of the people of these vast regions, and all having [illegible] with them.

"So far as the government of the United States is concerned, in its [illegible] with that portion of its territory [illegible] is deeply concerned) steam boats must continue to command its attention. For all the purposes of transportation, whether of army or of Indian supplies, or munitions of war, this mode is the best. It is the best, whether the progress of the expedition, the economy in the [illegible], or the certainty of the period of periods of arrival at the points of destination, be consulted. But these, however important in their place, are, in this [illegible] of the experiment, far outweighed in national point of view *(and this [illegible] never to be lost sight of.)* This [illegible] embraces the encouragement of one of the grandest and most useful inventions of man, which, whilst it delights the admiration of our countrymen, and [illegible] [illegible] to the advantage and [illegible] of the travelling parts of them, attracts at the same time, and rivets the attention of the old world to this wonderful contrivance; and sets monarchs at work to imitate the efforts and development of a REPUBLICAN genius.

"Who does not wish success to the whole scheme! Who does not think of the Herculean undertakings of the Johnsons with admiration? Who does not wish success to these men, not on account of their *enterprize*, only, but of their valor, their patriotism? No a wordy valor; not a boisterous patriotism, but practical and pure; such, I mean, as enveloped them in victory and has given renown to American [illegible] throughout the world; and which can never be forgotten till time shall moulder history down to the dust and bury the noblest deeds of man in one common ruin, with the final overthrow of the world. But I must come out of Moravian town, and from the banks of our Thames.

"When this expedition was fitting, I now and then heard of "*detention!*" of "*apprehension*," from their occasional recurrence, that the expedition must be abandoned. I thought I saw in some a half-willingness to abandon the steam-boat part of the design, and adopt the old song of "row brothers, row." But I put them all down to the ardor of the American character. I applauded the spirit, which, in *such a work*, became impatient of delay. But I knew that Atkinson, and Jessup, and Johnson, were there. And I doubted not but the two first, who are no less distinguished for their intelligence than their bravery, would see the vastness of the undertaking which rested on the shoulders of the third, that suitable allowance would be made for any accidental mishaps, to which such extended and diversified operations were liable, and which no mind but an Omniscient one could foresee; and no power, but Omnipotent power, could *immediately* control.

To my great gratification, the whole, at last, moved off. But what if they could only have *made ready* this year, it would only have been like a thing under orders for the next. As to the losses or evil consequences of such a delay, they would have been trivial, compared with the abandonment of the steam boat part of the great design. The year, however, is not lost; nor the steam boat part of the scheme abandoned; but the *Johnson* has passed Franklin in all the grandeur of her mysterious movements; full of health and spirits, pointing, as she goes, the attention of the thousands who witness her wonderful progress, to *the government* of a country, of which too many of the hapless beings who behold her, know too little, but who are approximating every year, nearer and nearer, to the point of a full observation, from which will be perceived the majesty and mildness of our laws, the justice and humanity of the government. And these must strike them with lessons of admiration and affection, that will eventuate in their attachment to them all.

Our youthful, but already ripened, secretary of war stands identified, specially so, with this grand expedition; under his guidance, we may look for the finest consequences of which it is susceptible." *Frank. Gaz.*

From the Illinois Spectator.

A statement of facts relative to the proceedings of a mob of slaveholders at Boon's Lick, in July, 1819. *By* Humphrey Smith.

At a camp-meeting held near Franklin, in the Missouri territory, in May or June last, in a conversation with a Mr. Sexton, I asked him how he could be a member of the methodist church, and at the same time hold negroes in slavery, as it was contrary to the discipline of the church; at which he was offended. Several slaveholders came near to defend their cause, who said that God made negroes for slaves, and white men for masters, or he would not suffer it to be so. By this time the preachers and hearers were all collected round, to hear what was said. No one said any thing on the part of freedom but myself. Several spoke in favor of slavery. A great fellow came up to us, and swore he would kill me—that he had killed two, and would kill me also. One of the preachers counted the number of oaths he took. The preachers came up to me, and requested me to be silent. I gave them assurances that I would. Some swore they would not suffer a man to stay in the country, that said so much against slavery; the principal part of which was, that I wished the restriction of congress might take place.

On the 17th of July, about 12 o'clock at night, a man called at my door for entertainment. I got out of my bed and went to the door. He asked me my name, which I told him. I then discovered that he had his face partly masked. He instantly caught hold of my right hand, and hauled me past the corner of the house. At this instant, three or four men rushed from behind the corner with clubs, and beat me on the head, and I fell to the ground. It was some time before I recovered my recollection, when I found them hauling me towards the fence. I caught hold of the fence, and hung to it with all my strength. All this time, some were beating me, and some endeavered to pull me over the fence. My wife came to my assistance, and threw a swingling-board at the man who had me by the hand, and broke his hold. My wife was struck across the eye with a club. We broke through the rioters, got into the house, and bolted the door. A short time after, a great shout was heard in the woods, thirty or forty rods from the house. I then fled into the cornfield, and staid until all was quiet. Upon returning to my bed, I could not sleep, in consequence of the wounds I had received. The next day, many of my neighbors came to see me, and said they were astonished at such conduct. Some of my friends warned me of another party that intended to make me a visit upon the same business. A few days after this riot, a camp-meeting was held about four miles from my place of residence. I neglected attending it, fearing some accident might take place. I was informed by a friend, that one of the slaveholders declared to him, that there were twenty at the meeting who would have beaten me, had I attended it.

HUMPHREY SMITH.

State of Illinois, Madison County, ss.

Personally appeared before me, Thornton Peeples, a justice of the peace, in & for Madison county, Humphrey Smith, who made oath that the above statement is true, according to the best of his knowledge and belief. Given under my hand this 15th day of September, 1819.

THORNTON PEEPLES, j. p.

Agricultural Society.

"The Kentucky society for promoting Agriculture," held its annual meeting on Thursday the 30th day of September, 1819, at Captain Fowler's garden. Col. Hubbard Taylor of Clarke county, one of the vice presidents, presided at the meeting. It attracted an immense concourse of respectable citizens from all quarters of the state, as well as many foreigners, during the two days of the exhibition. The society was numerously attended and a valuable addition of many members was made to it.

The spectators were highly gratified with the finest exhibition of the various objects brought forward for premiums that has ever been made in the state, as well as with many other specimens of industry and produce, for which no premiums were advertised. Among the objects of the latter description were an uncommonly fine eight months old calf, by a Buffaloe Bull, from a Cow the property of Col. Geo. Thompson, of Mercer, and a remarkably fine Sow, the property of Mrs. Shannon, and several samples of very excellent snuff, manufactured by Mr. Tho. J. Garret of Mount Sterling

Committees were appointed to examine the various descriptions of stock, and domestic manufactures, and to award premiums agreeably to the advertisement.

The committee appointed to report on the specimens of domestic fabrics exhibited for premiums, reported as follows:

That they have awarded a premium of a silver cup for the best piece of carpeting to Mrs. E. Warfield. Several pieces were exhibited by different persons of excellent carpeting. Mrs. John Hart's had the superiority in point of texture, but taking into consideration all the circumstances, particularly the important one of coloring, Mr. W's was preferred.

The best piece of Flax Linen was exhibited by Lewis Sanders, unbleached, spun by Mrs. Gillespie and wove by Mr. Gillespie, for which the premium of a silver cup was awarded. Mrs. John Hart offered a piece beautifully bleached.

To Mrs. John Hart was adjudged the premium of a Silver Cup for the best piece of Table Linen. It was beautifully bleeached.

Several pieces of Janes and Cassinets were exhibited. The premium of a silver Cup was awarded to Mrs. McKinney Jun. for the best piece of Jeans. *Mrs. John Hart's was deemed the next best.

Several samples of excellent Cheese were exhibited. The premium of a Silver Cup was awarded to Mrs. E. Warfield for the best. Mrs. Joshua Brown had the next best.

The premium of a Silver Cup for the best Wheat was awarded to John Stark.

H. Clay,
D. Harrison,
R. Frazer,
J. Brand. } Committee.

The committee appointed to adjudge the premiums for the best Gelding, and for the best Colt, reported,

That Mr. O. Keene exhibited a gelding, the property of Mr. Crittenden, much approved for figure and color. Mr. Anderson exhibited a gelding of fine size. Mr. M. Elder exhibited a very fine gelding. Mr. Bowman exhibited a gelding by Whip, which, for size, figure, and action, is deemed the best, and a Silver Cup is accordingly awarded to him.

The Colts exhibited were considered fine. Mr. Anderson's had superior size: Mr. Clay's was considered very fine; but, taking into view, size, action and figure, the committee award the premium of a Silver Cup to D. Bryan's mare colt exhibited by Wm. Bowman.

E. Warfield,
R. Higgins,
A. Blanchard,
R. Crockett,
W Brown, } Committee.

The committee appointed to adjudge the premiums for Cattle report as follows:

Wm. Smith exhibited imported Bull, Bright, of the long horn breed, 4 years old:

H. Clay exhibited an imported Bull, Ambassador, of the Herefordshire breed, 4 years old:

N. Hart exhibited an imported Bull, John Bull, of the short horn breed:

John Hart exhibited an imported Bull, Prince Regent, of the short horn breed.

The premium of a Silver Cup for the best imported Bull is awarded to Captain Smith for his imported long horn Bull.

Stephen Fisher of Lincoln county exhibited a fine red Bull, three years old, got by captain Fowler's Bull, Buzzard, for which a premium of a Silver Cup is awarded.

Robert Crockett exhibited a young red Bull, 2 years old 27th November next, out of capt. Smith's imported Cow of the Teeswater breed.

Wm. T. Banton exhibited a young Bull, beautifully marked red and white, 2 years old, 22d Dec. next, out of Mr. Mundays imported Cow, Mrs. Motte, of the Teeswater breed, got by Tecumseh, an imported Bull of the Holderness breed.

The committee deem it proper to state that they awarded the premium to Mr Crockett's young bull by a majority of one only.

Daniel Harrison exhibited a bull calf, 9 months old, got by Ambassador.

H. Clay exhibited a bull Calf six months old, got by the same, out of an imported cow.

Wm. Smith exhibited a bull calf six months old, got by San Martin, an imported bull of the Teeswater breed, out of an imported horn cow.

John Spears exhibited a bull calf 9 months old, of Patton's old breed.

E. Warfield exhibited a bull Calf 4 months old, by Comet, an imported bull of the short horn breed.

The committee award the premium of a Silver Cup to D. Harrison for his bull calf by a majority of ONE only.

Wm. Smith exhibited an imported Cow, 4 years old of the Durham breed.

Wm. T. Banton exhibited a red Cow, white back, by capt. Fowler's bull Buzzard, out of captain Smith's Virginia cow

John Spears exhibited a very fine and large Cow, 9 years old, of Patton's old breed.

Daniel Harrison exhibited his Cow, Puss got by Pluto, 11 years old.

E. Warfield exhibited a cow, four, another five, and another six years old.

The committee award the premium of a silver cup for the best cow to Wm. T. Banton.

S. Fisher exhibited a large red cow, 3 years old, got by capt. Fowler's Buzzard.

R. Crockett exhibited three cows, each 3 years old.

The committee award the premium of a silver cup, for the best three year old cow to Mr. Fisher.

The premium of a silver cup for the best 2 year old heifer was awarded to R. Crockett, *no competitor.*

Wm. T. Banton exhibited a yearling heifer by Comet, out of his cow, that obtained the premium at this meeting; also a yearling heifer by Robert Wickliffe's bull.

Wm. Smith exhibited a brindle heifer by Fowler's bull, 18 months old; also two half blood long horn heifers 14 months old.

Robert Crockett exhibited an heifer of the Herfordshire breed, bred by H. Clay, also an heifer 18 months old, raised by himself.

The premium of a silver cup is awarded to Wm. T. Banton for the best yearling heifer.

Wm. Smith exhibited a red heifer calf by San Martin out of his imported cow of the Teeswater breed; also an half blood long horn heifer calf.

Wm. Bowman exhibited an heifer calf by Comet.

Robert Crocket exhibited an heifer calf by Smith's long horn bull.

Wm. T. Banton exhibited an heifer calf by Smith's long horn bull, and of his cow that won the premium.

E. Warfield exhibited an heifer calf San Martin.

The premium of a silver cup is awarded to Wm. Bowman.

John Boyce exhibited three fat Bullocks.

John Spears exhibited two very fine Bullocks.

The premium of a silver cup is awarded to John Boyce for his four year old steer, bred by G. McKinney, treasurer of this Society.

M. D. Hardin,
B. P. Gay,
M. Anderson,
Geo. Coons,
J. Munday. } Committee.

A sample of excellent Whiskey was exhibited by Robert Crockett.

A sample of excellent Whiskey was exhibited by Robert Huston & Co.

A sample of excellent and fine flavored Whiskey was exhibited by John Spears.

For strength and flavor Mr. Crockett's was thought superior: the committe award to him the premium of a silver cup.

R. Higgins,
S. Fisher,
J. Morrison,
A. Blanchard, } Committee.

Officers of the Society for the next twelve months.

ISAAC SHELBY, President.
HUB'D TAYLOR, 1st Vice Pres't.
NATH'L HART, 2d do
JOHN FOWLER, 3d do
R. CROCKETT, 4th do
M. D. HARDIN, 5th do
LEWIS SANDERS, Sec'ry.
GERARD MCKINNEY, Treas.

ROBERT CROCKETT,
LEWIS SANDERS,
E. WARFIELD,
JOHN BRAND,
JOHN HART,
Corresponding Committee, and Committee of Arrangement for the next year.

* This lady deserves the highest [illegible] for the fine spirit which she has manifested on this, as well as former occasions.

Married,

On Thursday the 30th ult. Mr. GEORGE TRE[illegible], to Miss ELIZABETH ANN BROWN, both of this county.

On the same evening, Mr. CLARKE DERRIS, of this county, to Miss ELIZABETH STOCY, of Scott county.

Died,

In Jessamine county on the 2d inst. Mr. JOHN M. YOUNG.

At his residence in Henderson, General SAMUEL HOPKINS, a distinguished citizen of Kentucky.

PERSONS holding SUBSCRIPTION PAPERS for the "*CHRISTIAN ADVOCATE*," will please forward a list of the subscribers' names.

THOMAS J STEVENSON.

Lexington, Oct 7, 1819.

Medical School.

THE Medical School of Transylvania University will be opened at Lexington on the *second Monday in November next.* The following gentlemen are the professors, and will give lectures in their several departments:

Granville S. Pattison, M. D. *Anatomy.*
Samuel Brown, M. D. *Theory & Practice.*
Charles Caldwell, M. D. *Institutes & Materia Medica.*
Benjamin W. Dudley, M. D. *Surgery.*
William H. Richardson, M. D. *Obstetrics and Diseases of Women and Children.*
James Blythe, D. D. *Chemistry.*

The professor of Botany and Natural History in the University, C. S. RAFINESQUE, esq. will give lectures to such students as wish to attend upon his instructions. All these gentlemen, except Dr. Pattison, are already known to the American public, and need no remarks of ours, to recommend them to the confidence and regard of the friends of science in the west. Of Dr. Pattison, it is proper to give some information to our fellow-citizens. He has lately arrived in Philadelphia from Scotland, and brings with him the most ample and satisfactory testimonials from professional men of the first standing in Great Britain. His talents, attainments, and character, are spoken of in the highest terms by his European brethren. Dr. ASTLEY COOPER, of London, writes concerning him, that "*he has cultivated anatomy most ardently and with the greatest success. He is also exceedingly well informed on every branch of professional knowledge.*" Dr. Cooper adds, that he is capable of filling the chair of anatomy "*with the highest credit to himself, and the utmost possible advantage to those he is called upon to instruct.*" Dr. K[illegible] of Glasgow, says, that in his opinion, "*Dr. Pattison is at this moment one of the first anatomists in Europe.*" Dr. Brown, also of Glasgow, Doctors Barclay and Thompson of Edinburgh, Rev. Thomas Chalmers, D. D. Rev. John Dick, D. D. and Francis Jeffrey, Esq. a well known writer in the Edinburgh Review, express themselves most warmly and fully in favor of Dr. Pattison. He will bring with him to Lexington an ANATOMICAL MUSEUM, to which no other in this country can be compared. It is a complete collection of means for scientific demonstration, and also for popular illustration. Good rooms for lecturers are procured, and this town now furnishes, at a moderate expense, as good accommodations as can be found in the state.

The Medical School of Transylvania University being thus organized, and about to open under such auspices, the trustees would be unfaithful to the interests of the institution if they did not publish these advantages for the benefit of the community, and earnestly solicit the attention and patronage of all the friends of science in the west. It is confidently believed, that a better medical education cannot be obtained in any school in the United States than in that of Lexington. All the considerations of patriotism, a regard to the prosperity of our interior world, as well as the smaller considerations of economy and convenience, urge the young men of the west promptly to contribute their aid to the establishment and support of a good and a great medical school at home. We have made much effort to procure the gentlemen, whose talents and services are here offered to the public, and nothing but liberal encouragement can or ought to induce them to remain among us. We trust that the community will not suffer this encouragement to be wanting, and our common interest to be sacrificed by neglect.

R. WICKLIFFE,
Chairman of the Board of Trustees of Transylvania University.

Oct 4.—41

Document 5b. The *Kentucky Gazette*, newspaper, October 8, 1819. [National Archives]

Latest News by the Mails.

LATEST FROM ENGLAND.

IMPORTANT.

New-York, Sept. 20.

Capt. Webb, of the Schr. Athens, arrived last night in the very short passage of 28 days from Cork, has obligingly favored the Editors of the New-York Gazette with Cork papers to the 22d of August.

RIOTS AT MANCHESTER.

On Monday the 16th of August, the Reform meeting was held at Manchester. There were not less, at this Meeting than 100,000 people, collected from all the villages round for 20 miles.—Orator Hunt was the leader. The approach of the different bodies of the deluded populace, of which it was constituted, was made with all manner of outward display, in order to impose forbearance on the civil authorities. Banners and bands of music added their effect to the march of the different divisions of the refomers, which was conducted with something like military precision. Among the former were several bearing the following inscriptions and devices.—'Let us die like men, and not be sold as slaves!'—'No corn laws'—'Annual parliaments, and universal suffrage'—'Major Cartwright's bill'—The rose, supported on each side by the shamrock and thistle, with two hands united, and the word union among them. Three different flags, bearing the cap of liberty on the flag staff. 'Equal representation or death!—Taxation with false representation is unjust and tyranical.'

Women, in considerable numbers, were united in these processions, and advanced with them to the general place of meeting in Peter's Square. When every thing of preliminary arrangement had concluded, Hunt, with his immediate party, mounted a platform prepared for their reception, from whence he proceeded to address the multitude.—His harangue was suffered to go on for one hour after the riot act had been read in due form, and then he was interrupted by a body of cavalry, acting under the orders of the civil magistrates. They made a full charge in full gallop, amongst the crowd, to the platform on which he was placed, cut it down with their swords, and took Hunt and all on the stage prisoners. They then made a second charge to disperse the people, in which hundreds were thrown down and rode over. Five lost their lives, and about one hundred were severely wounded. All continued confusion till evening, when the mob broke some windows in the New-Cross. The 88th foot then fired on them and killed four men; they were then assailed by the mob with stones and brickbats, and one dragoon was knocked down from his horse senseless by a blow, and has since died. On the 17th all was alarm, and the streets crowded with militia. Orders were issued for all the shops to be closed, and it was reported that some thousands were coming to Manchester with pikes and arms. Cannon was placed in the streets, but the mob seemed desperate and determined to have revenge. [Our accounts are no later than the 17th.] Hunt, Johnson, Knight, Morehouse, Saxton, and the other leaders of the Reformers, were imprisoned in separate cells.

From the Bost. Daily Advertiser, Sept. 18.

Second Edition.—Last night we were favored by capt. Frost, of the ship Suffolk, with Liverpool papers to the 16th, and London to the 12th ult.

Important Occurrence.—The meeting of the Reformers, at Manchester, had been dispersed by several regiments and corps of cavalry; and between forty and fifty men, women and children, wounded; and three men killed. The meeting it was estimated, consisted of 70,000; and was headed by Mr. Hunt, who was taken into custody. All the flags, caps of liberty, &c. were taken, destroyed, or carried off in triumph by the cavalry. Two of the cavalry were wounded. The women who carried banners, it is said, fought most courageously to defend them, and one was cut down with the banner in her hand. Some accounts say the riot act was not read before the cavalry made their charges. Among the flags, was a black one bearing 'Universal Representation or Death.' The meeting is described in the Liverpool papers as very orderly, and Hunt had only addressed them, when they were dispersed. The wounded carried from the field filled six coaches, three carts, and three litters; five women, dreadfully wounded, were among them. The meeting was held the 16th Aug. Bills of indictment have been found against Major Cartwright, Mr. Wooler, Editor of the Black Dwarf, and others, concerned in the election of Sir Charles Wolseley, as an extra member of Parliament.

From the New York Gazette.

By the quick ship Robert Fulton, capt. Holdridge, who sailed from Liverpool on the 12th ult. the editors of the Gazette have received the London Courier of the evening of the 9th, two days later than by the arrivals at Boston.

By the Courier it appears, that the disaffected in the disturbed districts had been checked, but not subdued. Bold attempts were still made to hold meetings, but it was hoped that perseverance in that part of the government would accomplish tranquillity.

The king of England, by the last monthly report, had enjoyed a good state of health, but his disorder still remained unchanged.

German papers state, that the duke of Parma, (Cambaceres) set off from Brussels for Paris, on the 3d ult. and that Marat had permission to return to France.

The Prince Regent embarked on board the yatch at Margate on the 8th ult. on a water excursion, either for the Scottish coast on a visit to the Earl of Fife; or to Portsmouth, where the Persian embassador was to have been put on board—the Isle of Wight, Plymouth, &c.

Corn Exchange, Aug. 9.—The supply of wheat was small this morning, and the prices better than Monday last.—Barley went off more freely in consequence of the unfavorable report of the quality of the new crop.

LIVERPOOL, AUG. 11.

Our cotton market is very steady, and there is no appearance of any decline, and we have no doubt but 15d. will soon be realized for real good cotton, perhaps more; but we should caution you against being too sanguine. The India cotton is a roll over heads, and we must act with judgment. The sales of the last week were 13,000 bags of all sorts, and thus far in the present week (Wednesday) there is little doing in any thing else. Ashes are freely offered at our quotations. Tobacco has improved a little, and we hope it may further improve. There is no prospect of the ports opening for wheat and flour this year.

FROM ST. HELENA.

Extract of a letter, dated St. Helena, May 20.

The governor has been very busy lately at Longwood, superintending the placing of the iron palisadoes which he has brought up to surround the new house building for Bonaparte. About 500 men of the regiment are employed daily, at a shilling per day each, in carrying stones and other materials for completing it. The duty is very severe, as the men who are relieved from guard in the morning are obliged to go on working parties immediately on their return to Longwood; and those who mount guard in the evening are obliged to work until 4 o'clock. It is thought that it will be finished in eight or nine months. So little is known of Bonaparte, that the authorities here have no other mode of ascertaining either his actual presence or state of health, than by the reports of some person who obtains a casual glimpse of him at his window, or sitting on the steps of the billiard room. Whenever any person sees him, even through a telescope, he is obliged to report the circumstance, and is generally *made* to say that he looked very well, and appeared in perfect health.

The 20th regiment is at Francis Plain and is not yet allowed to mount guard at Longwood, as the governor does not wish that the prisoner should have any communication with persons lately arrived from Europe.

Madame Bertrand is well, but very seldom comes into camp now, as the governor sent word to Col. Dodgin to have her watched and followed wherever she went. It is said that Sir H. Lowe is to be removed, and that the government will devolve to Sir George Bingham.—We are anxious to hear a confirmation of this, as we are heartily sick of the present odious system. Mr. Baxter, the governor's body physician, who has been ill for a long time, has been sent home, it is supposed with dispatches.—The prohibition against the introduction of newspapers into the island is as rigidly enforced as ever, and I have only seen two for the last four months."

DON LOUIS DE ONIS.

From our late European papers (says the Boston Centinel) we gather the following facts respecting this diplomatist. He passed from the United States to England, and from thence to Paris, where he heard of the removal of the Spanish prime minister, the Marquis de Casa Yrujo, and immediately posted for Madrid. When he had reached Valladolid, more than half way from the frontier to the capital—he received a royal mandate to stop, and not approach nigher to Madrid. Afterwards he was arrested, and conducted to a convent near Avilla, not far from Madrid, where a court of enquiry was ordered to convene to investigate certain charges made against him and the above named marquis, who had been ordered to the same place of confinement. The general newspaper opinion in Spain was, that the charges alluded to the grants of lands in the Floridas, made during the negotiation of the late treaty for their cession to the United States, in which instrument there is a clause limiting their extent.—*Intel.*

ATTENTION!!

THOSE persons, who, during the late War, were redeemed from captivity with the Indians, by gentlemen residing in Detroit and the Michigan territory,—will confer a favour on the undersigned, by meeting him at Lanphear's Tavern in the town of Lexington, on the last Monday in this month. Those who cannot attend, will do him a favour, by sending their affidavits, sworn to before, and certified by, some Justice of the peace, in which is stated, the amount paid for their redemption, and by whom.

This application is made, because congress have lately made provision to discharge those claims; and it is to be hoped, that the soldiers here addressed, will not for a moment neglect the debt of gratitude which they owe to those humane and patriotic citizens, who, at a moment of extreme peril to themselves, saved all the prisoners redeemed, from the sufferings and horrors of Indian captivity, and many from certain death.

The following persons are particularly requested to attend to the above.—

Isaac L. Baker, Gustavus M. Bower, Spencer Shumate, Julius Turner, Jesse Green, Alexander Montgomery, Nathl. Chinn, Frederick M'Nill, Wm. Cook, Wm. Peacock, Abraham Estes, Robert Ellis, Henry Spoon, Peter Winchell, Wm. Goodlett.

CHARLES BRADFORD.

Lexington, Oct. 1st, 1819.——41

Tammany Election.

THE Sons of St. Tammany, or Brethren of the Columbian Order, who belong to Wigwam No. 1, are requested to be punctual in their attendance, at the place of meeting on Tuesday the 12th inst at 11 o'clock, A. M. being the Anniversary of the Discovery of America, for the purpose of electing officers for the ensuing twelve months.

By order of the Grand Sachem,

RICHARD H. CHINN, Sec'y.

Lost or Mislaid,

ON Saturday last, in or about the Court-house, on the public square, a small

Blue Morocco Pocket Book.

Containing, besides several receipts and other papers, 17 Dollars in bank notes: a $10 bill on a bank in Tennessee, one $5 do. on the Farmers' and Mechanics' bank of Springfield, 2 $1 do. the banks not recollected. Also a ticket in the Grand Masonic Hall Lottery, No. 15,934 with the names of the owners written on the back and face of the same. Any person having found the book and will leave it at this office, with its contents, will receive the thanks of the owner. The consciousness of having performed a just and honorable act is a satisfactory reward to an honest man. A rogue never hesitates to reward himself, when in his power so to do.

NATHL. S. PORTER.

Oct. 8th, 1819—41

List of Letters,

REMAINING in the Post-office at Lexington, on the first of October, 1819, which if not taken out by the 1st of January, will be sent to the General Post-office as dead letters.

A.

Ashton S. S.	Auberry R.
Allen Rebecca W.	Anderson James
Annis Nancy	Adkins Allen S.
Anderson William C.	Anshutz C.
Atchison John 2	Allen Elvin
Ausberry Henry	Adams Absolem
Adams Larkin	Archer Stephen C. 2
Austin Jas. E. B.	Adams Robert
Alexander Robert 2	Ayer Theodore
Abernathy Richard L.	Atchinson Richard
Alsop William	Anderson Henry
Armstead Robert D.	Armstrong Mary
Ault Frederick	Armstrong William
Atchison Hamilton	

B.

Bell Mary P.	Bailey Joshua
Boin William	Barry Catharine A.
Brunn George	Bolan William
Beach John	Bradley Keeling
Bruin Joseph	Boyle John
Blair Will. W. 4	Bond Joshua
Beltch Gabriel	Breckenridge W. T.
Bender George	Bean Isaac 4
Brown Jinks	Brownlee George
Breckinridge Wm. L.	Brooks Benjamin 2
Bradford Daniel 2	Bachrel Benjamin
Bosworth David	Baker William
Brown Nancy	Bastide Mr.
Bullock Waller	Beaver Peter
Butler Jane H.	Burnett Isaac
Boston Thomas W.	Brumbarger John
Boone Samuel	Brown George M.
Robb William	Banks Charles
Bishop Purnell	Butler Mr. A.
Butler P. 2	Brock Thomas
Beatty James	Bitchael John 4
Booth William	Brown George
Barrett William P.	Booth William
Butler Eliza A.	Bobbard Wiett
Barbee Clarissa	Brock Thomas
Ball John	Burrell George
Barrey James T.	Baits Ephraim
Bean Abner	Butcher Solomon
Beatty John 3	Busanl Solomon
Bell Benjamin	Buford J. 2
Berry Richard	Bryants Messrs.
Butler Anthony	Brock Thomas
Byers James	Belam James
Bullock Mary A.	Bradley Nancey
Buckner A. W.	Black John B.
Bullock Ann	Bryan William T.
Brewer Nathaniel	Bryant Jesse
Brown Doct. P.	Buts John
Brown Samuel	Boyd Thomas
Bertrand Hubert	Boyce John
Banks Simeon	Boon Nathaniel R. 2
Bryan William P.	Benston Isaac
Brent Richard	Baker Joshua 2
Bullock Waller	Bowlin William
Bale John	Barnett Isaac
Barbee Amanda	Bost Charles C.
Baxter Elizabeth	Bascomb Henry B.
Bowles T.	Bonhomme Charles
Berrey Benjamin	Brice Samuel

C.

Cannons John	Chapman John
Chambers James	Colden David C.
Cropper Thomas 2	Cookshott A. R.
Crockett Louisa	Crider Mary
Cannon Burton	Cassey Nicholas
Cavwood Michael	Calvert Levi
Caldwell John C. 2	Cox George
Cochran William	Carr Sarah A.
Clanens David	Carr Frances
Clarkson James P. S.	Clemson E. B.
Collins Thomas	Coffman David
Carson James	Coburn Robert
Clark Enoch 2	Clark John B.
Clark James S.	Clift Powell
Clark Elizabeth	Coons Thomas
Craig Saunders W.	Cunningham Robert
Caldwell Susannah W.	Cartmell Elijah
Chamblin Elizabeth C.	Cavendish Wm. H.
Collins E. U.	Chamberlain Thomas
Cook Will. W.	Crockett Robert
Christopher William	Chaney Leonard
Caruthers William A.	Cosby Eliza J.
Coughorn Thomas F.	Caslett Eli
Caldwell Samuel	Chawl Jacob
Culbertson Robert	Chin Samuel
Curry William	Carey Thomas
Colman Isaac J. 2	Craig Samuel 2
Clugett John	Coats William C. 5
Crider Maryann M.	

D.

Dodd Thomas	Davall Thomas
Doomas John	Darimple Roger
Dodge Ann	Dabney John Q.
Dunn John	Deadman John
Develly George	Day John H.
Dodge Nancy A.	Delaney James W.
Dudley M. V.	Dezard Mr.
Duke Thomas M. 3	Dickinson John B.
Ducire A. 2	Dinfast Frances
Dunlap William 2	Doxey N. N.
Dolettel Thomas	Dickey William
Deines Matthew	

E.

Estes Thorp. R.	Essex William
Ewing Putnam	Epes Daniel
Eddleman Peter	Elliott Benjamin T.
Ellis William	Ellis Armstrong
Earp Richard	Eddy E. D.
Earp Robert 3	Eastham James
Evans Nathaniel	Eoncks John
Earley James	Elmaker David 5

F.

Fishel Michael 3	Fink John
Finley & Vanasear	Fishback Samuel D. 2
Fisher John	Fleming John 2
Frost William	Fidler William 2
Ferguson Alexander	Flournoy Frances 2
Ferguson Priscilla	Ford Thomas
Fowler Samuel	Fry Aaron
Faulconer Nelson	Fry William
Ford [illegible] 2	Flournoy Ferdinand
Fife Thomas 2	Franklin Henry
Foote George	Fisher William
Fosdick [illegible] B.	Ferrell William T.
Fauquier John B.	Fleming James
Ferguson Daniel	Farrar Dr. 2
[illegible]	

G.

Gest John	Gaines Miller
Griffith [illegible]	Gran William
Garrison John	Grayson Alfred
Graves John C.	Gaines Catharine
Gray John	Graham Reubin
Gray George	Guynn Josiah
Gess Mrs.	Givin Dickinson 2
Birrett Thomas 2	Gilway Patrick
Goldner David	Garrard Depthah
Grant Mary W.	Gaines Ellen
Gibson James	Gibson William
Graves Samuel	Gilbert ——
Graves William	Gregory William
Grates James 2	Grimes William Jr.
Gerdlet Samuel	Garisch Mr.
Grimes Stephen	Barnett Richard 2
Guthrty Machl.	Grimes Stephen

H.

Hunt William	Head James
Hunt John	Hawkins Christianna
Hawkins John W. 2	Harris Notley
Hopkins Thompson	Hopkins Edmund H.
Hayden Mr.	Hunter John D.
Hill James H.	Hancock Higginson
Haney John	Hays Thomas
Hopkins Silas	Harvie John
Hahn [illegible] R.	Hurst James
Hannah [illegible] A. 3	Wiggins James
Hartley William	Hamilton Robert
Hardman [illegible]	Harrison Cabell M.
[illegible] L.	Hill John
Hess [illegible]	Halleyman Thomas
Hanley [illegible]	Hurst John
Hoover [illegible]	Hogeland Solomon
Henry [illegible] 2	Halstead Daniel 2
Hendricks John T.	Humphreys Mary
Hampton Andrew	Hays William
Hopkins Charles	Hull John
Hudson Philip	Humphreys Charles 4
Hamilton John	Henderson James
Hubbard John	Harriss Samuel
Hill Mrs. or John	Houghton Reubin
Hord Benj. F.	Hawes R. H.
Hill Isaac	Hazlerigg Alexander
Hawkins John	Hopkins John
Hastings Oliver	Hampton Andrew
Hall Jas.	Hoover William
Hall Jacob	Hamilton William
Hoover Elizabeth	Hartman Peter
Hawkins Julius	Halloway Elizabeth
Hull Catharine	Hillox James
Hefley Jacob	

J.

Jones Ann	Johnson Thomas
Jones Ann	Johnson Samuel
Jones Thomas	Johnson Solomon
Johnson [illegible] 3	Johnson Simpson
Jones Nicholas	James Peter
Jones Joseph	Jackson John
Jones Thomas	Joyce John 3
Jones Jonathan	Ingle Richard
Johnson Jacob 3	Inskeep Joseph
Johnson John 2	Irwin Stephenson
Johnson Nicholas 2	Ingles Anna Mariah
Johnson Nelson C.	

K.

Kermeer James	Kincaid Robert
Ker John 2	Kitchen Anthony
King Ely	Ketley James
Kilburn George	Kenning William
Kennedy Richard	Kern Oliver
Kemberlin John	Ker Sarah

L.

Lingisfelter John	Logan Alexander
Leroy Hugh	Lindsay Thomas
Lewis Lucinda	Lingisfelter George
Lewis John	Lucas Zachariah
Logan James	Lafferty William 2
Lloyd Marshall 3	Luck Garland D.
Laird Samuel	Looney Robert Q.
Lawrence John	Link Adam
Littlejohn John	Long William
Lyman John W.	Logan William
Lewis Stephen D.	Lowry Mr.
Laughlin Lucy D.	Latham Allen 2
Lewis J. O.	Lea Elijah
Lewis John	Lewis Hector
Lewis William	Long Samuel

M.

Monroe Nancey	Minter A. & J.
Moore Frances	Markee James
Moore John H.	Moore Samuel
[illegible] & Tresson	Miller John B.
Merrill William	Miller Anderson
Marquis John	Mayrick Joseph
Matron Alexander	Matheney James R.
Meredith William	Miles William
Moore John	Maddox Nancy
Menifee Jarrett	Morris John M.
Maxwell Joseph L.	Miller Eli R. 2
Mather Joseph T. 2	Myers Barbary
Metcalf Samuel L. 3	Muir John
Mallory Ambrose	Moxley Thomas
Maxwell Rebecca	Milligan William
Marchel James	Magnor Jeremiah
Martin Martha W.	Morton David
Muir John	Murray Robert W.
Matchaar Jos.	Marshall J. J.
Meredith Elisha	Mosbey Littlebury H.
Montgomery Wm.	Mason Lydiann
Martin Isaiah 2	Moore Nathaniel
Minter James	Moore Richard S.
Martin Samuel	Moore Nimrod H.
Minor George	Moore Benjamin
Mills Edmund 2	Moore John W.
Morison James	Mitchel & Trotter
Mathiney Rachael	McLaughlin George

Mc.

M'Gruder Samuel W.	M'Conathy Jacob
M'Gibney John	M'Farlain William
M'Cray Wm. & Steel	M'Haffey Alfred
James H.	M'Guire Douglas
M'Carter Dennis	M'Pheeters Nancy
M'Donald G.	M'Isaac Isaac
M'Guire Sarah	M'Cracken Thomas
M'Millen James	M'Garvin James
M'Lanahan Elijah	M'Quie J. & W.
M'Duet James	M'Dowell James
M'Dowell Martha	

N.

Nichols Pheldan	Noble Garsdus
Newhall Oren	Nelson Matilda J.
Newman Jacob	Noble Elijah
Newman Arthur	Nape Prosper
Nyfong Michael	North William

O.

Offutt Fieldin	Oxley Mehala
O'Neill Francis	Oxley Nancey
O'Brian Daniel	Outten Thomas
Oaid & Jos. Bickley 2	

P.

Pusard Noah	Page Thomas
Patterson James	Peacher Jonathan
Pervine Mrs. 2	Poindexter Zacheriah
Pike Robert	Poage Polley
Parr William L.	Patterson Ezekiel
Paxson Richard	Prince Preston
Prentice James	Prewett Willis
Parrott John Q.	Palmateer William
Poage Thomas	Potter Peter Sogich
Price William	Plumer Abiazer
Potter Charles 2	Paul Peter
Patterson Samuel	Pleasants Ann C.
Payne Asa	Palmer Samuel
Perry Elbert 2	Patterson Nicholas
Parrish Sidney W.	Patterson Thomas
Patterson Leonard	Plum Archibald
Peebles Robert	Perkins Bustis
Pilcher Mason	Parlow John G.
Payne John	Pigret David
Parks John	Prentiss John
Parks Margaret	Patterson Elizabeth
Phillips & Stout	Proprietors of the Cotton Factory
Pratt Enos	

Q.

Quarles Rowger	Quarles John

R.

Reed Isaac	Rankins Martha
Reid Frances Jane	Russell Thomas A.
Robb Joseph	Richards Alexd. C.
Russell Samuel P.	Ricketts Thomas
Richardson Mary B. 2	Ramsey Thomas
Robinson Kitsey	Rucker Jerrey
Richardson [illegible]	Reid James
Rhinelander John S.	Rubey Jane
Rucker Lewis D.	Reed William
Russell Sylvester	Reakin Harrison
Rucker James	Ryman John
Robinson David	Robinson Joseph 2
Reynolds or Taylor	Russell Wm. H.
Berrey	Rowgers C. W.
Russell Mary Ann	Respess Robert C.
Robb James	Rogers Chas. W.
Richards Wm. P.	Randall William P.
Robinson Susannah	Rhoads Christopher
Rigesbey James L. 3	

S.

Smith Matthew 2	Seth Joseph
Smith Samuel H.	Sanders Clark
Smith Creed T.	Saunders George A.
Smith Elijah M.	Sergent Dabney
Smith John R.	Simmons Solomon
Smith Thomas	Steele John
Smith Ann	Simmons T.
Smith A. 3	Shields James C.
Summers Caleb	Steele Hannaniah D. 2
Scofield Martha	Stout Jediah
Studman Maria	Schnebley James
Stout Benjamin 2	Stockam Thomas
Smith Wm.	Scantlin Wm.
Stout Robert	Stephenson Andrew P.
Sharp Linefield	Spiers Samuel
Salsigiver L. 3	Steele John
Shelby Thomas	Sanders Samuel
Shropshire Abner	Stout Ashton
Sullivan Wm.	Spilman Sylvester
Spiers Samuel	Stockdell Wm.
Steele Mary Jane	Sorrell John
Stewart Robert 2	Scott Thomas
Sanders Caleb J.	Shephard Dickey
Sinclair John	Steele Jane
Sawyier N. 2	Stout Elinor
Stevenson Thomas	Sanders Robert
South Elizabeth 2	Southard Isaac
Steele Oliver	Steele Isaac
South Samuel	Stout Ira
Simrall Joseph K.	Steele Solomon
Stinnett Henry	

T.

Trotter James	Thompson M.
Trott John	Turnbull James
Tanners Sampson	Taylor Ann
Trimble C. W.	Taylor Eliza
Tulley Jacob A.	Tulam Paul
Tyler Wm.	Thornton John
Taul Samuel 2	Talbott Charlotte S.
Tomlin Charles	Tedman Frances
Thompson Stapler	Tyler Benjamin
Talley Nelson	Thorns Elizabeth
Taylor Acquiller	True James
Thompson Ann	Taylor Mary O.
Todd James C.	Thomas Nancy
Turner J. A.	Talbott George W.
Taylor Richard	Tucker William
Trumbull Mr.	Tams Wm.
Trimble Robert	Tutt Benjamin
Tait Bacon	Thuston Algernon S.
Tindle Isaac	Turner Jane
Tyler Charles	Tilford Nicholas

U. V.

Usher Luke	Vanlear John 2
Utt John F.	Vaughan James
Upp Jacob	Vansant Christopher
Vantrouxberson G. 2	Vawter Richard
Von Mushack	

W.

Wilson John I. Jr.	Wallace James
Warnack George	Worthington Vachel
Williams Benjamin	Wellfort Robert
Wheeler George and	Weathers James
Warren	Wallace George H.
Weber George A.	Whiting Warner W.
Wright Benjamin	Wingfield Hudson M.
Wilson Reed	Williamson Lelly
Wilson William	Wymore Martin
Watson Wm. G. 4	Whittley C. Gen.
Woodson Joseph	Watkins Elisha
Williams O. J.	Williams George W.
Woodman Dan.	Wilkinson Wm.
Whitcomb James	Ward Geo. T.
Wilson J. & D.	Willers John
Wells David T. 3	Ward James
Wells Matthew	Waston James M.
Wight Spencer	Walker Chas.
Warfield Thos. B. 2	Walker Matthew 2
Wright John	Wingter Chas.
Wilsh James	Wilch Edward
Walker Adam R.	Ward David L.
Winter Gabriel	Williamson Richard
Wyatt Walter 4	Wilson Robert 2
Walsh N.	Wright Thomas C.
Wagley Isaac Q.	Wright Spencer
Wooley John	Watey Richard
Wilson James 5	Wells Frank
Wattson Patsey	White Minor
Welch Edwin	Webb Edward
Ward James	Wilson & Owings
Woodruff Aron 2	Wilson Moses
Wilson John	Worley Joshua

Y. Z.

Young Rubin	Zink Mr.
Young Ambrose	Clerk of the Fayette
Young Stephen	Circuit Court.

☞ Persons having letters advertised in the above list, will please name it on making application.

JOHN FOWLER, P. M.

N. B. No persons will be credited at the post office on any pretence whatever. 41-3

List of Letters,

REMAINING in the post-office at Versailles, Ky. which if not taken out before the first of January next, will be sent to the General post-office as dead letters.

A.

Jane Allen	Elliott Armstrong
And. Anderson	Ann Alloway
Lewis Arnold	Wm. Ashing
John Ashford	B
Buck & Cotton 2	Robt. Bell
Allen W. Berry	Wm. Blackburn 2
Richard Birins	Buck & Mitcham
Thos. C. Bailey	Branham & Marsham
Charles Buck 3	John H. Berryman 2
Alex'r. Bell & Co. 3	Doct. R. B. Berry 2
Capt. B. Berry	Soloman Boon
Jerry Buckley	Mr. Bivens

C.

James Craig 2	Daniel Clarke
Clerk Woodford C. C.	Samuel H. Claggett 2
Wm. H. Cosby	Joseph Collins
David Clarkson	N. B. Cooke & Co.
Nathan Compton	James Cox
Peter Conover	Seth Cook
N. B. Cooke 2	Geo. T. Cotton
Lewis Craig 2	Thos. Cary
Genl. M. Calames	A. C. Carlisle
David Campbell	Wm. Christopher
H. Crittenden 2	Jonas Christman
Wm. Cunningham	Loftus Ngel
John Cleavland 2	Wm. M. Coleman
Martin Coons	George Chittit

D.

Thos. Davis 2	Richard Dawson
Henry Davis	Joseph P. Davis
John Dennis	Walker Deering
Elizabeth Arnold	Lary Deering

E. F.

Wm. Edger	John Foster
Frederick Elgin	Martha T. Fox
John Elliott	John Ford
Josiah Elkin	Leonard Fleming
And Elliott	

G

Elizabeth T. Gaway 2	Samuel Gwinn
James Gardner	Robert Gwyn
Elijah Groomes	John George
Gabriel Gaines	Wm. Garnett
Mary Gerdon	

H

Walter R. Hurst	Lewis Haller
William Hill	Rebecca Huffman
Solomon Hufford	Jane Harris
John Hanna & Co.	James G. Hiter
Wilford G. Hagin	William Harper
Willis Hall	

Edward Johnson	[illegible] Jinkins
Wm. Johnson	John Jackson
Hedgeman Jinkins	Ephraim January
Dennis Inglehart	Elizabeth Johnson

K.

Archd. Kinkead 2	Jos. & Jno. Kinkead
Jos. Kinkead & Son 5	George W. Kinney

L.

Wm. B. Long 2	Elijah Lacy
H. & W. B. Long	Zach Long
James C. Long	G. Long & brothers
John H. Lee	Richard Lake
Jane Lightfoot	Wm. Lisenby

M

Major Jno. McKinney	Sally Morton
Dr. Littleb'ry Mosby 5	Wm. Masde
Wm. Mayo & Co. 4	Dr. L. Marshall
Samuel Miller	Colbit Maxsey
Richard M'Carty	James Martin
Eliza W. Majors	James Meek
M'Knight & Cosby	Johnson Malone
Jas. G. M'Kinney	Caroline F. Mayo

N. O.

Samuel Nuckols	Wm. O'Banion 2
James Norris	Hillery Offutt 2
James O'Hara	Fielder Offutt

P.

Patrick & Weir 4	John P. Porter
Wm. Powell 2	Mary Parker 2
Jacob Payne	Geo. F. Preston

R.

Judy Ralton 2	Wm. Robertson
Thos. Ramsey	Robert Rush
Samuel Ritchey	Richard Robertson
Joel Rice	Elizabeth Reed
Benj. Redd,	Charles Railey
Hanson Rush	

S.

Jacob Stewart	Catharine Steel
Sarah Stamper	Robt. Stevenson
Beverly Searcy	Robert Scott
John H. Smith	David D. Sites
Col. Wm. Steel	Allen Smith
John Swingle 2	Margaret Stevenson
James Scott	David Searcy
Robert Searcey	

T.

Claibourne L. Thomas	Samuel Torbitt
Chas. B. Thurston 2	Peggy Toler
Presley Ferrell	Henry Toler
Abraham Todd	Willis Thornton
Isham Talbot	Reuben Twyman

V. W.

Martha J. Vance	George S. Ward
Ben Vance	Absalom Wells
Benj. Wood	Thos. Wooldridge
Dr. J. Watson	George Woodward
Matilda A. Wallace	Richard Wiggs
Jos. H. Watkins	Jos. Wallace
Samuel B. Wallace	John Wiseman
Jos. White 2	Thomas Woolfolk
David Warford	John Watkins
Jefferson Williams	

JOS. W. BRYSON, D. P. M.

Versailles, October 1, 1819—41-3t

To John Spence and Mary his wife, late Mary Tebbs, Thomas Triplett and Margaret his wife, late Margaret Tebbs, Ann F. Tebbs and Thomas Tebbs, Fouchee Tebbs, Willoughby Tebbs and Samuel Tebbs, heirs of Willoughby Tebbs, deceased, who was sole heir at law of John Tebbs, deceased.

Jesse L. Holman and Elizabeth his wife, late Elizabeth Masterson, Thomas Peniston and Sally his wife, late Sally Masterson, William Scandevitt and Mary his wife, late Mary Masterson, Wesly P. Masterson, Lucy Masterson and Eleanor Masterson, heirs at law of Richard Masterson, decd. and George Evans,

Take Notice,

THAT on the 6th day of November next, at the Court-house in Lexington I shall take the depositions of Gen. Thomas Bodley, Gen. James Taylor and Capt. Thomas Young; and on the second Monday in November next, and also on the second Saturday in November next, at the Court house in Washington, I shall take the depositions of Gen. Henry Lee, David Blanchard, William Beckly, Peter Lee and Moses Daulton, as evidence in the suit in chancery, depending in the Mason Circuit Court, in which I am complainant and you are defendants.

JOHN FOWLER.

Oct. 8th, 1819.—41-4t

State of Kentucky,

Fayette Circuit, Set.—August Term, 1819.

Hiram Wortham, Complainant,

Against

John Keiser's children, John Boulware and others, Defendants,

IN CHANCERY.

THIS day came the complainant aforesaid by his counsel, and it appearing to the satisfaction of the court, that the defendants, John Boulware and Jacob Boulware, are no inhabitants of this commonwealth, and they having failed to enter their appearance herein agreeably to Law, and the rules of this court: On motion of the complainant by his counsel, it is ordered, that unless the said defendants, John and Jacob Boulware do appear here on or before the first day of the next February term, and answer the complainant's bill herein, the same will be taken for confessed against them, and it is further ordered, that a copy of this order be inserted in some authorised newspaper published in this state for two months successively. A copy. Att.

41 THOS. BODLEY, c. f. c. c.

Document 5c. The *Kentucky Gazette*, newspaper, October 8, 1819. [National Archives]

Document 5d. The *Kentucky Gazette*, newspaper, October 8, 1819. [National Archives]

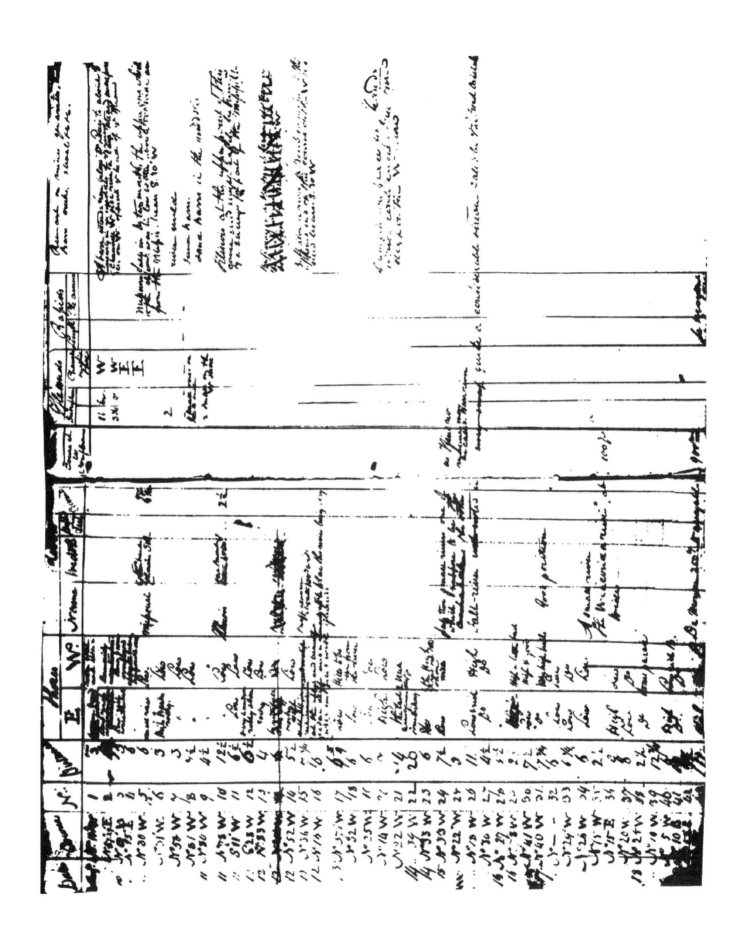

Document 6. Zebulon Pike's exploration notebook, 1805-1807. [National Archives]

Orders.

Pursuant to order of the Hon Secretary of War, Major Long assumes command of the Expedition about to engage in exploring the Mississippi, Missouri and their navagable Tributaries on board of the United States Steam Boat "Western Engineer" —

The Commanding Officer will direct the movements and operations of the Expedition, both in relation to Military and Scientific pursuits. — A strict observance of all orders whether written or verbal, emanating from him, will be required of all connected with the expedition.

The prime object of the expedition being a military survey of the Country about to be explored — the Com Officer will avail himself of any assistance he may require of any persons on board to aid in taking the necessary observations for an Astronomical and Barometrical Survey of the Country. — In this branch of duty Lt Graham and Cadet Swift will officiate as his immediate Assistants.

The Journal of the Expedition will be kept by Major Biddle, whose duty, it will be to record all transactions of the party that concern the objects of the expedition — to describe the manners, customs, &c, of the Inhabitants of the Countries thro' which we may pass. to trace in a compendious manner the histories of the Towns, villages, and tribes of Indians we may visit. to review the writings

Document 7a. Instructions from John C. Calhoun to Major
Stephen Long, March 30, 1819. [National Archives]

of other travellers and compare their statements with our own observations. and in general to record whatever may be of interest to the community in a civil point of view not interfering with the records to be kept by the Naturalist attached to the expedition.

Dr Baldwin will act as Botanist for the Expedition — a description of all the products of vegetation whether common or peculiar to the Countries we may traverse will be required of him — Also the diseases prevailing among the Inhabitants civilized & savage. and their probable causes will be subjects for his investigation — Any varieties in the Anatomy of the human frame, or any other phenomena observable in our species, will be particularly noticed by him.

Dr Baldwin will also officiate as Physician and Sur-geon for the expedition.

Mr Say will examine and describe any subjects in Zoology and its several branches that may come under our observation — a classification of all Land and Water Animals and a particular description of the animal remains found in a concrete state, will be required of him.

Geology. so far as it relates to Earths. Minerals. & Fossils distinguishing the Primitive, Transition. Secondary. and alluvial Formations and deposits will afford subjects for the invest--igation of Mr Jessup. — in this science. as also in Botany, & Zoology. facts will be required without regard to the The-

Document 7b. Instructions from John C. Calhoun to Major Stephen Long, March 30, 1819. [National Archives]

ories or hypotheses that have been advanced on numerous occasions by men of science.

Mr Peale will officiate as Assistant Naturalist in the several departments above enumerated, his services will be required in collecting specimens suitable to be preserved in drafting or delineating them in preserving the skins &c of Animals, and in sketching the Stratifications of Rocks Earths &c as presented on the declivities of Precipices.

Mr Seymour, as Painter for the Expedition will furnish sketches of Landscapes whenever we meet with any distinguished for their beauty or grandeur – he will also paint miniature likenesses, or Portraits if required of distinguished Indians and exhibit groups of savages, engaged in celebrating their festivals or sitting in council and in general illustrate any subject that may be deemed appropriate in his art.

Lt Graham and Cadet Swift, in addition to the duties they may perform in the capacity of Assistant Topographers – will attend to drilling the Boats Crew in the exercise of the Musket, the Field Pieces and the Sabre – their duties will be assigned them from time to time by the Com Officer.

All records kept on board of the Steam Boat, all subjects of Natural History, Geology and Botany – all drawings, as also all documents of every kind, relating to the expedition will at all times be subject to the inspection

Document 7c. Instructions from John C. Calhoun to Major
Stephen Long, March 30, 1819. [National Archives]

of the Commanding Officer, and at the conclusion of each Trip or voyage will be placed at his disposal as agent for the U. S Government.

Orders will be given from time to time whenever the Commanding Officer may deem them expedient.

(Signed)

S. H. Long. Maj. U. S. Eng.
Comg Expedition.

Pittsburgh 30th March 1819.

RATES OF TOLL

TO BE CHARGED ON THE

CHESAPEAKE AND OHIO CANAL,

From and after the 1st of July, 1857.

Copy of original from the Chesapeake and Ohio Canal records

Document 8. Chart of Chesapeake and Ohio Canal toll rates, July 1, 1857. [National Archives]

An act

giving the assent of this state to an act of congress for laying out & making a road from the Potomac river to the state of Ohio

Whereas by an act of the congress of the U. S. passed on the twenty ninth day of march one thousand eight hundred & six, entitled "an act to regulate the laying out and making a road from Cumberland in the state of maryland to the state of Ohio" the President of the united states was empowered to lay out a road from the potomac to the ohio rivers, and to take measures for making the same, so soon as the consent of the legislatures of the several states, through which the said road should pass, could be obtained: and whereas application hath been made to this present general assembly, by the president of the united states, for its consent to the measures aforesaid:

Be it therefore enacted by the general assembly, that the president of the united states be, and is hereby authorized to cause so much of the said road as will be within this state, to be cut out from the place where the same may enter the territory of this state, to such point or place on the Ohio river as now is or hereafter may be agreed upon by the president or congress of the united States, and to cause the said road to be made, regulated & completed within the limits, and according to the true intent and meaning of the before recited act of congress, or any future act by them to be passed in relation thereto.

Be it further enacted, that such person or persons as are or shall be appointed for the purpose of laying out and completing the said road, under the authority of the united States, shall have full power and authority to enter upon the lands through which the same may pass, and upon any lands near or adjacent thereto, and therefrom to take, dig, cut & carry away such materials of earth, stone, gravel, timber & sand, as may be necessary for completing the said road.

Provided, Nevertheless, that such materials shall be valued & appraised in the same manner as materials taken for similar purposes, under the authority of this commonwealth are by the laws thereof directed to be valued and appraised and a certificate of the amount thereof shall, by the person or persons appointed, or hereafter to be appointed under the authority of the U.S. for the purpose aforesaid, be delivered to each party entitled thereto, for any materials to be taken by virtue of this act, to entitle him or her to receive payment therefor from the united States.

This act shall be in force from the passing thereof.

I certify, that the preceding is a correct copy of an act passed by the general assembly of Virginia, on the twelfth day of January one thousand eight hundred & seven. Given under my hand (there being no official seal) at Richmond, this twenty third day of January in the year of our Lord one thousand eight hundred and twenty two, and of the commonwealth the forty sixth.

Signd { Wm Mumford } Keeper of the Rolls,

for the post at Chickasaw Bluffs, to whom you will please to address the Goods intended for the Factory established at that place. Mr. Peterkin leaves the Seat of Government tomorrow for the place of his destination.

I am &c. H.D.

To. Thomas Peterkin Esquire.

Sir,

The Goods placed under your care, are intended exclusively for supplying the Indians, within the jurisdiction of the United States.

In your intercourse with the Indians you will cherish and cultivate a spirit of friendship and harmony, carefully avoiding on your part every cause of offence. Your conduct at all times should be temperate, kindind, and conciliatory proper respect should be paid to the Chiefs, and other men of distinction.

The prices of the several articles of merchandize should be as uniform as possible, and to avoid disputes and ultimate losses no credit should be given, excepting in extraordinary cases, and to men of note and distinction. No sales should be made but to natives. You will not supply white traders with merchandize on any terms, or conditions. The sale of ardent spirits are strictly prohibited.

Care should be taken to prevent frauds in relation to the skins or furs you may receive in payment for Goods: and no means should be neglected for the preservation of them when received.

Remittances are to be made by you to the order and under the direction of General Irvine Superintendant of Military Stores and Agent for Indian Trading Houses. "It

It is presumed that merchandize will bear an advance of from seventy five to one hundred pr. Centum upon the Invoices, and by which you will govern yourself until you shall receive further instructions

You will keep correct accounts of all sales and receipts, and of every species of expence attending the business Losses of property should be carefully guarded against

A suitable guard will be furnished you by the Officer commanding the Garrison; you will how ever absent yourself as little as possible from the stores. An Interpreter when necessary will be furnished you (on application) by Colonel Mitchell or in his absence by the Officer commanding the Garrison. It is important that your interpreter should be a person of sober and discreet habits.

It is deemed incompatible with your public agency to be employed in private trade or commerce.

War Office 28th July 1802
H. Dearborn

Wm Irvine

War Department
29th July 1802

Sir,

Payments have been made at the seat of Government to the following persons the sums respectively annexed to their names, Viz,

John Johnston United States Factor, Fort Wayne .... $500.
Joseph Chambers .... Do .... Do .... Choctaw .... "200.
Robert Munson .... Do .... Do .... Detroit .... 350.
Thomas Peterkin .... Do .... Do .... Chickasaw Bluffs 200.

With which you will please to debit each of the Gentlemen in your books, and hold them accountable therefor in the adjustment of their accounts.

Iam &c H.D

Document 10b. Letter from H. Dearborn to Thomas Peterkin, July 28, 1802. [National Archives]

To the Honourable the Senate and House of Representatives in Congress assembled,

The Memorial of Eli Whitney.

Respectfully sheweth,

That your memorialist is the inventor of the machine with which the principal part of the Cotton raised in the United States is cleaned & prepared for market. — That being in the State of Georgia in the year 1793, he was informed by the planters, that the agriculture of that State was unproductive, especially in the interior, where it produced little or nothing, for exportation. — That attempts had been made to cultivate cotton; but that the prospect of success was not flattering. — That of the various kinds which had been tried in the interior, none of them were productive, except the Green seed Cotton, which was so extremely dif-

difficult to clean, as to discourage all further attempts to raise it. — That it was generally believed this species of cotton might be cultivated with great advantage, if any cheap and expeditious method of separating it from its seeds could be discovered — and that such a discovery would be highly beneficial both to the public and the inventor. —

These remarks first drew the attention of your memorialist to this subject and after considerable reflection he became impressed with a belief that this desireable object might be accomplished. —
At the same time he could not but entertain doubts, whether he ought to suffer any prospect of so precarious a nature, as that which depends upon the success of new projects, to divert his attention from a regular profession —

About this time Congress passed a New Patent Law, which your memorialist

Document 11b. Memorial of Eli Whitney, April 16, 1812. [National Archives]

considered as a premium offered to any citizen who should devote his attention to useful improvements and as a pledge from his country, that in case he should be successful, his rights and his property would be protected. ———

Under these impressions your memorialist relinquished every other object of pursuit — and devoted his utmost exersions to reduce his invention, which, as yet was little more than a floating image of the mind, to practical use — and fortunately for the Country he succeeded in giving form to the conceptions of his imagination and to matter a new mode of existence — and the result of this new modification of matter, was every thing that could be wished

After reducing his theory to practice, by effectual & successful experiments your memorialist took out a Patent.

So alluring were the advantages developed by this invention that in a short time the whole attention of the planters of the middle and upper country, of the Southern States, was turned to planting the Green Seed Cotton—

The means furnished by this discovery of cleaning, that species of cotton, were at once so cheap and expeditious, and the prospect of advantage so alluring, that it suddenly became the general crop of the country

Little or no regard, however, was paid to the claims of your memorialist—and the infringment of his rights became almost as extensive as the cultivation of cotton—— He was soon reduced to the disagreable necessity of resorting to courts of Justice for the protection of his property——

After the unavoidable delays which usually attend prosecutions of this kind and a laboured trial, it was discovered that the Defendents had only used — and that as the law then stood they must both make and use the machine, or they could not be liable — the Court decided that it was a fatal, though inadvertant defect in the law and gave judgment for the Defendents. —

It was not untill the year 1800. that this defect in the law was amended. — Immediately after the amendment of the law, your memorialist commenced a number of suits; but so effectual were the means of procrastination and delay, resorted to, by the Defendents, that he was unable to obtain any decision on the merits of his claim untill the year 1807 — not untill he had been eleven years in the Law & thirteen years of his patent term had expired. —

A compromise has been made with several of the States, to which your memorialist has assigned his right and relinquished all further claim; but from the state in which he first made and introduced his invention, and which has derived the most signal benefits from it, he has realized nothing — and from no state has he received the amount of half a Cent pr pound, on the cotton cleaned with his machine, within that state, in one year. —

Estimating the value of the labour of one man at twenty cents pr Day, the whole amount which has been realized by your memorialist for his invention, is not equal to the value of the labour saved in one hour by his machines, now in use, in the U. States. —

Permit your memorialist further to remark that by far the greatest part of the cotton raised in the United States has been & must of necessity continue to be the Green Seed. That, before the invention of your memorialist, the value of this species of cotton, after it was cleaned, was not equal to the expence of cleaning it — that since, the cultivation of this species has been a great —

source of wealth to the community & of riches to thousands of her citizens — That as a labour-saving machine it is an invention which enables <u>one man</u> to perform in a given time <u>that</u> which would require a <u>thousand men</u>, without its aid, to perform in the same time — in short that it furnishes to the whole family of mankind the means of procuring the article of cotton, that important raw material, which constitutes a great part of their cloathing at a much cheaper rate —

Your memorialist begs leave further to state that a confident-expectation that his case would be embraced in the general law which Congress has, for several years, had under consideration, has prevented his making an earlier application. — That the expences incurred by him in making and introducing this useful improvement and establishing his claim to its invention, have absorbed a great proportion of what he has received, from those states with which he has made a compromise —

Document 11g. Memorial of Eli Whitney, April 16, 1812. [National Archives]

That he humbly conceives himself fairly intitled to a further remuneration from his Country — and that he ought to be admitted to a more liberal participation with his fellow citizens, in the benefits of his invention.

He therefore prays your Honourable Body, to take his case into consideration, and authorize the renewal of his Patent, or grant such other relief, as Congress in their wisdom and their justice may deem meet, and proper —

Eli Whitney

Washington 16th Aprl. 1812.

Captain John Kendrick   Duplicate   [Madison]

Sir, The Ship Columbia & Sloop Washing-
ton, being Compleatly equipt for a Voyage to the Pacific Ocean, and the
Sea, We place such confidence in you, as to give you the entire comman[d]
the Enterprise————— It would be impossible, upon a Voyage of this Natu[re]
give with propriety, any binding Instructions, and such is our reliance o[n]
your Honor, Integrity, and good conduct, that it would be needless at an[y]
time, you will be on the spot, and as circumstances turn up, you must improve th[em]
but We cannot forbear to impress upon your mind, our wish, and expectatio[n]
that the most inviolable Harmony & Friendship, may subsist, between yo[u]
and the Natives, and that no advantage, may be taken of them in Trade [but]
but that you endeavour, by Honest conduct, to impress upon their minds, [a]
Friendship, for Americans.————— We recommend your stoping on the Coast
and from thence continue your trade, as you find opherture-
nity. If in the course of the first season you have collected furrs suficient o[r]
five hundred Sea Otters & others in proportion, We would have you send t[hem]
by the Sloop to China, and Let the Sloop return to you in the Spring wit[h]
such supplys as you may find necessary both for your trade, and the us[e]
of your men, but at all events, We depend the Ship will winter on the Coas[t]
and the Sloop also, unless Furrs suficient are procured, to send her to Chin[a]
and if ——— the second season, there should not be more than Furrs suffic[ient]
to load the Sloop, say Four Thousand sea Otters, and you find it agreeab[le]
We would have you send the Sloop to China, and tarry over in the Ship
a second season; and in Short, We leave it intirely to you to remain on
the Coast as long as you find it advantageous, and convenient, and in that
case every season We expect you send what Furrs you have procured to Market and you will bear in mind, that you can have from China, all th[e]
supplies you may want from time to time ———— When you are coming of[f]

Document 12a. Letter from Joseph Barrett to Captain John Kendrick, ca. 1786-1787. [National Archives]

the Coast yourself, if you find a perfect safety in it, and twelve of your men or as many as you can spare, are willing to stay behind. it is our wish they may be gratified, and for their further encouragement. We agree, either to double their Wages, and find them provisions, Or. to find them Provisions only, and throw in all the remainder of your Cargo out; which they shall trade with and the Furrs produced therefrom shall be one half their property and the other half the property of the Owners of this Enterprize. In this Case you will make a firm Agreement in writing with them, you will see the men are properly arranged, and leave a good man to command them; you will leave them all the Boats you can spare, and if you find it necessary the Sloop also. or We will engage to send a Vessel to take them off whenever you shall agree to do it. We mean if any stay behind they shall also be intitled to receive the Gratuity if the Voyage prospers, as much as if they returned in the Ship, and it shall be paid to their order, as soon as the Voyage is made up in America.

If you make any Fort or any improvement of land on the Coast, be sure you purchase the Soil of the Natives and it would not be amiss if you purchased some advantageous tract of land in the name of the Owners, if you should, let the Instrument of conveyance bear every authentic mark the circumstance will admit of.

The Medals & the Copper Coins you have, you will on no terms terms part with me, until you have doubled Cape Horn, after which you will distribute them in every place you stop at either as presents or Traffic and you will as occasion offers, distribute such presents to the Natives as you think will be advantageous to us, and pleasing to them

You will constantly bear in mind, that no trade is to be allowed on the Coast, on any pretence whatever but for the Benefit of the Owners.

When you send the Sloop to China, you are to give her orders to stop at Maccau, and enquire for Letters, which will be lodged there, for her, and also for you and whatever orders you find there are to be followed, as far as they can be with propriety —

If you think adviseable, when you come off the Coast in the Ship, you may touch at Japan, but not Anchor unless you can do it with perfect security, but if you find that can be done, and the trade is better there than in China (w.ch you will be able to know when the Sloop returns to you) you will trade there —

Be sure that you omit no opportunity of writing by all Vessels you may meet and any Letters you may write by the way of China to the care of Mess.rs Shaw & Randall. by the way of France to the care of Mess.rs Le Coutiaulx & Co. Paris, by the way of Portugal to Mess.rs Dohrman, & Co. Lisbon. by the way of London to Mess.rs Lane Son & Frazier.

We propose to consign you to Mess.rs Shaw, and Randall at Canton, you will therefore if you meet no orders at Macao, apply to them at Canton, & if they have the Consignment, follow their orders. —

You are strictly enjoined not to touch at any part of the Spanish Dominions on the Western Coast of America, unless drawn there by an avoidable Accident in which case you will stay no longer than is necessary, & while there, be carefull to give no offence to any of the Subjects of his Catholic Majesty — and if you meet with any subjects of any European Prince, you are to treat them with friendship & civility. —

The Certificates you have from the French and Dutch Consul you will make use of if you meet with any ships of those Nations, & you will pay them every respect that is due to them.

The Sea Letters from Congress & this State you will also use on every proper Occasion, and altho' we expect you will treat all Nations with respect & civility, yet We depend you will suffer Insult and Injury from none, without shewing that Spirit w.ch ever become a free and Independent American. —

You will give to Cap.t Gray the proper directions where to meet you, if you should be seperated from him and how to proceed upon the Coast if he should not meet you there — In case of sickness & God forbid and you should find yourself dangerous, We leave it with you to appoint a

Successor, in dᵗʰ case We should prefer your giving that Charge to the two most suitable, on board, at the present it appears to us, that this command had best be given to Capt. Gray, and Mr. Howe, and it is our idea if such an event as here mention'd should take place without your appointing other persons, that they may Jointly have the command so far as it respects the trading upon this Enterprize —

You will take from Capt. Gray a Receipt similar to what you gave us, for the Cargo he has on board the Sloop makeing him in case of your Death Accountable for the Proceeds & his conduct —

You will procure every sort of seeds & plants wᶜʰ you meet with in the Country you may visit —

We wish a Prosperous Voyage

These are the orders I have received from the Owners of the Columbia & Washington to Promise Honorably to follow

John Kendrick

For your Encouragement, if you ..... it with him. We agree to allow you Five pounds lawful ₱ mo. &c. & a commission of five ₱₡ on the Neat Proceeds of the Voyage when it is made up in America; and We agree to Advance on Account of your Wages & the six men on board for wᶜʰ you represent ' at the rate of two hundred Dollars ₱ Annum .... favourable Accounts from you — and We agree to allow to R.S. Howe & John Breck Treat, if they conduct faithfully, to each of them or above their Wages, One half per Cent on the Neat Proceeds of the Voyage in America

In behalf of the Owners

Joseph Barrell

I am in behalf of the Owners
Your friend & Servt

Joseph Barrell

At a Court of Chancery held for the State of New York at the City of Albany on the twenty first day of October in the year of our Lord one thousand eight hundred and Eighteen

Present

The Honourable James Kent Esquire Chancellor

Aaron Ogden
vs
Thomas Gibbons

On reading the complainants bill of complaint in this cause verified by his oath and on motion of Josiah Ogden Hoffman Esquire Solicitor for the said Complainant it is Ordered that the said bill be filed with one of the Clerks of this court and that thereupon a writ or writs of Injunction issue out of and under the seal of this court, to be directed to the above named defendant Thomas Gibbons and to all and every his confederates, agents, Captains, Pilots Engineers, Mariners & Servants commanding them and every of them under a certain penalty therein to be expressed, absolutely to desist from Using, employing and navigating the two steam boats in the said bill particularly mentioned, the one named the Stoutington but usually called the Mouse, and the other named the Bellona, or either of them or any other steam boat, or steam boats purchased or built by the said Thomas Gibbons on the waters of this State, lying between Elizabeth town in the State of New Jersey, or any place within the township of Elizabeth town aforesaid, and the City of New York, until the said defendant shall have fully answered the said bill, and until the further order of this court in the premises according to the prayer of the said bill

a Copy   Isaac S Kip
                              Assistant Register

Muscle Shoals January 25th 1807

Sir

I have lately been informed that some ill disposed persons in the Cumberland Country have tried at the last Federal Court held at Nashville to have presented to the grand jurors of sd Court certain citizens supposed to have purchased Lands from Doublehead. I am informed that the attempt failed for the want of authentic testimony — Well might it do so, for I do assure you Sir that he Doublehead has not sold one acre of ground — it is true that he has rented or leased some of the ground reserved for him & those that live on it with him to some respectable farmers, who I conceive will be of essencial Service to the Indians by setting the Pattern of industry & true farming, I have long conceiv -ed that it was the wish of our Government to cause the Indians to become farmers & quit the hunting life — If so Sir, there can nothing be devised that will sooner lead to the object than the very thing done by Doublehead. Cer= =tainly Sir the United States must intend.. that such Indians as fall into the plan that Government has so strenuously impressed on their minds attended with large expences, should become indivirdual proffesors of Land — for this purpose I conceive government has given those reserves of land that are recognised by the treaty at Tellico 25 & 27 of October 1805 & by the Convention made at the city Washington on the 7th day of January 1806.

Document 14a. Letter from John Chisholm to Colonel Meigs, January 25, 1807. [National Archives]

Which Treaties have been ratified by the Government agreable to the constitution, & as such I have judged that they are part of the Supreme Laws of the land, & therefore I shall rest satisfied & assured that those lands are completely out of the grasp of our Greedy minded & inhuman Speculators & that such honest citizens as may serve & settle on those Reserves of land will be perfectly safe under the Auspecies, & protection of the Government of the United States — You Sir I flatter myself are no stranger to my Indeavor in this question, to promote Civilization & the, Invaluable & virtuous Views of the Government, — I shall continue that line of conduct untill I am desired by Authority to desist — I hope Sir that you will take a view of my Neighborhood & make a comparative view of their neighbors, I am sorry to say that our laws & business are pestered with ill matured Stories propogated & circulated on the upper Towns, as we suppose by some white persons residing their & are no friends to the Government of the United States & wish to prevent the improvement & civilization on Indians ———

Since I have heard of the affair of Mr Burr, it brings to my mind Recollection a circumstance that happened some time in October — it is as follows an unknown young Man passing thro the Settlement of this place — he was asked by an Indian who he was & where he was going he replied he was travelling had been lost & was very hungry ———

Document 14b. Letter from John Chisholm to Colonel Meigs, January 25, 1807. [National Archives]

The Indian brought him to me were there were some other people of my Neighbors Collected, I asked him some Questions he told me he was a Mill Wright by Trade, that he had been unfortunate, had got in debt, was put into Nashville Jail, that Col⁰ Burr had paid his Debt gave him a horse & advised him to the Creek Nation, that he had been lost & wanted some provision, that he had no money except a fifty dollar bank bill, he shew me the Bill I looked on the bill to be bad—

I asked him if he had got a passport to travel thro the Indian Nations he answered no — I then told him that he appeared some what suspicious & that he must return I got a piece of Meat from an Indian, gave him & he went off. he appeared to keep his saddle bags very close on his arm — Some of the people observed to me that he ought to be taken up that were of opinion that if his saddle bags were searched he would be found to Contain a Quantity of Counterfeit Bills — as I had no authority to do so I omitted it & he went off — I am of opinion that perhaps he was upon other business. & I think by applying to the Jailor at Nashville that a discovery can be found perhaps to a valuable purpose —

I have been gout for some time with the commissioners from the State of Tennessee viewing the road that is recognized by the Treaty of Tellico from Franklin to the Tombigbee

Document 14c. Letter from John Chisholm to Colonel Meigs, January 25, 1807. [National Archives]

river, so far as we have viewed it it is a most excelent way for a load — this road it will be a most excelent acquisition to the Citizens of Tennessee & to the government of the United States by opening a very short & safe Communication to the post near Mobile & the Choctaw Nation — I will thank you to give your aid on this Business so far as is Consistent — it will not exceed 180 Miles from Nashville to the navigation were Vesels of very considerable burden can come — as I have no opportunity of writing their Honors Messers Smith & Campbell on this subject — I will thank you to mention it — to them if you think it proper

I am Sir your most obedient

John D. Chisholm —

Col: deTrumbs Meigs

Document 14d. Letter from John Chisholm to Colonel Meigs, January 25, 1807. [National Archives]

the ground, that they had been specially attached to Major General Porter's command & were to communicate with & receive orders from him alone. To check at once a distinction so hostile to military order - so fatal to the views of the President - I hasten to inform you, to the end that you may inform our Indian friends, that the command in chief on the Niagara frontier is vested in Major General Brown - & that of course he, who commands all, will command them also - and that their services can only be accepted on condition of their entire willingness to receive & obey the orders of the said Major Genl Brown, & in case of his death, of the Officer who would com= mand in his stead, according to the rules & usages of the Army.

War Department.
June 11th 1814.

Sir,
The President of the United States has been pleased His Excellency to appoint you Commissioner to confer with the Indian Nations
Isaac Shelby of the West and north and to conclude with them a treaty
& & of Peace and alliance - The treaty will be held at
The same letter Greenville in the State of Ohio and at such time as may
to Gov Harrison have been fixed in the invitation given to the Indians by
& His Exc'y Govr General Harrison. - The object to be attained will be
Cass - indicated under the following heads viz:

1st A Peace sincere and lasting between the Contracting parties: -

2d An alliance between the said parties in prosecuting the present War against Great Britain - and

3. An arrangement for the extinction of the Indian title to the tract of Land lying between the Michigan Territory on the north, the Western limits of the State of Ohio on the West, the Indian boundary line as settled by General Wayne on the South, and the line by treaty of the 4th of July 1805, on the East.

In the first of these objects the parties have a common

and obvious interest. —

To engage the Indians in the second, their warriors will be taken into the Service of the United States, and will receive the monthly pay or subsistence of Soldiers of our Army — Such as bring good and efficient arms will be entitled to a reasonable Compensation for their use. — Such as have not arms of this description to bring, will be supplied with musquets. To those serving faithfully certain articles of Clothing will be furnished viz: Blankets and Cloth for leggins and breech Clouts — They will be specially commanded by their own Chiefs, (who will be subject to the Orders of the General Officer and Officers of the United States Army assigned to the command of the Division or Brigade with which they may act &) who will be commissioned by medals presented to them by order of the President. —

The arrangement with regard to the exchange of Lands is deemed important by some of the Inhabitants of the State of Ohio — If the suggestion can be made and the arrangement effected, without exciting in the Indians any disagreeable Sensations — this object may be prosecuted otherwise it is not to be touched.

The Lands proposed to be given in exchange, is a tract of equal dimensions, lying between Lake Michigan and the Mississippi —

His Excy
Isaac Shelby
&c —

The same letter
Gen. Harrison
Gov. Lewis Cass

War Department.
June 11th 1814.

Sir,

On more mature deliberation two alterations in the instructions forwarded to you in relation to the proposed treaty, have been adopted.

1st. That instead of an article stipulating alliance and subsidy by pay &c. one shall be substituted, simply obligatory on the Indians to assist in prosecuting the War, against Great Britain if so required to do by the United States — and — 2d. That nothing

Peorias, 18. Feb. 1812

May it please Your Excellency,

I have had the honor to receive your two letters of 13th & 16th December last, and am sorry that I was not at home to answer your letters by Governor Edwards' Messenger, who left this a few days before I arrived from Chicago. It appears from Indian information that the Prophets' party was dispersed only for a moment, as I am informed that he, the Prophet was not more than two or three miles from the battle-ground, for several days after the army left the Prophets' village. When I was first informed of the battle, the Indians said that Governor Harrison was killed, and they, Indians, appear to be very inveterate against Governor Harrison, and should think it advisable to acquaint G.H. to be on his guard.

I have it from good information that only two of Catfish's party committed the murder on Coles' party in 1810, and they are both at the Prophets' village, and they must be now on the Wabash. Those who killed Cox on Kaskaskia river are now about six miles above this place. Those Indians who killed Price are Folsovoins, and are at their

(village)

Document 16a. Letter from Thomas Forsyth to Governor Howard, February 18, 1812. [National Archives]

village near Puant's bay. As all the chiefs of the Potowatimie nation will be at the council at Vincennes, I think it would be a proper time and place, to demand all those murderers. Sheguenaby who is a considerable man among the Indians of this Country sent word to those chiefs who are going to Vincennes that he would not go to Vincennes, but was ready to go down to Kaskaskia, to settle their business there. Therefore I expect that on their return home from Vincennes, they will go down. The main Poc is expected early in the Spring from Detroit, & he, no doubt, will turn the scale of affairs, either better or worse. —

On my way from Chicago to this place, I fell in with Indians from the Kankeekee river, who informed that there were not more than 300 men in the Prophets' village, and not more than 80 or 90 in the battle; that 31 were killed dead (some say only 24) from 40 to 50 wounded: that most all the wounded were already well. That they had no ammunition, or they would have followed the army towards Vincennes and cut many off. I have wrote Genl. Clarke fully on the

(subject)

subject of Indian affairs, and I refer you to my letter to him of this day's date. —

Please accept my best thanks for your goodness in recommending me for the agency of this Post, and I hope I shall always merit the confidence that may be entrusted to me by my Country. —

Should any thing particular occur I shall acquaint you by express. I have wrote Major Whiteside to make himself easy while the Chiefs are at Vincennes, and that they have promised me faithfully to go down to bear Governor Edward's talk, after they return from Vincennes. —

I remain, Yr. Excellency's
Mo: ob: Servant
(Signed) Thomas Forsyth.
—— // ——

His Excy.
Governor Howard
St. Louis'

New-york July 24th 1790

Sir

I left Muskingum the 2d instant; northing new
in that quarter since Mr Morgan came on, except,
that a number of Horses have been stolen & one man
killed at Belleville (a Virginia settlement about three
miles below the great Hockhocking) which appears to be
a mischief altogether unprovoked. also about the 20th
of last month a woman was taken near the mouth of
Buffaloe Creek, and was afterward murdered; but this
business was preceded by the white people stealing a
number of Horses from the the Indians & refuseing
to deliver them up when demanded: ————

The Muskingum settlements have lost many Horses, the
last fall & this Summer, some stollen by white people
but more by the Indians, and their is sufficient evidence
that some of the Delawares and Wyndots who attended the

Treaty at Fort Harmar, as well as the Shawonees have been concerned in the theift — their is also good reason to beleve that several belonging to the Dellaware & Wyndot Nations, have been concerned in Murdering the people and plundering the boats, going down the ohio; the last winter and Spring, & it is likewise said, that a number of white men weare among that gang of robbe.

It seems that they are possessed of some boats or other Craft on the Sioto, in which they Issue out of that river into the ohio, and haueing obtained their boot retire again with feistly — : would not a small detachment of Troops stationed at the mouth of the Sioto in great measure, if not wholly, put a stop to this kind of business, and at the same time giue confider to the people in the new settlements on the the ohio, whi are commencieing between the Sioto and the Great Kenhawa

By letters recived at Muskingum, from Mr

Document 17b. Letter from Judge Rufus Putnam to President George Washington, July 24, 1790. [National Archives]

Secretary Sargent, and also from Major Doughty, information: I learnt that Governor St Clair was still in the Illinois Country & would not probably, return to Muskingum till october, & that Messieurs Symes & Turner, left the Miamis in the month of May. to attend the governor — under these circumstances I concieved it best to to return imedately for my family. I leave this on monday morning, I shall be in Town again the first or 2d week in September on my way to the Western world —

I have the honour to be Sir with every posable sentiments of the most perfect esteem your Excellencys most obeadent Humble Servent

Rufus Putnam

The President

~~To the Senate & House of Representatives of the United States.~~

In pursuance ~~of measures proposed~~ to Congress by ~~a message~~ of Jan. 18. 1803. and ~~sanctioned by their~~ appropriation for carrying it into execution, Capt. ~~Meriwether~~ Lewis of the 1st. regiment of in-fantry was appointed, with a party of men, to explore the river Missouri, from it's mouth to it's source; & ~~crossing~~ the highlands by the shortest portage, to seek the best water communication thence to the Pacific ocean: & Lieu^t. Clarke was appointed second in command. they were to enter into conference with the Indian nations on their route, with a view to the ~~establishment of~~ commerce with them. they entered the Missouri May 14. 1804. and on the 1st. of Nov. took up their winter quarters near the Mandan towns, 1609 miles above the mouth of the river, in Lat. 47°-21'-47" North, & Long. 99°-24'-45" West from Greenwich. on the 8th. ~~of~~ April 1805. they proceeded up the river in pursuance of the objects ~~prescribed~~ to them. a letter of the preceding day Apr. 7. from Capt. Lewis, is herewith communicated. during his stay among the Mandans, he ~~had~~ been able to lay down the Missouri, accord-ing to courses & distances taken on his passage up it, corrected by frequent observations of Longitude & Latitude, & to add to the actual survey of this portion of the river, a general map of the country between the Missisipi & Pacific, from the 34th. to the 54th. degrees of Latitude. these additions are from information collected from Indians with whom he had oppor-tunities of communicating ~~during~~ his journey & residence with them.

Document 18a. Message from President Thomas Jefferson to Congress, February 19, 1806. [National Archives]

copies of this map are now presented to both houses of Congress. With these I communicate also a statistical view, procured and forwarded by him, of the Indian nations inhabiting the territory of Louisiana, & the countries adjacent to it's Northern and Western borders, of their commerce, & of other interesting circumstances res-pecting them.

In order to render the statement, as compleat as may be, of the Indians inhabiting the country West of the Missisipi, I add Doctr. Sibley's account of those residing in & adjacent to the Territory of Orleans.

I communicate also from the same person, an account of the Red river, according to the best information he had been able to collect.

Having been disappointed, after considerable preparation, in the purpose of sending an exploring party up that river in the summer of 1804. it was thought best to employ the autumn of that year in procuring a knowledge of an interesting branch of the river called the Washita. this was undertaken under the direction of mr Dunbar of Natchez, a citizen of distinguished science, who had aided, and continues to aid us, with his disinterested & valuable ser-vices in the prosecution of these enterprizes. he ascended the river to the remarkeable Hotsprings near it, in Lat. 34.-31-4.16 Long. 92-50.45" West from Greenwich, taking it's courses & distances, & correcting them by frequent celestial observations. Extracts from his observations, and

Document 18b. Message from President Thomas Jefferson to Congress, February 19, 1806. [National Archives]

copies of his map of the river, from it's mouth to the Hot-springs, make part of the present communications. the examination of the Red river itself, is but now commencing.

Th Jefferson
Feb. 19. 1806.

Message from the Pr. of U.S.
communicating information of Capt.
Lewis; progress in exploring the western
Country. &

1806. Feb. 19. to be

Document 18d. Message from President Thomas Jefferson to Congress, February 19, 1806. [National Archives]

Packing note of Pettries to be received of Mr. Pelajon by Mr George Johnston at Drummond Islands — viz —

1 78 Beaver Skins 100 ℔,
2 82 — " — " — 100 „
3 89 = " — " — 100 „
4 85 — " — " — 100 „
5 86 — " — " — 100 „
6 85 — " — " — 100 „
7 76 — " — " — 100 „
8 712 Muskrats and 2 Beaver Skins 4 ℔,
9 736 — ditto — " 2 — ditto — " — 4 ℔,
10 665 — ditto — " 2 — ditto — " 3 ℔,
11 8 Bears
   80 Martens
   50 Otters
   ~~50 Minks~~
   5 Fishers
12 3 Bears
   90 Lynx

Mr Crooks would beg of Mr Johnston to open every Pack, examine the condition of the Skins, count the whole, and weigh the Beaver. all the Skins are to be received, but Mr Johnston will have the goodness in meeting to say how the different kinds are, as to quality; and the order a condition in which he finds them

Michilimackinac — 30 July 1818

Document 19. Packing list for pelts, July 30, 1818. [National Archives]

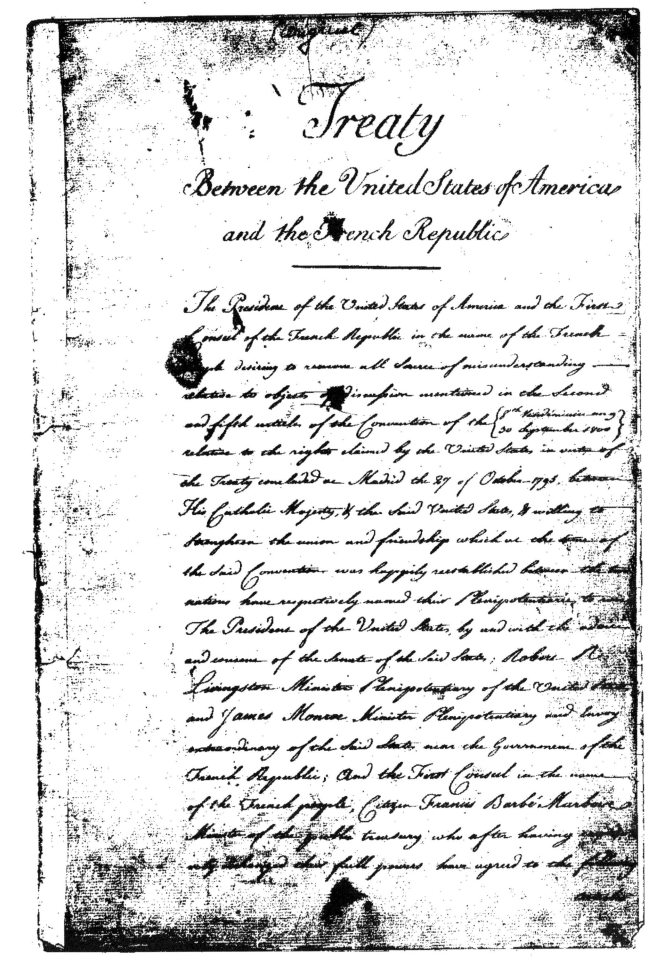

Treaty

Between the United States of America and the French Republic

The President of the United States of America and the First Consul of the French Republic in the name of the French people desiring to remove all Source of misunderstanding relative to objects of discussion mentioned in the Second and fifth articles of the Convention of the 8th Vendémiaire an 9 / 30 September 1800 relative to the rights claimed by the United States in virtue of the Treaty concluded at Madrid the 27 of October 1795, between His Catholic Majesty, & the Said United States, & willing to strengthen the union and friendship which at the time of the Said Convention was happily reestablished between the two nations have respectively named their Plenipotentiaries, to wit The President of the United States, by and with the advice and consent of the Senate of the Said States; Robert R. Livingston Minister Plenipotentiary of the United States and James Monroe Minister Plenipotentiary and Envoy extraordinary of the Said States near the Government of the French Republic; And the First Consul in the name of the French people, Citizen Francis Barbé Marbois Minister of the public treasury who after having respectively exchanged their full powers have agreed to the following

Article. —

Article I

Whereas by the Article the third of the Treaty concluded at St Ildefonso the {9 Vendémiaire an 9 / 1st October 1800} between the First Consul of the French Republic and his Catholic Majesty it was agreed as follows. —

"His Catholic Majesty promises and engages on his part to cede to the French Republic six months after the full and entire execution of the conditions and Stipulations herein relative to his Royal Highness the Duke of Parma, the Colony or Province of Louisiana with the Same extent that it now has in the hands of Spain, & that it had when France possessed it; and Such as it Should be after the Treaty subsequently "entered into between Spain and other States. —

And whereas in pursuance of the Treaty, and particularly of the third article the French Republic has an incontestible title to the domain and to the possession of the said Territory — The First Consul of the French Republic desiring to give to the United States a strong proof of his friendship doth hereby cede to the said United States in the name of the French Republic for ever and in full Sovereignty the said territory with all its rights and appurtenances as fully and in the Same manner as they have been acquired by the French Republic in virtue of the above mentioned Treaty concluded with his Catholic Majesty. —

Art. II

In the cession made by the preceding article are included the adjacent Islands belonging to Louisiana all public lots and Squares and Squares, vacant lands and all public buildings, fortifications, barracks and other edifices which are not private property. — The Archives, papers & Documents relative to the domain and Sovereignty of Louisiana and its dependances, will be left in the possession of the Commissaries of the United States, and copies will be afterwards given in due form to the Magistrates and Municipal officers, of such of the said papers and documents as may be necessary to them. —

Art. III

The inhabitants of the ceded territory shall be incorporated in the Union of the United States, and admitted as soon as possible according to the principles of the federal Constitution, to the enjoyment of all the rights, advantages and immunities of citizens of the United States; and in the mean time they shall be maintained and protected in the free enjoyment of their liberty, property and the Religion which they profess. —

Art. IV

There shall be sent by the Government of France a Commissary to Louisiana to the end that he do every act necessary as well to receive from the Officers of his Catholic Majesty the said country and its dependances in the name of the French Republic if it has not been already done as to transmit it in the name of the French Republic to the Commissary or agent of the United States. —

Art. V

Immediately after the ratification of the present —

Treaty

Treaty by the President of the United States and in case either of the said french Consuls shall have been previously obtained, the Commissary of the french Republic shall remit all military posts of New Orleans and other parts of the said territory to the Commissary or Commissaries named by the President to take possession; the troops, whether of France or Spain who may be there shall cease to occupy any military post from the time of taking possession, and shall be embarked as soon as possible in the course of three months after the ratification of this treaty. —

Art: VI

The United States promise to execute such treaties and articles as may have been agreed between Spain and the tribes and nations of Indians, until by mutual consent of the United States and the said tribes or nations other suitable articles shall have been agreed upon. —

Art: VII

As it is reciprocally advantageous to the commerce of France and the United States to encourage the commerce both nations for a limited time in the country ceded by the present treaty until general arrangements relative to the commerce of both nations may be agreed on; it has been agreed between the contracting parties that the french ships coming directly from France or any of her colonies loaded only with the produce and manufactures of France or her said Colonies; and the Ships of Spain coming directly from Spain or any of her colonies loaded only with the

produce

produce or manufactures of Spain or her Colonies, shall be admitted during the space of twelve years in the Port of New Orleans, and in all other legal ports of entry within the ceded territory, in the same manner as the Ships of the United States coming directly from France or Spain, or any of their Colonies, without being subject to any other or greater duty on merchandize, or other or greater tonnage than that paid by the citizens of the United States. —

During the space of time above mentioned, no other nation shall have a right to the same privileges in the Ports of the ceded territory. — the twelve years shall commence three month after the exchange of ratifications if it shall take place in France or three months after it shall have been notified at Paris to the French Government if it shall take place in the United States. It is however well understood that the object of the above article is to favour the manufactures, Commerce, freight and navigation of France and of Spain, so far as relates to the importations that the French and Spanish shall make into the said Ports of the United States, without in any sort affecting the regulations that the United States may make concerning the exportation of the produce and merchandize of the United States, or any right they may have to make such regulations. —

Art: VIII

In future and for ever after the expiration of the twelve years, the Ships of France shall be treated upon the footing

the faculty of the same [...] in the ports above mentioned —

Art. IX

The particular Convention signed this day by the respective Ministers, having for its object to provide for the payment of debts due to the Citizens of the United States by the said Republic, prior to the 30th Sept.r 1800 (8th Vendémiaire [...]) is approved and [...] Convention in the same manner as if it had been inserted in this present treaty; and it Shall be ratified in the Same form and in the Same time, So that the one Shall not be ratified distinct from the other. ——

Another particular Convention Signed at the + Same date as the present treaty relative to a definitive rule between the contracting parties, is in the like manner approved, and will be ratified in the Same form, and in the Same time, and jointly. —

Art X

The present treaty Shall be ratified in good and due form, and the ratifications Shall be exchanged in the Space of Six months after the date of the Signature by the Ministers Plenipotentiary, or Sooner if possible.

In faith whereof, the respective Plenipo = tentiaries have Signed these articles in the French and English languages; declaring nevertheless that the present Treaty was originally agreed to in the French language; and have thereunto affixed their Seals. ——

Done

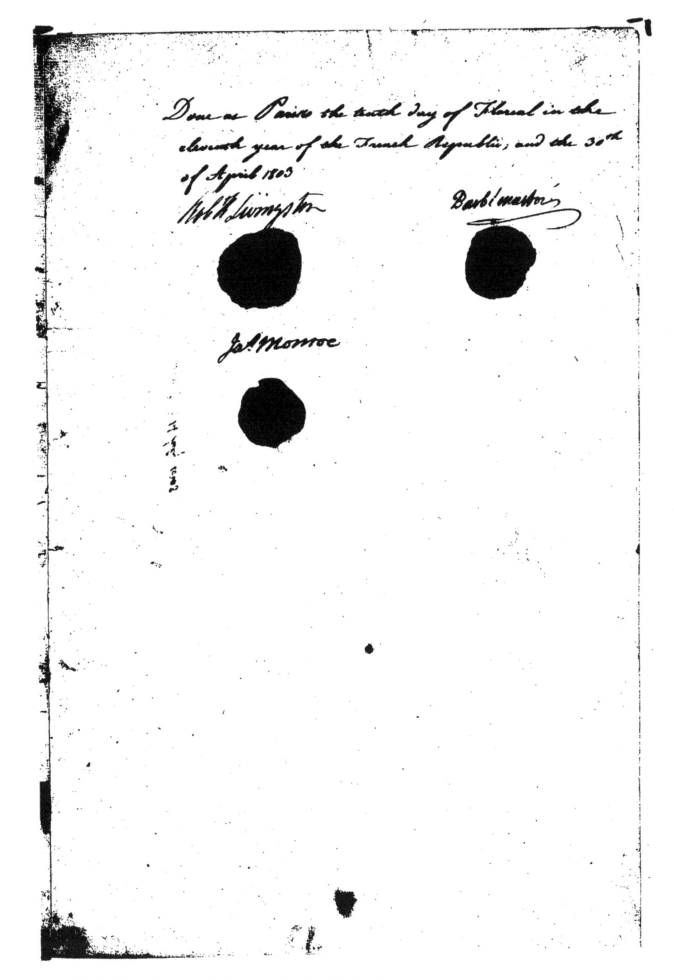

Done at Paris the tenth day of Floreal in the eleventh year of the French Republic; and the 30th of April 1803

Robt R Livingston   *Barbé Marbois*

Jas Monroe

Document 20g. The Louisiana Purchase, April 30, 1803. [National Archives]

To Albert Gallatin, Secretary of the Treasury of the United States.

Whereas by an Act, passed the tenth day of November, in the year one thousand eight hundred and three, entitled "An Act authorizing the creation of a stock to the amount of eleven millions two hundred and fifty thousand dollars for the purpose of carrying into effect the Convention of the 30th of April one thousand eight hundred and three, between the United States of America, and the French Republic; and making provision for the payment of the same" it is, among other things, enacted "That for the purpose of carrying into effect the Convention of the thirtieth day of April 1803 between the United States of America and the French Republic, the Secretary of the Treasury be, and he is hereby, authorized to cause to be constituted Certificates of Stock signed by the Register of the treasury, in favor of the French Republic or of its Assignees, for the sum of Eleven Millions two hundred and fifty thousand dollars, bearing an interest of six per centum per annum, from the time when possession of Louisiana shall have been obtained in conformity with the treaty of the thirtieth day of April 1803, between the United States of America and the French Republic, and in other respects conformable with the tenor of the Convention aforesaid: And the President of the United States is authorized to cause the said Certificates of Stock to be delivered to the Government of France, or to such Person or Persons as shall be authorized to receive them, in three months at most after the exchange of ratifications of the treaty aforesaid and after Louisiana shall be taken possession of in the name of the Government of the United States" _____ Now therefore Be it Known, that, I, Thomas Jefferson, President of the United States of America, by virtue of the power in me vested by the Act before recited, I hereby authorize and require you, Albert Gallatin, Secretary of the Treasury, to cause to be delivered to the Government of France, or to such person or persons as have been authorized to receive the same, the Certificates of Stock which have been constituted in conformity with the Convention of the thirtieth day of April 1803, between the United States of America and the French Republic ———: And for so doing this shall be your sufficient Warrant.

In testimony whereof, I have hereunto subscribed my hand at the City of Washington the sixteenth day of January one thousand eight hundred and four.

Th. Jefferson

That it shall not be lawful for any person or persons to import or bring into the said territory from any port or place within the limits of the united states, or to cause or procure to be so imported or brought, or knowingly to aid or assist in so importing or bringing any slave or slaves which shall have been imported since the

day of   into any port

or place within the limits of the united states from any port or place without the limits of the united states — and every person so offending and being thereof convicted before any court within said territory, having competent jurisdiction, shall forfeit and pay for each and every slave so imported or brought the sum of

Dollars, one moiety for the use of the person or persons who shall sue for the same — and no slave or slaves shall directly or indirectly be introduced into said territory, except by a person or persons removed into said territory for actual settlement, and being at the time of such removal, bona fide owner of such Slave or Slaves; and every Slave imported or brought into the said territory contrary to the provisions of this Act shall thereupon be entitled to and receive his or her freedom —

original to be returned — with the printed Blues
WB

Document 22b. Proposed amendment to Louisiana territorial organization to restrict slavery, December 30, 1803. [National Archives]

B.

New Orleans 10th February

Sir

In the letter of the attorney General of the
United States of the 10th of December, addressed to
you in relation to the pirates or smugglers of Barataria, and which you did me the honour to hand
to me for perusal, it is remarked, I am directed
by him "(the President) "to say to you, that a
discrimination between the cases proper, and improper
for lenity, may be made, by the District Attorney,
with your approbation." The course that it was
deemed necessary to pursue with regard to the
captain of pirates in a threatened
invasion of this State, the promise of pardon,
intercession for Pardon that was then held out to
them, and their subsequent good conduct, during
a period of difficulty and danger, are circumstances well known to you, and which, if known

Document 23a. Letter from Louisiana District Attorney John Dick to Governor
Claiborne about Jean Lafitte, February 10, 1815. [National Archives]

the Government, would doubtless increase the disposition to limits that is manifested by the letter already referred to. Under the impression of this belief, and as you have suggested to me, in conversation the propriety of entering Nolle prose-quis in the cases of all these offenders, I think it proper to hand you the names of those against whom prosecutions have been commenced or presentments found with an indication of the offences alledged against each; and I have to acquire the favour of you to signify your approbation of my entering a Nolle prosequi in each cause, or to make...

...in the course pointed out by the Attorney General, under the direction of the President

    I have the honor to be

His Excellency
Governor Claiborne

Sir very Respectfully
Yr obedient Servt
John Dick
attorney of the U S for
the Louisiana District

Document 23b. Letter from Louisiana District Attorney John Dick to Governor Claiborne about Jean Lafitte, February 10, 1815. [National Archives]

"Enumeration" of prosecutions in the Court of the United States, for the Louisiana district "against persons committed from Barataria, &c."

The U. States vs Johannes & Peter Lafitte.	Piracy.— The first, as principal; the second, as accessory before the fact.

The U. States vs Sans, alias Sausette, and Peter Lafitte.	Piracy. — The first as principal. Second, as accessory before the fact.

The U.S. vs Joachim Santos	Piracy.	4.	The U. States vs Manuel Joachim	Piracy.
5. The U. States vs. Juan Smarilles, alias Sapien.	Piracy.	6.	The U. States vs Fernand Lafon.	Piracy.
7 The U. States vs Gaspar Casson.	Piracy	8.	The U. States vs René Piland.	Piracy.
The U. States vs Dominique alias Frederick Youx.	Piracy.	10	The U. States vs Alext St Elme.	Piracy.

Document 23c. Letter from Louisiana District Attorney John Dick to Governor Claiborne about Jean Lafitte, February 10, 1815. [National Archives]

Several Counters } Piracy.

12. The U. States vs. John Rudolph } Piracy.

The U. States vs. Alex. Bonavial } Piracy.

14. The U. States vs. Antoine Saroyae, alias Count Belle Coupee. } accompany Piracy. Illegally out.

The U. States, vs. J. J. Coules } Fitting out, within the territory of the U.S. with intent to cruize and commit hostilities against States with whom U.S. were at peace.

The U. States, vs. Capt. Fleming } Illegally fitting out.

vs. Henry St. Gême } [illegible] Commdg without the aid of the U.S. with intent to cruize & commit hostilities upon the subjects and property of Princes and States, with whom the U. S. were then at peace, with a view to share in the profit thereof.

Document 23d. Letter from Louisiana District Attorney John Dick to Governor Claiborne about Jean Lafitte, February 10, 1815. [National Archives]

By WILLIAM CHARLES COLE CLAIBORNE,

Governor of the Territory of Orleans,

A PROCLAMATION.

———◦:◦:◦:◦:◦:◦:◦:◦:◦:◦:◦:———

WHEREAS, the senate and house of representatives of the United States of America, in congress assembled, did, on the second day of March of this present year, pass " An act further providing for the government of the territory of Orleans," which act was approved and signed by the President of the United States, and is now in force—And whereas by the second section of the said act, it is directed, " that the governor of the said territory shall cause to be elected twenty-five representatives, for which purpose, he shall lay off the said territory into convenient election districts, on or before the first Monday in October next, and give due notice thereof throughout the same, and appoint the most convenient time and place within each of the said districts for holding the elections; and shall nominate a proper officer or officers to preside at and conduct the same, and to return to him the names of the persons, who may have been duly elected"—Now therefore, I, WILLIAM CHARLES COLE CLAIBORNE, governor of the territory of Orleans, by virtue of and in obedience to the above mentioned act, do hereby declare and ordain, that the county of Orleans, shall form the first election district, and be entitled to seven representatives ; that the election shall be holden on the third Monday in September next, and the two succeeding days ;—on the first day, the election shall be holden at the house of M. Riviere : on the second day at the Hotel de Ville, in the city of New-Orleans, and on the third day, at the house of John Baptist Macarty. The polls on each day shall remain open from the hour of ten in the morning, until three in the afternoon.—And I do nominate and authorize the mayor of New-Orleans, the recorder of said city, and the sheriff of the said county of Orleans, or any one or more of them, to preside at, and conduct the said election.

The county of German Coast, shall form the second election district, and be entitled to two representatives ; the election shall be holden at the usual place of holding the court for said county, on the third Monday in September next, and the following day ; and I do nominate and authorize the judge, clerk and sheriff of the said county of German Coast, or any one or more of them, to preside at, and conduct the said election.

The county of Acadia, shall form the third election district, and be entitled to two representatives, the election shall be holden on the third Monday in September next, and the following day, at the usual place of holding the court of said county ; and I do nominate and authorise the judge, clerk and sheriff of said county of Acadia, or any one or more of them, to preside at, and conduct the said election.

The county of La Fourche shall form the fourth election district, and be entitled to two representatives ; the election shall take place at the usual place of holding the court of said county, on the third Monday in September next, and the following day ; and I do nominate and authorize the judge, clerk and sheriff of the said county of La-fourche, or any one or more of them, to preside at, and conduct the said election.

The county of Iberville shall form the fifth election district, and be entitled to two representatives ; the election shall be holden at the usual place of holding the court for said county, on the third Monday in September next, and the following day ; and I do nominate and authorize the judge, clerk and sheriff of the said county of Iberville, or any one or more of them, to preside at, and conduct the said election.

The county of Attacapas shall form the sixth election district, and be entitled to two representatives ; the election shall be holden on the third Monday in September next, and the following day, at the usual place of holding the court for said county : and I do hereby nominate and authorise the judge, clerk and sheriff of said county of Attacapas, or any one or more of them, to preside at and conduct the said election.

The county of Opelousas shall form the seventh election district, and be entitled to two Representatives ; the election shall be holden at the usual place of holding the court of said county, on the third Monday in September next, and the following day ; and I do nominate and authorise the judge, clerk and sheriff of said county of Opelousas, or any one or more of them, to preside at and conduct the said election.

The county of Point Coupee shall form the eighth election district, and be entitled to two representatives ; the election shall be holden at the usual place of holding the court for said county, on the third Monday in September next, and the following day : and I do nominate the judge, clerk and sheriff of said county of Point Coupee, or any one or more of them, to preside at and conduct the said election.

The county of Rapide shall form the ninth election district, and be entitled to one Representative ; the election shall be holden at the usual place of holding the court for said county, on the third Monday in September next, and the following day ; and I do nominate and authorise the judge, clerk and sheriff of said county of Rapide, or any one or more of them, to preside at and conduct the said election.

The county of Nachitoches shall form the tenth election district, and be entitled to one Representative ; the election shall be holden at the usual place of holding the court for said county, on the third Monday in September next, and the following day ; and I do nominate and authorise the judge, clerk and sheriff of said county of Nachitoches, or any one or more of them, to preside at and conduct the said election.

The county of Ouachitta shall form the eleventh election district, and be entitled to one Representative ; the election shall be holden at the usual place of holding the court for said county, on the third Monday in September next, and the following day ; and I do nominate and authorise the judge, clerk and sheriff of said county of Ouachitta, or any one or more of them, to preside at and conduct the said election.

The county of Concordia shall form the twelfth election district, and be entitled to one Rprefentative ; the election shall be holden on the third Monday in September next, and the following day, at the usual place of holding the court for said county ; and I do nominate and authorise the judge, clerk and sheriff of said county of Concordia, or any one or more of them, to preside at and conduct the said election.

And I do require of the officers who are nominated and authorised to preside at and conduct the respective elections, hereby directed, to make a return to the undersigned in writing, under their hands and seals, on or before the thirtieth day of October next, of the names of the persons who to them shall appear to have been duly elected—And I do further by virtue of the powers in me vested, require all and singular the Representatives, who shall be elected as aforesaid, to convene in the city of New-Orleans on the first Monday in November next, at the hour of eleven in the forenoon, in the Hall lately occupied by the Legislative Council.

{L. S.} Given under my hand, and the seal of the Territory, at the City of New-Orleans, on the twenty-sixth day of July, in the year of our Lord one thousand, eight hundred and five, and of the Independence of the United States the thirtieth.

WILLIAM CHARLES COLE CLAIBORNE.

Document 24. Proclamation about territorial elections, July 26, 1805. [National Archives]

General Orders.

Head Quarters

Parole – Sabine.
C. Sign – Addais.

Camp Addais October 25th 1806

Officer for the day tomorrow Capt. Sparks.
Adjutant .... " .... " .... Mead.

General Orders.

Head Quarters

Parole – Matta.
C. Sign – Romer.

Camp Addais October 26th 1806

Officer for the day tomorrow Colonel Cushing
Adjutant .... " .... " .... Knight

John Corns a private of Captain Houses is transferred to Capt.
Many's Company of Artillerists.

General Orders,

Head Quarters

Parole – Courage.
C. Sign – Constancy.

Camp La Pedria October 27th 1806.

Officer for the day tomorrow Lt. Col. Kingsbury.
Adjutant .... " .... " .... Knight.

General Orders,

Head Quarters

Parole – Caution.
C. Sign – Vigilance

Camp La Pedrias October 28th 1806
Twenty Six miles from Natchitoches.

Officer for the day tomorrow Major Porter.
Adjutant .... " .... " .... Mead.

The depending movement of the Troops, is not to seek an
enemy, but to assert a right of Sovereignty; This right is denied
by the Spanish Commander in our front, who has recently warned

Document 25a. General Orders from General Wilkinson's letterbook, October 28, 1806. [National Archives]

the General, that he considers his advance an Act of Hostility which his orders compel him to resist: whatever then may be the Calculation or their result, the safety and honor of the Corps, and the National interests require that every individual attached to the expedition, should move and act as if an Engagement was Certain and innevatable — we are obliged to wait the attack, and our Opponents being all mounted may give or refuse themselves at their discretion, and of Consequence will avail themselves of any advantage we may Offer them.

+ The Signal to prepare for Action when encamped will be a Gun from the left, on which every man who bears Arms will take his place in the line, and the whole wait orders — The signal to form when under march will be a Gun from the front — The Infantry with their field pieces will immediately form two lines, at two hundred yards distance, and on the flanks of the road — Farar's Dragoons will retire by the road to the rear, and form Column prepared to charge — Major Welch's mounted Infantry will skirmish and fall back, on the right or left of the Front line, as the Ground and other circumstances may render most advantageous — The moment the signal is given, the rear Guard, Pioneers, and every man of the line are to join their Corps leaving their packs and teams in charge of Mr. Kagan and the Engagees of the Quarter Masters & Contractors department; should an attempt be made to turn our flank which is probable, the Infantry will form the Hollow square, and the Artillery take post on the Angles, to enfelade the Enemy with Grape and Cannister. Major Welch's men to retire towards the rear and endeavour to out flank our assailants, keeping up as

quick

quick and deadly a fire as possible.—— An Officer to each division of the Infantry will take post with the front rank, every other Officer will be in the rear, to see the men do not throw away their fire, and if one should be found so dastardly as to give back to put him to instant death.

Under all circumstances the Artillery will receive orders when to fire. —— But the Infantry with Shouldered Arms are to wait the approach of the Enemy, until within forty Yards, when the front Rank is to present, level well, fire and charge Bayonet, —— If the Enemy are not broken or staggered, the second Rank are to take aim at their Breasts, and when at fifteen yards are to pour in their fire, and should they still come on are to be received by both ranks with dauntless resolution on their Bayonets — The Dragoons are reserved for a critical effort, and will receive orders when and where to make it; the Gentlemen will bear in mind that whatever may be the order of the charge the instant they close with the enemy, the action will become Pell-Mell; they should be careful to level their blows at the neck, rather horizontally than Perpendicularly, and in General to cut and pass from Man to Man.

The Spanish force is greatly superior and all mounted, but it is made up of an undiciplined rabble. Their attack will be made in great disorder, and probably with velocity and an Air of Boldness, because they will depend more on noise and appearance; than the solid shock; It will be our part to present a rampart of Bayonets wherever attacked — Let the Officers be attentive to their men, and the men silent and Obedient to their Officers — Let each individual put confidence in his

his own strength and the Cooperation of his flank files — above all let us avoid hurry, which always produces Confusion — & superiority of numbers will serve but to augment our triumph, and increase the Honor of our Arms.

The whole train of transport and the men attached to it, whether Soldier or Citizen, are subject to the order of the Quarter Masters Captain Hooke and his subordinates, and every person engaged on the expedition is subject to the Martial law — But the Agent of the Contractor and his Assistants, are to be supported in the proper execution of their duties.

An Orderly Drum to attend at Head Quarters, Day & Night.

Until further orders the Taps will be given at the Inspectors Tent, to be followed from right to left, fifteen minutes after, the Revellies will commence — at the first stroke of which, the Gun is to be fired. The Troops turn out at the Taps.

The General to beat this morning at nine O'Clock in place of the Troop.

The Arms & Ammunition of the Troops are to be critically inspected this evening at Roll Call.

General Orders
Parole — Patriotism.
C. Sign — Patience.

Head Quarters
Camp
October 29" 1806.

Officer for the day tomorrow Capt. Sparks.
Adjutant .... " .... Knight.

Document 25d. General Orders from General Wilkinson's letterbook, October 28, 1806. [National Archives]

PATENT CERTIFICATE.

No. ____

LAND OFFICE AT OPELOUSAS,
STATE OF LOUISIANA,
10th day of January 1831

It is hereby certified, That in pursuance of the Act of Congress, passed on the 3d day of March, 1807, entitled "AN ACT respecting claims to Land in the Territories of Orleans and Louisiana"

Pierre Arsoneau of the County of Attakapas, claiming as one of the heirs of the late Pierre Arsoneau dec'd, in virtue of a Spanish Order of Survey to said dec'd by the Governor Miro, bearing date the 14 day of January in the year A.D. 1796 on the 15th day of May 1811, filed with the **REGISTER OF THE LAND OFFICE** for the **WESTERN DISTRICT** of the (now) **State of Louisiana,** a Certificate of the COMMISSIONERS appointed for the purpose of ascertaining the rights of persons claiming Lands in the said District, No. B. 392 confirming his claim to a certain tract of Land, containing 277 57/100 acres, situated in the County of Opelousas, on the East side of the Bayon Plaquemine Boulé, having 23 40/100 front by ho before depth, bounded above by Francis Laurent, below by Eulalie Pagé, designated as being Section No. 53 ____ in Township No. Ten y S. of Range No. One W as per plat herewith. 277.57

NOW, THEREFORE, BE IT KNOWN, That on presentation of this Certificate to the COMMISSIONER OF THE GENERAL LAND-OFFICE, the said Pierre Arseneau, his heirs of ____ shall be entitled to receive a patent for the land above described.

Valentine King
Register of the Land Office.

This claim being among the early informations of the Board, I suspect the commissioners were received. The original title of Pierre Arseneau, as recited in the within Certificate calls for the River Nementas — the Requête or Application of the claimant runs thus — "Sur la rive orientale de la rivière et centas de soisante et dix a quatre-vingt arpens — c'est a dire, depuis la borne de S' Leblanc jusqu'a l'endroit vulgairement appellé le Conti de l'aigle" — On the E bank of the River Nementas, having a front of from 70 to 80 arpens — that is to say — from the boundary of M' Leblanc to the place commonly called the eagle creek.. The spanish order of survey directs the survey to be made as petitioned for " Sobre los setenta ó ochenta arpanes que encuentran desde el limite del nombrado Leblanc "&c

Leblanc's claim calls for the Point Nementas on the Nementas River at the Indian village which is believed to be 12 miles lower down —

Valentine King
R.S.

See note by Register ~
Certif. N° 602 —

No 603.
Pierre Arseneau.
B. 39°

Patent dated 1st
November 1833

Recorded Vol. E
Recorded Page 76.

AVIS.

La SOUSSIGNÉ Vendra à des conditions raisonnables une TERRE située sur le bayou La Fourche, de vingt arpens de face sur quarante de profondeur, sur la rive gauche de la rivière, à dix sept lieues du Mississipi, appartenant précédemment à M. Daniel Clark, & aujourd'hui à M. Wm. Brown, ci-devant Collecteur à la Nouvelle-Orléans. Il y a environ cent arpens défrichés sur cette habitation. Si elle n'est pas vendue à l'amiable avant le second Lundi de Juillet prochain, elle sera alors exposée en Vente Publique à Donaldsonville, à un, deux, & trois ans de crédit, l'acheteur donnant une caution de toute satisfaction pour le prix d'achat.

Nlle.-Orléans, 28 Mai 1810.

P. Grymes,
Agent pour les Etats-Unis.

NOTICE.

The SUBSCRIBER will sell upon accommodating terms a TRACT of LAND situated on the bayou La Fourche, of twenty arpents front, by forty in depth, on the left bank of the river, and seventeen leagues from the Mississipi, formerly the property of M. Daniel Clark, and now belonging to Wm. Brown late Collector at New Orleans. There are about one hundred arpents cleared on this plantation. If not sold by private contract before the second Monday in July next, it will then be exposed to Public Sale at Donaldsonville, on a credit of one, two and three years, the purchaser giving approved security for the purchase money.

New Orleans, May 28th. 1810.

P. Grymes,
Agent for the United States.

Vincennes 29ᵗ July 1790

Sir

       Mr Joseph St. Marie a citizen of Vincennes of good character, has made representation to me of a seizure upon his property by an officer of his catholic Majesty, and within what is understood to be the Territory of the united States, which I beg leave to lay before your Excellency.

       With very great respect I have the honor to be your Excellency's

       most humble & devoted Servant

       Winthrop Sargent

The President of the
United States

To the honorable Winthrop Sargent esquire Secretary in and for the Territory of the united States north. west of the River Ohio and vested with all the powers of Governor and Commander in chief.

       Joseph St. Marie of St. Vincennes in the County of Knox in the said Territory, begs leave to acquaint your honor that on the 23ᵈ day of August 1788 he took the liberty of addressing a letter to John Francis Hamtramck esquire Major in the first united States Regiment, and Commandant at Post Vincennes, of which the following is a copy. "Sir. In pursuance to the ancient usage and

custom

Document 28a. Letter from Joseph St. Marie to Territorial
Secretary Sargent, July 29, 1790. [National Archives]

custom of this Country, I in the month of November last applied for and obtained leave of absence on a trading voyage. In consequence of which and of my right as a Freeman and Citizen of the United States of America, I loaded a Pettiauger with several goods and merchandize to the amount of five thousand nine hundred and forty one Livres and fifteen sols in Peltry, Currency of this place, equal to one thousand nine hundred and eighty dollars and forty two ninetieths of a dollar, and sent them under the care and management of my Clerk Mr. Swimmer, with directions to proceed down the Missisippi River, and trade them off with the Indian nations living within the bounds of the United States of America. Mr. Swimmer accordingly set out and went down that River to a place called the Chicasaw Lake, which is situate about ninety leagues down from the River Ohio, about twenty leagues higher than where the English Fort of the Arquanças formerly stood and in about 34°. 40′ of north Latitude according to Hutchin's map, where he pitched his Camp on the East or American side of the Missisippi, in the neighbourhood of some friendly Indians who were there hunting. Here after a few days stay he was taken up by an order from Mr. Valliere the Spanish Commandant at the Post of the Arquanças by a party of Spanish Soldiers sent from that Fort, who at the same time seized the Pettiauger and the goods, and carried them together with my Clerk and the other hands in the Boat to the

Spanish

Document 28b. Letter from Joseph St. Marie to Territorial Secretary Sargent, July 29, 1790. [National Archives]

Spanish Fort, where M. Vallière the Commandant - seized and confiscated the property for the use of the Spanish King, at the same time informing the men, that his orders from the Governor of Lousiana at New Orleans were express, to seize and confiscate all the property which might be found on the Mississippi or on either of it's shores any where below the mouth of the Ohio, and to send the persons of those with such goods, prisoners to him at New Orleans. Being very soon after informed of this transaction, I went to the Arquanças and applied to the Spanish Commandant for a restoration of my property, who in very peremptory terms refused giving them up alledging his beforementioned orders and adding that I might take it as a great favour that my clerk and hands as well as myself were not confined and sent in irons to Orleans as prisoners. When I reasoned on my right as an american subject to traffic in the American Dominions, and that my property was seized in the Territory to which I conceived America had an undoubted right, he stopped me short by informing me that the Country on both sides of the River Mississippi as high up as the mouth of the River Ohio belonged to Spain, and that the whole of the Country on the East side of the Mississippi from the mouth of Ohio downwards was then under the Spanish Government."

"Surprised at this information and not being
satisfied

satisfied that the Governor had really given such orders. I went to New Orleans, and about the 4th day of May last obtained an audience of the Governor. Don Meto, who as soon as informed of my name, asked me in very haughty terms how I could have the audacity to appear before him on the subject of the seizure of my property; that although I was a Frenchman born, yet that I then was an American subject, and that if he the Governor was to follow his orders from the Court of Spain, he would send me prisoner to the mines of Brazil, and then concluded in a threatening manner with bidding me depart from thence and be no more seen, which last orders I was glad to obey, and withdraw myself as soon and as far as possible from such despots, without receiving any satisfaction. Thus circumstanced my only and last resourse is to the honorable the Congress of the United States of America, as guardians of the rights and liberties of her subjects, whose persons have been seized and properties confiscated on her acknowledged Territory by an armed force in pursuance to the orders of a foreign Prince. From the time that the name of an American has been known in this Country I have been a subject of the United States; I have fought in defence of that Country whose subjects a Spanish Commandant is hardy enough to oppress. And I am now, unless Government interferes, without any remedy for a loss which will reduce me with a wife and a numerous family to the utmost distress

70

"I must beg of you, Sir, to make known my case to Congress in such manner as you shall think proper and as speedily as possible, as in me the right of Sovereignty of America, as well to a very extensive Territory as to the navigation of the Mississippi any where below the mouth of the Ohio has been invaded: my cause is become a public cause and will in it's consequences determine a grand national question. I dare hope and trust that as an ancient inhabitant of this Country, and as one of the first subjects of America in it, I shall be thought worthy the protection of Congress, and that they will adopt some means to give satisfaction and recompence for my losses. To convince you and the world of the justice of my cause, I propose to make oath before a Magistrate of the truth of the whole of the case as before stated, and shall whenever called upon produce proper vouchers and proofs to authenticate the same. I am Sir &c."

"This letter was accompanied with the oath proposed, and with the invoice hereto annexed, and also with an affidavit of Mr. Wm. McIntosh who is now on a voyage, testifying that he had seen and had read to him by Mr. Valliere the Spanish Commandant at the Post of the Arquanças the original letter or orders from Don Moro Governor of Louisiana at New Orleans, directing the said Mr. Valliere to seize and confiscate the property of all those who should be found on the

Mississippi

Document 28e. Letter from Joseph St. Marie to Territorial
Secretary Sargent, July 29, 1790. [National Archives]

Mississippi or on either shore thereof from the mouth of the Ohio downwards, as the whole of that country belonged to Spain. These letters and papers Major Hamtramck forwarded to General Harmar, who sent them to Congress; but as they were delivered that honorable Body when their dissolution was about taking place, and as the many public affairs since the adoption of the new Constitution have in a manner entirely engaged the attention of the new Congress, he begs leave to address himself to your honor, as vested with the Governor and Commander in Chief's power in this country, begging you to lay his case before Congress and to procure him such redress as his distressed situation as well as that of his family requires. He also begs permission to testify the truth of what is herein before setforth by his own oath, and he also proffers to adduce other sufficient and satisfactory proofs thereof whenever thereto requested. He begs leave to subscribe himself your honor's

Most obedient & very hum. Serv.
Joseph St. Marie

St Vincennes July 22d 1790.

On the 22d July 1790 personally appeared before us, two of the Justices of the Peace for the County of Knox. Joseph St Marie above named, who made oath on the holy Evangelists according to law, that the

above

above statement of his case is just and true. In witness whereof we have hereunto set our hands and
seals the day and year aforesaid.

Paul Gamelin   (ss)

Antoine Gamelin   (ss)

An Invoice of the Merchandize &c that were
seized by orders of Mr Valliere, Commandant at the
Arquancas.

February 6th				
To 6 pieces of Stroud a	150 livres in peltry			900.
To 46 Blankets of 2½ points	a	12'		552
To 6 pair Blankets of 2 points	a	9'		54
To 7 Blankets of 1½ Do	a	6'		42
To 2 pair Do of 3 Do	a	15+		30
To 6 Do Do of 4 Do	a	4' 10		27
To 2 doz Callicoe Shirts	a	12' p.puce		288
To 4 Do white Do Ruffled	a	12' p		144
To 1 Do Callicoe Do	a	7" 10 p		90
To 3 small Shirts	a	4' 10		13. 10
To 1 doz bc stkfs	a	12' p.puce		144
To 1 puce & 3 Ells of Callicoe	a	9'		157. 10
To 36 lb Powder	a	6'		216
To 130 lb Ball	a	1'		130
To 1½ doz large Knives	a	1' 10		18
To 6 spring clasp knives	a	1' 10		9
To 10 Looking Glasses	a	1' 10		15
To 3 pieces holland Lace	a	30'		90
To 3 Do in Rolls	a	12'		36
To 6 Rolls Ribband	a	20'		120
To 23 Ells Scarlet Cloth	a	20+		50
To 5 pieces save ½ Ells of Scarlet Cloth				300

Item	Rate	Amount
To 11 lb Vermilion	a 15ʳ	165..
To 1 packet of Beads		9.
To 1 Dº of white		9.
To 4 papers Rings	a 1: 10	6..
To 6 Combs	a 1ʳ	6..
To 6 coloured silk Hkfs	a 12ʳ	72.
To 12 lb worsted	a 12ʳ	18..
To 4 paper needles		6..
To 3 dozⁿ Thimbles	a 6ʳ	18..
To 3 pairs Scissars	a 1ʳ	3.
To 4 Traps	a 30ʳ	120..
To 3 Kersey Cloaks	a 9ᵈ	27.
To 19¼ lb brass Kettles	a 3ʳ	57. 15.
To 12 lb Tobacco	a 1ʳ 10	18...
To 3200 large silver Broaches	a 30ᵈ	960.
To 120 pairs small dº Ear bobs	a 1ʳ 10	180.
To 8 pair Bracelets of dº	a 6ʳ	48..
To 3 setts Silver Hair Bands	a 15ʳ	45..
To 2 pair of small arm bracelets	a 45ʳ	90..
To 1 dº large Dº		30..
To 1 small Dº		22.. 10.
To 4 large concave Broaches	a 6ʳ	24..
To 2 Ear wheels	a 6ʳ	12.
To 50 fashioned Broaches		30..
To 150 small Dº	a 20ᵈ	30..
To 6 dº fashioned on	a 1ʳ 10	9.
To 3 Reliques	a 6ʳ	18..
To 10 large Crosses	a 9ʳ	90.
To 2 setts silver Gorgets, 5 in each sett	a 90	180..
To 1 Pot 30ᵈ. To 1 Tent contᵍ 20 Ells Linen 100ᵈ		130..
To 5 Bear Skins	a 3ʳ	15..
To 1 Axe 20ᵈ. To 1 Tomahawk 6ʳ. To 1 Peroque 100ᵈ		126..
To 4 Package Cloths	a 10ᵈ	40..
Equal to 1956..15		5941.. 15..

Joseph St. Marie

Document 28h. Letter from Joseph St. Marie to Territorial
Secretary Sargent, July 29, 1790. [National Archives]

New Orleans 24th January 1806.

Sir,

I have the honor to enclose you a Copy of a statement made me on Oath, by Stephen a free black man; I do not credit it in whole. ~~I however have no doubt but that the free~~ people of Color have been tampered with, and that some of them are devoted to the spanish Interest.

Mr. Morales is yet in this City, and should I not on Tomorrow learn that his preparations for a departure are in forwardness, I shall remind him of the President's Orders, and add, that a Compliance therewith will be expected in the course of the present month.

Good order prevails in this City, and I believe thro' out the Territory; — my vigilence shall be unceasing, and I pray you to be persuaded, that the Public Peace and safety will be maintained.

I am Sir
with very great respect
Your Obt. Hum Sert.
William C. C. Claiborne

The Secretary of State.

Stephen, a free Black Man, informs the Governor of the Territory of Orleans, as follows:

That he is privy to the hostile intentions of certain Creoles of color in the City of New Orleans:

That the said people of color, with the exceptions of John Sadu and Vallefois Trudeau, and a few others, consist of every free man of that description, in the town and in the neighbourhood:

That they hold nightly meetings at certain places, towit; at Clavare's a free Negro opposite la Nuce's; at Francis Dorvill's a mulatto man who is called Captain and wears a spanish Cockade, opposite to Moralle's; at Beekes a mulatto's place near the Bayou St. John; and at several other places, — at which meetings they hold Counsels, and concert plans of hostility against the Americans:

That these people have, all, the possession of Guns and other military arms, and of powder and Ball:

He has frequently overheard their conversations, and heard them mention particularly the names of, the Marquis Casa Calvo, Medsinger, Morales, Charles Lawe a mulatto man, Joseph Cabaree a mulatto man, Charles Brulet a yellow man called Captain of the Granadies, Landau a mulatto man whose Brother is married to Julia Bryan and is the person who carries about the paper to ascertain those who are friendly to the Spaniards, and a considerable number of others whose names he does not recollect: They only wait the return of the Marquis to give the Whoop, to commence the Massacre.

He understands that these people expect the Marquis

to

To Chariot Officer.

Document 29b. Letter from Governor Claiborne to Secretary of State Madison, January 24, 1806. [National Archives]

to arrive shortly with three or four thousand troops, and that he is to bring one or two nations of Indians with him, or that they are to follow him:

They offer to set all the Black People free who will join them:

He gives a caution, that if the Americans should hear the cry of Fire, not to go out, but to stand upon their guard.

Sworn to the 23. of January 1806.

of March last by the Spanish Secretary of State to the Minister Plenipotentiary of the United States at Madrid, on the subject of the decree of the Intendant at New Orleans interrupting the American right of deposit at that place; and communicating the disinclination of his Catholic Majesty to enter into arrangements with the United States for annexing to them adjoining territories of Spain.

The communication made by Mr. Cevallos on the 31st of March had

[The above beginning of a letter was addressed to the Messieurs Livingston but by mistake was inserted there as being to Charles King when it was only an inclosure to him]

Robert R. Livingston Esqr.   Department of State
                    Sir,   July 29th 1803.

Since the date of my last which was May 24 I have received your several letters of April 11. 13 & 17 & May 12th. As they relate almost wholly to the subject which was happily terminated on the 30th of April a particular answer is rendered unnecessary by that event, and by the answer which goes by this conveyance to the joint letter from yourself and Mr. Monroe of the 13th of May. It will only be observed first — that the difference in the diplomatic titles given to Mr. Monroe from that given to you, and which you understood to have ranked him above you was the result merely of an error in the clerk who copied the document and which escaped attention when they were signed. It was not the intention of the President that any distinction of grade should be made between you. Indeed according to the authority of Vattel the characters of Minister Plenipotentiary and Envoy Extraordinary are precisely of the same grade, altho' it is said that the usage, in France particularly, does not correspond with this idea. Secondly, that the relation of the First Consul to the Italian Republic received the compliment deemed sufficient in the answer to a Note of Mr. Pichon, communicating the flag of that Nation. A copy of the communication and of the answer are now inclosed.

The boundaries of Louisiana seems to be so imperfectly understood and are of so much importance, that the President wishes them to be investigated wherever information is likely to be obtained. You will be pleased to attend particularly to this object as it relates to the Spanish possessions both on the West and on the East side of the Mississippi. The proofs countenancing our claim to a part of West Florida may be of immediate use in the negotiations which are to take place at Madrid. Should Mr. Monroe have proceeded thither, as is probable, and any such proofs should after his

departure

Document 30a. Letter from Secretary of State Madison to Robert
Livingston and James Monroe, July 29, 1803. [National Archives]

departure have come to your knowledge, you will of course have transmitted them to him.

You will find by our Gazettes that your memorial drawn up about a year ago on the subject of Louisiana, has found its way into public circulation. The passages in it which strike at G. Britain have undergone some comments, and will probably be conveyed to the attention of that Government. The document appears to have been sent from Paris, where you will be able no doubt to trace the indiscretion to its author.

No answer has yet been received either from you or Mr Monroe to the diplomatic arrangement for London and Paris. The importance of shortening the interval at the former, and preventing one at the latter, makes us anxious on this point. As your late letters have not repeated your intention of returning home this fall, it is hoped that the interesting scenes which have since supervened may reconcile you to a longer stay in Europe

I have the honor to be &c &c &c

James Madison

Charles Pinckney Esq.   Department of State
Sir,   July 29 ~ 1803

My last letter was of the   day of
Those received from you since that date are of

You will have learnt doubtless from Paris, that a Treaty has been signed there by which New Orleans and the rest of Louisiana is conveyed to the United States. The Floridas are not included in the Treaty, being, it appears still held by Spain. The inclosed copy of a communication from the Spanish Minister here contains a refusal of his Catholic Majesty to alienate any part of his Colonial possessions. A copy of the answer to it is also inclosed.

At the date of this refusal it was probably unknown that the Cession by France to the United States, had been or would be made. This consideration with the kind of reasons given for the refusal and the situation of Spain resulting from the war between Great Britain and France, lead to a calculation that at present there may be less repugnance to our views. The Letter herewith addressed to Mr Monroe gives the instructions under which the negociations are to be pursued. Being for your use as well as his, it is unsealed and in your cypher; a copy in his having been forwarded to Paris.

In case Mr Monroe should not have arrived, but be expected at Madrid, you will forbear to enter into negociations on this subject, unless they should be brought on by the Spanish Government, and the moment should be critical

critical for securing our object on favorable terms. The maximum of price contemplated by the President will be found in the instructions. At this price the bargain cannot be a bad one. But considering the motives which Spain ought now to feel for making the arrangement easy and satisfactory, the certainty that the Floridas must at no distant period find a way into our hands, and the tax on our finances resulting from the purchase of Louisiana which makes a further purchase immediately less convenient, it may be hoped as it is to be wished, that the bargain will be considerably cheapened. Under such circumstances it would not be proper to accede to terms, which under others might have been admissible.

In case Mr Monroe should be obliged to decline or postpone his visit to Spain, I have requested him to give you his ideas on the expediency of your proceeding or not in the negotiation. The advantage given him by his opportunities of scanning the policy of Great Britain and France in relation to Spain, and of estimating the course of the war, will render his opinion on that point particularly worthy of your confidence.

You will observe in the answer to the Marquis D'yrujo communication, a merited animadversion on the motives assigned for the restoration of the deposit. The United States can never admit that this was a favor, not of right, nor receive as a favor what they demand as a right.

As the indemnifications claimed from Spain are to be incorporated in the overtures for the Floridas, it will be advisable to leave them, altho' within your ordinary functions, for the joint negotiations of yourself and Mr Monroe. In these, as proceeding from an extraordinary mission the subject can be pressed with greater force, and more probable effect. Should Mr Monroe however, not be likely soon to join you, and there be a prospect of extending the Convention not acceded here, to the claims omitted in it, you will continue to urge them on the justice of the Spanish government, and in terms and a tone that will make it sensible of the impolicy of disappointing the reasonable expectations of the United States.

I have the honor to be &c

James Madison

James Monroe Esq.
&c

Department of State
July — 29 1803

The communications by Mr Hughes including the treaty
and

SIXTEENTH CONGRESS OF THE UNITED STATES;

AT THE FIRST SESSION,

Begun and held in the City of Washington, in the Territory of Columbia, on Monday, the sixth day of December, one thousand eight hundred and nineteen.

———

AN ACT to authorize the people of the Missouri territory to form a constitution and state government and for the admission of such state into the union on an equal footing with the original states, and to prohibit slavery in certain territories

———

BE it enacted by the Senate and House of Representatives of the United States of America in Congress assembled, That the inhabitants of that portion of the Missouri Territory included within the boundaries herein after designated be, and they are hereby authorized to form for themselves a constitution and state government and to assume such name as they shall deem proper, and the said state when formed, shall be admitted into the Union upon an equal footing with the original states in all respects whatsoever. And be it further enacted, That the said state shall consist of all the territory included within the following boundaries, to wit: Beginning in the middle of the Mississippi river on the parallel of thirty six degrees of North latitude, thence west along that parallel of latitude to the St. Francis river; thence up and following the course of that river in the middle of the main channel thereof to the parallel of latitude of thirty six degrees and thirty minutes; thence west along the same, to a point where the said parallel is intersected by a meridian line passing through the middle of the mouth of the Kansas river, where the same empties into the Missouri river; thence, from the point aforesaid north, along the said meridian line to the intersection of the parallel of latitude which passes through the rapids of the river Des Moines, making the said line to correspond with the Indian boundary line; thence east, from the point of intersection last aforesaid, along the said parallel of latitude to the middle of the channel of the main fork of the said river Des Moines; thence down, and along the middle of the main channel of the said river Des Moines to the mouth of the same, where it empties into the Mississippi river; thence, due east, to the middle of the main channel of the Mississippi river thence, down and following the course of the Mississippi river, in the middle of the main channel thereof, to the place of beginning: Provided the said state shall ratify the boundaries aforesaid: And provided also, That the said state shall have concurrent jurisdiction on the river Mississippi, and every other river bordering on the said state, so far as the said rivers shall form a common boundary to the said state, and any other state or states now or hereafter to be formed and bounded by the same; such rivers to be common to both; and that the river Mississippi, and the navigable rivers and waters leading into the same, shall be common highways, and for ever free, as well to the inhabitants of the said state, as to other citizens of the United States, without any tax, duty, impost, or toll, therefore, imposed by the said state. Sec. 2. And be it further enacted, That all free white male citizens of the United States, who shall have arrived at the age of twenty one years, and have resided in said Territory three months previous to the day of election, and all other persons qualified to vote for representatives to the general Assembly of the said territory, shall be qualified to be elected, and they are hereby qualified and authorized to vote, and choose representatives to form a convention, who shall be apportioned amongst the several counties as follows: From the county of Howard, five representatives; From the county of Cooper, three representatives; From the county of Montgomery, two representatives; From the county of Pike, one representative; From the county of Lincoln, one representative; From the county of St. Charles, three representatives; From the county of Franklin, one representative; From the county of St. Louis, eight representatives; From the county of Jefferson, one representative; From the county of Washington, three representatives; From the county of St. Genevieve, four representatives; From the county of Madison, one representative; From the county of Cape Girardeau, five representatives; From the county of New Madrid, two representatives; From the county of Wayne, and that portion of the county of Lawrence that falls within the boundaries herein designated, one representative; and the elections for the representatives aforesaid shall be holden on the first Monday, and two succeeding days of May next, throughout the several counties aforesaid in the said territory; and shall be in every respect held and conducted in the same manner, and under the same regulations, as is prescribed by the laws of the said territory regulating elections therein for members of the General Assembly, except that the returns of the election in that portion of Lawrence county included in the boundaries aforesaid, shall be made to the county of Wayne, as is provided in other cases under the laws of said territory. Sec. 4. And be it further enacted, That the members of the convention thus duly elected shall be, and they are hereby authorized, to meet at the seat of government of said territory, on the second Monday of the month of June next; and the said convention, when so assembled, shall have power and authority to adjourn to any other place in the said territory which to them shall seem best for the convenient transaction of their business; and whichsoever convention, when so met, shall first determine, by a majority of the whole number elected, whether it be, or be not, expedient, at that time, to form a constitution and state government for the people within the said territory, as included within the boundaries above designated; and if it be deemed expedient, the convention shall be, and hereby is, authorized to form a constitution and state government; or if it be deemed more expedient the said convention shall provide by ordinance for electing representatives to form a constitution or frame of government, which said representatives shall be chosen in such manner, and in such proportion, as they shall designate, and shall meet at such time and place, as shall be prescribed by the said ordinance ... and shall then form ... for the people ... territory within the boundaries aforesaid, a constitution and state government: Provided, That ... when formed, shall be republican, and not repugnant to the constitution of the United States ...

———

Document 31a. The Missouri Compromise, March 6, 1820. [National Archives]

Document 32. Committee draft report on Indian affairs, October 15, 1783. [National Archives]

(Copy.)

Speech of the United Indian Nations, at their confederate Council held near the mouth of the Detroit River, the 28th. November & 18th Dec: 1786.

Present.

The five Nations, the Hurons, Delawares, Shawanese, Ottawas, Chippewas, Powtewattimies, Twichtwees, Cherokees, and the Wabash Confederates.

To the Congress of the United States of America—

Brethren of the United States of America.

It is now more than three years since peace was made between the King of Great Britain and you, but we the Indians were disappointed finding ourselves not included in that peace according to our expectations, for we thought that its conclusion would have promoted a friendship between the United States and Indians, and that we might enjoy that happiness that formerly subsisted between us and our elder brethren— We have received two very agreeable messages from the Thirteen United States— we also received a message from the King, whose war we were engaged in, desiring us to remain quiet; which we accordingly complied with— During the time of this tranquility, we were deliberating the best method we could to form a lasting reconciliation with the Thirteen United States— Pleased at the same time

Document 33a. Address from Confederated Tribes to the Confederation Congress, December 18, 1786. [National Archives]

time, we thought we were entering upon a reconciliation and friendship with a set of people born on the same continent with ourselves, certain that the quarrel between us was not of our own making — In the course of our councils we imagined we hit upon an expedient that would promote a lasting peace between us.

Brothers. — We still are of the same opinion as to the means which may tend to reconcile us to each other; and we are sorry to find, altho' we had the best thoughts in our minds, during the before-mentioned period; mischief has nevertheless happened between you and us — We are still anxious of putting our plan of accommodation into execution; and we shall briefly inform you of the means that seem most probable to us of effecting a firm and lasting peace and reconciliation. The first step towards which should, in our opinion, be, that all treaties carried on with the United States, on our part, should be with the general voice of the whole confederacy, and carried on in the most open manner, without any restraint on either side — And especially as landed matters are often the subject of our councils with you, a matter of the greatest importance and of general concern to us, in this case we hold it indispensably necessary that any cession of our lands should be made in the most public manner, and by the united voice of the Confederacy — Holding all partial treaties as void and of no effect.

Brothers — We think it is owing to you that the tranquility which since the peace between us has not lasted, and that that essential good has been followed by mischief, and confusion, having

managed

managed every thing respecting your own way — You kindled your council fires where you thought proper without consulting us, at which you held seperate treaties, and have entirely neglected our plan of having a general conference with the different nations of the confederacy — Had this happened we have reason to believe every thing would now have been settled between us in a most friendly manner — We did every thing in our power at the treaty of Fort Stanwix, to induce you to follow this plan, as our real intentions were at that very time to promote peace and concord between us, and that we might look upon each other as friends having given you no cause or provocation to be otherwise.

Brothers — Notwithstanding the mischief that has happened, we are still sincere in our wishes to have peace and tranquillity established between us, earnestly hoping to find the same inclination in you — We wish therefore you would take it into serious consideration, and let us speak to you in the manner we proposed — Let us have a treaty with you early in the spring — let us pursue reasonable steps — let us meet half ways for our mutual convenience — we shall then bring in oblivion the missfortunes that have happened, and meet each other on a footing of friendship.

Brothers — We say let us meet half way, and let us pursue such steps as become upright and honest men — We beg that you will prevent your Surveyors, and other people from coming upon our side the Ohio River — We have told you before, we wished to pursue just steps, and we are determined they shall appear just

and

Document 33c. Address from Confederated Tribes to the
Confederation Congress, December 18, 1786. [National Archives]

and reasonable, in the eyes of the world. This is the determination of all the chiefs of our confederacy now assembled here, notwithstanding the accidents that have happened in our villages, even when in council, where several innocent chiefs were killed when absolutely engaged in promoting a peace with you — the Thirteen United States.

Although then interrupted, the chiefs here present still wish to meet you in the spring, for the before-mentioned good purposes; when we hope to speak to each other without either haughtiness or menaces.

Brothers — We again request of you in the most earnest manner, to order your surveyors, and others that mark out lands, to cease from crossing the Ohio, until we shall have spoken to you because the mischief that has recently happened has originated in that quarter; we shall likewise prevent our people from going over until that time.

Brothers — It shall not be our faults, if the plans which we have suggested to you, should not be carried into execution; in that case the event will be very precarious, and if fresh ruptures ensue, we hope to be able to exculpate ourselves; and shall most assuredly with our united force, be obliged to defend those rights and privileges which have been transmitted to us by our Ancestors — And if we should be thereby reduced to misfortunes, the world will pity us when they think of the amicable proposals we now make to prevent the unnecessary effusion of blood. These are our thoughts, and firm resolves, and we earnestly desire that you

will

Document 33d. Address from Confederated Tribes to the
Confederation Congress, December 18, 1786. [National Archives]

will transmit to us, as soon as possible your answer, be it what it may.

Done at our Confederated Council Fire, at the Huron Village, near the mouth of the Detroit River, December 18th 1786

(Signed)   The five Nations.
              Hurons.
              Shawanese
              Delawares.
              Ottawaas.
              Chippewas.
              Powtewatimies.
              Twichtwees.
              Cherokees.
              The Wabash Confederates.

A true Copy
(Signed) Jos: Brant.

War Office 23rd May 1789
compared with the original. Knox—

Chaktaw Trading house July 10th 1811

Bartered with Indians
1¼lb Powder @1 . . . . . 1.25
4½lb Lead 25 . . . . . 1.12½
1 Stran Beads 12½ 2 50
Received in Payment
6 Dee. Skins 10lb @20 — 2.
2½lb Beeswax " . .50 . . . 2.50

" Sold for Cash
1¼lb Powder @125 . . . 1.56¼
⅓ Doz: Flints 18¾ . . . 6¼
1 Barlow Knife 25
1 Looking Glass 18¾
Peltry &c 2.06
3 Carrots Tobacco @50 1.50 3 56

11th Bartered with Indians
5/8lb Powder . . . @1 . . .62½
2½lb Lead 25 . .62½
3 oz: Vermillion " .75
1⅔ Doz: Flints . 18¾ .31¼
6 yds Binding 6¼ .37½ 2 69
Received in payment
12½lb Beeswax @20 — 250
1 Fox Skin . .19 2.69

" Sold for Cash
2½ yds C. Checks @75 . . . 1.87½
3 " Mamoody 50 . . . 1.50
1lb Powder 1.25
1¾lb Lead 28 49
Peltry &c 5.12
1 Dressed Deer Skin . . . . . .88 6 —

Document 34. Choctaw factory daybook, July 10, 1811. [National Archives]

Washington City,
March 5th 1819.

Father,

The delegation of your red children
the Cherokees has heard your talk with attention
~~and sattisfaction the hearts of their people have been~~
~~filled with grief and oppression when they left their~~
Nation — You can justly imagine what was and ought
to have been the feelings of the delegation on that
occasion — but now the scene we hope will be changed
and that the burthen will be lightened and their hearts
relieved from that grief and oppression, by the
illuminations of justice and humanity which have
~~been produced by the magnanimous kind of the~~
~~government We have long since been convinced~~
— lieve that civilized life was preferable to that of
the hunters — but circumstances arising from the
situation of our people, require time to make the
change — the Cherokees do not depend on hunting
for a livelihood, and they are fully sensible that
game cannot always exist — experience has clearly
demonstrated this matter to them — had they

been insensible of that fact – they would not have ex
=pected to follow those of their fellow Countrymen who
have seperated themselves from the soil of their Nat
=ivity and emigrated to the West – the establishmen
of schools in our Nation has been productive of the
greatest good, there are now two missionary estab.
– lishments in our Nation, one at spring place unde
the patronage of the moravian society, and the othe
at Brainerd on Chickamaugah, under that of the
American Board of foreign Missions – and they
are both in a flattering and progressive situation –
the numerous public roads leading through our
Nation in various directions, have also been a
great cause of stimulating the Cherokees to the
industrious pursuits of ~~husba~~ Agriculture and husba
=ry – the habitations of the Cherokees are also progress in
in comfort – many of their improvements and farms are
extensive, and their circumstances in relation to domestica
property, such as horses, Cattle, hogs sheep &c.are sufficiently
abundant to produce comfort. – this we have comm
=nicated for your more comprehensive knowledge of ou
true situations – As the Chief magistrate of this extensi
Republic and as the Father and protector of the Ame
=rican Aborigines, we feel ourselves bound to make
known to you our sentiments and actual situations
with Frankness. – We have now surrendered to t

United States a large portion of our Country for the benefit of those of our Countrymen who have emigrated to the Arkansas and we hope that the Government will now strictly protect us from the intrusions of her bad Citizens and not solicit us for more land— As we positively believe that the comfort and convenience of our Nation requires us to retain our present limits—

Father, there is one great existing cause which has hitherto placed our Nation under a peculiar disadvan=tage and inconvenience and incurred much unnecessa=ry trouble and expence to the United States, to which we beg leave to call your attention— When treaties for lands have been contemplated to be held with us, by the consent of the government, Our National Council have been summoned together on the spur of the occa=sion, without any previous knowledge of the object. had we refused to attend the call, we would have been represented as obstinate and unfriendly, this We believe ~~has operated as an~~ evil, and hope you will view it as an object worthy to be remedied by the friendly interposition of Your Fatherly hand. May the Great Spirit keep the chains of friendship between the United States and the Red Children of America, in perpetual brightness—And that the conditions of the American Aborigines be made prosperous and happy, under the fostering hands of the Government of this great Republic——And that Your life may be preserved many years in peace prosperity and happiness are the sincere wishes of your Cherokee Children

Ch. Hicks
Jno. Ross
James Brown
John Martin
Geo. Lowry
Cabbin × Smith
his mark
Sleeping × Rabbit
Small Wood ×

Washington City
5 March 1819
Cherokee Deputation

To His Excellency
James Monroe
President of the U. States.

Document 35d. Letter from chiefs of the Cherokee Nation to President James Monroe, March 5, 1819. [National Archives]

Novr 18th 1830

Dr Sir

In reply to your note of this morning
[illegible] the Govr of
be derived to the State of Georgia, or the
United States, by the enrolling plan,
but an accumulation of expense to the
Government, & a constant drain to
our Treasury. suppose 1000 enrolled
for emigration, this does not lessen
the claim of the Cherokees, as a tribe
[illegible] claimed by them
within Ge [illegible]
that has lately appeared amongst them
to emigrate, it is evident to my mind,
that the chiefs, shortly will propose a
treaty, under which the whole will emi-
:grate, that do not intend to remain as
Citizens; but if the enrolling system
is commenced, it will have the effect
to [illegible] the order that now an begins
[illegible] emigrating to the
west. Thus, [illegible]
[illegible] will have [illegible]
they, Indians, will compel their chiefs
to send Deputies duly authorised to
treat for the whole Country — Therefore
you will answer the Govr of Georgia
that this enrolling scheme ought to be

Document 36a. Letter from President Andrew Jackson to Secretary
of War Eaton, November 18, 1830. [National Archives]

postponed for the present until the
course the Legislature of Georgia, may
take on this subject, and until it is
seen what effect the late suspension for
emigration, by many of them, may
produce upon the whole is seen—
    I have no doubt but the common
Indian on seeing that their chiefs have
become wealthy by the course pursued
by them whilst the common Indians
have been reduced to beggary, will
soon burst their bonds of slavery,
& compel their chiefs to propose—
terms for their removal, for the
present the enrolling scheme ought
to be postponed
            yrs, Andrew Jackson

The Honble
    J. H. Eaton.
        Sec, of war—

Document 36b. Letter from President Andrew Jackson to Secretary
of War Eaton, November 18, 1830. [National Archives]

Worcester
Georgia

This Cause came the

On consideration whereof it is the opinion of this Court, that the act of the Legislature of the State of Georgia, upon which the indictment in this case is founded is contrary to the Constitution ~~Treaties~~ & Laws of the United ~~States;~~ the special plea in bar pleaded by the said Samuel A Worcester in manner aforesaid, ~~by~~ relying upon the Constitution, Treaties, & Laws of the United States aforesaid is a good bar & defence to the said Indictment by the said Samuel A Worcester; & as such ought to have been allowed & admitted by the said Superior Court for the County of Gwinnett in the State of Georgia before which the said Indictment was pending; & that there was error in the said Superior Court of the State of Georgia in overruling the plea ~~aforesaid~~ so pleaded as aforesaid. It is therefore ordered & adjudged, That the Judgment rendered in the premises by the said Superior Court of Georgia upon the plea of not guilty afterwards pleaded by the said Samuel A. Worcester, whereby the said Samuel A Worcester is sentenced to hard labour in the penitentiary of the State of Georgia, ought to

17

be ~~detrasagris~~ reversed & annulled. And this Court proceeding to render such judgment as the said Superior Court of the State of Georgia should have rendered, it is hereby ordered & adjudged that the said judgment of the said Superior Court, be ~~reversed~~ & hereby is reversed & annulled; & that judgment be & hereby is awarded that the special plea in bar so as aforesaid ^pleaded^ is a good & sufficient plea in bar in ~~Law~~ to the indictment aforesaid, & that all ~~persons~~ proceedings on the said Indictment do ~~recease~~ for ever surcease, & that the said Samuel A. Worcester be & hereby is henceforth dismissed ~~from~~ therefrom, & that he go thereof quit without day — And that a special mandate do go from this Court to the said Superior Court to carry this judgment into execution —

Document 37b. Court order in *Worcester v. Georgia*, January 1832. [National Archives]

Executive Department
Milledgeville April 20. 1831.

Sir,

I am desirous of receiving from you such information in answer to the following enquiries as your official station may enable you to obtain.

What effect has the late decision of the Supreme Court of the U. States in dismissing their Bill of Injunction against Georgia had upon the Cherokea

Are their Chiefs disposed to make a Treaty, if so what means will be most efficient to secure that result.

If their Chiefs are not so disposed, is the temper of the Middle and lower Classes different? — Could they be induced to have a general meeting of the whole Tribe without the Concurrence of their Chiefs

If a Treaty cannot be made with the whole Tribe thro' their Chiefs or the body of the People would those who reside in Georgia be disposed immediately to sell the Lands within its limits either by Treaty or by the Government agreeing to pay each Individual the Value for his improvements?

How can the Opinions and wishes and designs of the Chiefs and the People upon this subject

Document 39a. Letter from Governor Gilmer to Colonel Sanford, April 20, 1831. [National Archives]

subject be most Certainly ascertained.

What Whitemen residing among the Indians or elsewhere can with the greatest probability of success be employed to explain to them the policy of the General Government in desiring their removal to the Arkansas and the rights of the State which induced the extension of its jurisdiction over them and to Convince them of the great advantage they will derive from an immediate removal? —

Are there any individuals so situated that they could be employed for this object without exciting the suspicions of the Indians that they were the Agents of the Government? —

Are there any of the half breeds who could be trusted with such an employment?

What Portion of the Indians will probably remain in this State if a Treaty should be formed and Individuals allowed to take reservations? —

Are the Indians now prepared for the appointment of Commissioners to treat with them, or would further delay more Certainly accomplish the object?

You are also requested to Communicate to me whatever information you may have of the Conduct of the Missionary Worcester and

Document 39b. Letter from Governor Gilmer to Colonel Sanford, April 20, 1831. [National Archives]

Thompson or either of them in opposing the removal of the Indians to the West of the Mississippi — Creating opposition to the Laws of Georgia or inducing the Indians to persist in their attempt to establish an independent Government — What has been their conduct since their discharge? — What is the name of the White Man whose appointment you recommend should Worcester be removed from the Post Office at Echota?

Should Mr Bryan cease to be Post Master at Spring-Place, can any respectable Whiteman be found to succeed him.

Very Respectfully
Yours &c

George R Gilmer

Col: John W. A Sanford
Commander of the Guard &c

Document 40. Enrolled Cherokee immigrants, March 31, 1832. [National Archives]

Abstract of the number of deaths, with the Ages and diseases that occured in the Detachment of Cherokee emigrating to the nation West, from the 15 Octr until the 30 Decr 1837

Date of Death	Ages Years	Ages Month	Cholera Infantum	Dysentery	Typhus Fever	Inflammation of the lungs	Convulsions	Flours	Total	Remarks
October 25		"	1	"	"	"	"	"	1	Killed by the use of astringent Roots
Novr 1st	1	"	1	"	"	"	"	"	1	Would not take Medicine
" 8th	2	"	"	"	"	"	"	"	1	Ditto
" 13th	"	6	"	"	"	"	1	"	1	Diseases brought on by exposure, fatigue and exposure from scanty & would not take medicine
" 28	"	9	1	"	"	"	"	"	1	
" 30	"	18	"	"	"	1	"	"	1	
Decr 3	29	"	"	"	"	"	"	"	1	
" 7	8	"	"	"	1	"	"	"	1	
" 16	23	"	"	"	1	"	"	"	1	
" 16	20	"	"	"	"	1	"	"	1	
" 18	65	"	"	"	"	"	"	1	1	
" 21	"	6	1	"	"	"	"	"	1	
" 22	9	"	"	"	"	"	"	"	1	
" 26	13	"	"	"	"	"	"	"	1	
" 27	"	18	"	"	"	"	"	1	1	
			5	3	2	2	1	2	15	

G. S. Townsend. attending
Physician

f o 1

Mr. John Ross of the Cherokee Tribe

ARTICLES OF A TREATY

AGREED UPON

AT THE CITY OF WASHINGTON, MARCH 14, 1835,

BY

J. F. SCHERMERHORN,

ON THE PART OF

THE UNITED STATES OF AMERICA,

AND A

DELEGATION OF THE CHEROKEE TRIBE OF INDIANS;

WHICH,

BY THE PRESIDENT OF THE UNITED STATES, IS DIRECTED TO BE SUBMIT-
TED TO THE CHEROKEE NATION OF INDIANS FOR THEIR
CONSIDERATION AND APPROBATION.

Articles of a Treaty agreed upon at the City of Washington, March 14th, 1835, between J. F. Schermerhorn, on the part of the United States, and a Delegation of the Cherokee Tribe of Indians, which, by the President of the United States, is directed to be submitted to the Cherokee Nation of Indians, for their consideration and approbation.

WHEREAS, several persons of the Cherokee Nation of Indians, east of the Mississippi river, have visited the City of Washington, as delegates from that part of their Nation, in favor of emigration, with a hope and desire of making some arrangements which might be acceptable to the Government of the United States, and to their Nation generally, and thereby terminating the difficulties which they have experienced during a residence within the settled portion of the United States, under the jurisdiction and laws of the State Governments, and with a view of re-uniting their people in one body, and securing to themselves and their descendents the country selected by their forefathers, and sufficient for all their wants, and whereon they can establish and perpetuate such a state of society as may be most consonant with their habits and views, and as may tend to their individual comfort and their advancement in civilization:

AND WHEREAS, the President of the United States, animated with a sincere desire to relieve them from their embarrassments, and to provide for them a permanent establishment; and being willing, as far as his Constitutional power extends, to use all his efforts to accomplish these objects, has yielded to the wishes thus expressed to him in behalf of the Cherokees, and has authorized John F. Schermerhorn to meet the said members of the Cherokee Nation, and to arrange with them such terms as may be just and proper, between the parties:

AND WHEREAS, the said John F. Schermerhorn and the said Delegation of the Cherokee Nation of Indians, have met together and have taken the whole matter into consideration, and have agreed upon certain articles, which are to be considered merely as propositions to be made to the Cherokee people, on behalf of the United States, and to be utterly invalid until approved by them; it being distinctly understood that the said Cherokee people are not in the slightest manner committed by the formation of this provisional arrangement—

Now, THEREFORE, in consideration of the premises, and with a view to the final adjustment of all claims, and demands of every kind, of the Cherokees east of the Mississippi river, upon the United States, it is agreed as follows:

ARTICLE 1. This treaty shall be submitted to the people of the Cherokee Nation, for that purpose, to be assembled at New Echota, after due notice being given of the time of meeting by the Commissioner appointed by the President of the United States, whose duty it shall be fully to explain all its contents to them, and the views of the Government in regard to it, for their concurrence and adoption; and if it shall appear, after a fair, free, and full expression of their sentiments, that a majority of the people are in favor of the treaty, it shall be considered as approved and confirmed by the Nation; and their whole country shall be deemed to be ceded, and their claim and title to it to cease. But it is always understood that the treaty stipulations in former treaties, that have not been annulled or superseded by this, shall continue in full force.

ART. 2. The Cherokee Nation of Indians, for and in consideration of the additional quantity of land guarantied and secured to them by the third article of this treaty, and of the fulfilment of the covenants and stipulations hereinafter mentioned, and also of the sum of four millions five hundred thousand dollars, to be expended, paid, and invested, as agreed in the following articles, do hereby cede, relinquish, and convey to the United States, all their right and title to all the lands owned, claimed, and possessed by them, including the lands reserved by them for a school fund, east of the Mississippi river.

ART. 3. Whereas, by the treaty of May 6th, 1828, and the supplementary treaty thereto, of February 14th, 1833, with the Cherokees west of the Mississippi, the United States guarantied and secured, to be conveyed by patent, to the Cherokee Nation of Indians, the following tract of country: " Beginning at a point on the old western territorial line of Arkansas territory, being twenty-five miles north from the point where the territorial line crosses Arkansas river; thence running from said north point south on the said territorial line to the place where the said territorial line crosses Verdegris river; thence down said Verdegris river, to the Arkansas river; thence down said Arkansas to a point where a stone is placed, opposite to the east or lower bank of Grand river, at its junction with the Arkansas; thence running south forty-four degrees west, one mile; thence in a straight line to a point four miles northerly, from the mouth of the north fork of the Canadian; thence along the said four miles line to, the Canadian; thence down the Canadian to the Arkansas; thence down the Arkansas to that point on the Arkansas where the eastern Choctaw boundary strikes said river, and running thence with the western line of Arkansas territory, as now defined, to the southwest corner of Missouri; thence along the western Missouri line to the land assigned the Senecas; thence on the south line of the Senecas to Grand river; thence up said Grand river as far as the south line of the Osage reservation, extended if necessary; thence up and between said south Osage line, extended west if necessary, and a line drawn due west from the point of beginning to a certain distance west, at which a line running north and south from said Osage line to said due west line, will make seven millions of acres within the whole described boundaries. In addition to the seven millions of acres of land thus provided for and bounded, the United States further guaranty to the Cherokee Nation a perpetual outlet west, and a free and unmolested use of all the country lying west of the western boundary of said seven millions of acres, as far west as the sovereignty of the United States and their right of soil extend: *Provided however*, that if the saline or salt plain on the western prairie shall fall within said limits prescribed for said outlet, the right is reserved to the United States to permit other tribes of red men to get salt on said plain, in common with the Cherokees; and letters patent shall be issued by the United States, as soon as practicable, for the land hereby guarantied."

And whereas it is apprehended by the Cherokees, that in the above cession there is not contained a sufficient quantity of land for the accommodation of the whole nation, on their removal west

of the Mississippi, the United States, therefore, hereby covenant and agree to convey to the said Indians, and their descendants, by patent, in fee simple, the following additional tract of country, situated between the west line of the State of Missouri and the Osage reservation, beginning at the southeast corner of the same, and runs north along the east line of the Osage lands, fifty miles, to the northeast corner thereof; and thence east to the west line of the State of Missouri; thence with said line, south fifty miles; thence west to the place of beginning; estimated to contain 800,000 acres of land; but it is expressly understood, that if any of the lands assigned the Quapaws shall fall within the aforesaid bounds, the same shall be reserved and excepted out of the lands above granted. c

ART. 4. The United States also agree that the lands above ceded by the treaty of February 14, 1833, including the outlet and those ceded by this treaty, shall all be included in one patent, to be executed to the Cherokee Nation of Indians, by the President of the United States, according to the provisions of the act of May 28, 1830. It is, however, understood and agreed that the Union Missionary Station shall be held by the American Board for Foreign Missions, and the Military Reservation at Fort Gibson shall be held by the United States. But should the United States abandon said post, and have no further use for the same, it shall revert to the Cherokee nation. The United States shall always have the right to make and establish such post and military roads, and forts, in any part of the Cherokee country, as they may deem proper for the interest and protection of the same, and the free use of as much land, timber, fuel, and materials of all kinds for the construction and support of the same as may be necessary; provided, that if the private rights of individuals are interfered with, a just compensation therefor shall be made. With regard to the Union Missionary Reservation, it is understood that the American Board of Foreign Missions will continue to occupy the same, for the benefit of the Cherokee nation; and if, at any time hereafter, they shall abandon the same, upon payment for their improvements by the United States, it shall revert to the Cherokee Nation.

ART. 5. The United States also stipulate and agree to extinguish, for the benefit of the Cherokees, the title to the reservations within their country, made in the Osage treaty of 1825, to certain half breeds, and for this purpose they hereby agree to pay to the persons to whom the same belong or have been assigned, or to their agents or guardians, whenever they shall execute, after the ratification of this treaty, a satisfactory conveyance for the same, to the United States, the sum of fifteen thousand dollars, according to a schedule accompanying this treaty, of the relative value of the several reservations.

ART. 6. The United States hereby covenant and agree, that the lands ceded to the Cherokee nation, in the foregoing article, shall, in no future time, without their consent, be included within the territorial limits or jurisdiction of any State or Territory; but they shall secure to the Cherokee Nation the right, by their National Councils, to make and carry into effect all such laws as they may deem necessary for the government and protection of the persons and property within their own country, belonging to their people, or such persons as have connected themselves with them: *Provided always*, That they shall not be inconsistent with the Constitution of the United States, and such acts of Congress as have been or may be passed for the regulation of Indian affairs; and also, that they shall not be considered as extending to such citizens and army of the United States, as may travel or reside in the Indian country, according to the laws and regulations established by the government of the same.

ART. 7. Perpetual peace and friendship shall exist between the citizens of the United States and the Cherokee Indians. The United States agree to protect the Cherokee Nation from domestic strife and foreign enemies, and against intestine wars between the several tribes. They shall endeavor to preserve and maintain the peace of the country, and not make war upon their neighbors; and should hostilities commence by one or more tribes, upon another, the Cherokee Council of the Nation, when called upon by the authority of the President of the United States, shall aid the United States with as many warriors as may be deemed necessary to protect and restore peace in the Indian country; and while in service, they shall be entitled to the pay and rations of the army of the United States. They shall also be protected against all interruption and intrusion from citizens of the United States, who may attempt to settle in the country without their consent; and all

such persons shall be removed from the same by order of the President of the United States. But this is not intended to prevent the residence among them of useful farmers, mechanics, and teachers, for the instruction of the Indians, according to the treaty stipulations, and the regulations of the Government of the United States.

ART. 8. The Cherokee Nation, having already made great progress in civilization, and deeming it important that every proper and laudable inducement should be offered to their people to improve their condition, as well as to guard and secure, in the most effectual manner, the rights guarantied to them in this treaty, and with a view to illustrate the liberal and enlarged policy of the Government of the United States towards the Indians, in their removal beyond the territorial limits of the States, it is stipulated that they shall be entitled to a delegate in the House of Representatives of the United States, whenever Congress shall make provision for the same.

ART. 9. The United States also agree and stipulate to remove the Cherokees to their new homes, and to subsist them one year after their arrival there, and that a sufficient number of steamboats and baggage-wagons shall be furnished to remove them comfortably, and so as not to endanger their health; and that a physician, well supplied with medicines, shall accompany each detachment of emigrants removed by the Government. They shall also be furnished with blankets, kettles, and rifles, as stipulated in the treaty of 1828. The blankets shall be delivered before their removal, and the kettles and rifles after their removal in their new country. Such persons and families as, in the opinion of the Emigrating Agent, are capable of subsisting and removing themselves, shall be permitted to do so; and they shall be allowed in full for all claims for the same, twenty-five dollars for each member of their family, slaves excepted, for whom (those now owned in the Nation,) they shall be allowed eighteen dollars each; and in lieu of their one year's rations, they shall be paid the sum of thirty-three dollars, thirty-three cents, if they prefer it. And, in order to encourage immediate removal, and with a view to benefitting the poorer class of their people, the United States agree and promise to pay each member of the Cherokee Nation one hundred and fifty dollars on his removal, at the Cherokee Agency West, provided they enrol and remove within one year from the ratification of this treaty: and one hundred dollars to each person that removes within two years; and after this no *per capita* allowance whatever will be made; and it is expressly understood, that the whole Nation shall remove within two years from the ratification of the treaty. There shall also be paid to each emigrant since June 1833, one hundred and fifty dollars, according to the assurances given them by the Secretary of War, that they should be entitled to all the advantages and provisions of the treaty which should be finally concluded with their Nation. They shall also be paid for the improvements, according to their appraised value before they removed, where fraud has not already been shown in the valuation.

Such Cherokees, also, as reside at present out of the Nation, and shall remove with them, in two years, west of the Mississippi, shall be entitled to *per capita* allowance, removal, and subsistence, as above provided.

ART. 10. The United States agree to appoint suitable agents, who shall make a just and fair valuation of all such improvements now in the possession of the Cherokees, as add any value to the lands; and, also, of the ferries owned by them, according to their nett income; and such improvements and ferries from which they have been dispossessed in a lawless manner, or under any existing laws of the State where the same may be situated. The just debts of the Indians shall be paid out of any moneys due them for their improvements and claims; and they shall also be furnished, at the discretion of the President, with a sufficient sum to enable them to obtain the necessary means to remove themselves to their new homes, and the balance of their dues shall be paid them at the Cherokee Agency west of the Mississippi. The Missionary establishments shall also be valued and appraised in like manner, and the amount of them paid over by the United States to the treasurers of the respective Missionary Societies by whom they have been established and improved, in order to enable them to erect such buildings, and make such improvements, among the Cherokees west of the Mississippi, as they may deem necessary for their benefit. Such teachers at present among the Cherokees as their Council shall select and designate, shall be removed west of the Mississippi with the Cherokee Nation, and on the same terms allowed to them. It is, however, understood, that from the valuation of the Missionary establishments shall be deducted the *pro rata* amount advanced and expended for the same by the United States.

ART. 11. The President of the United States shall invest in some safe and most productive public stocks of the country, for the benefit of the whole Cherokee Nation, who have removed or shall remove to the lands assigned by this treaty to the Cherokee Nation west of the Mississippi, the following sums, as a permanent fund, for purposes hereinafter specified, and pay over the nett income of the same annually, to such person or persons as shall be authorized or appointed by the Cherokee Nation to receive the same, and their receipt shall be a full discharge for the amount paid to them, viz.: The sum of four hundred thousand dollars, to constitute a general fund, the interest of which shall be applied annually by the Council of the Nation to such purposes as they may deem best for the general interest of their people. The sum of fifty thousand dollars, to constitute an orphans' fund, the annual income of which shall be expended towards the support and education of such orphan children as are destitute of the means of subsistence. The sum of one hundred and sixty thousand dollars, to constitute a permanent school fund, the interest of which shall be applied annually by the Council of the Nation for the support of common schools, and such a literary institution of a higher order as may be established in the Indian country, and in order to secure, as far as possible, the true and beneficial application of the orphans' and school fund, the Council of the Cherokee Nation, when required by the President of the United States, shall make a report of the application of those funds; and he shall at all times have the right, if the funds have been misapplied, to correct any abuses of them, and to direct the manner of their application, for the purposes for which they were intended. The Council of the Nation may, by giving two years' notice of their intention, withdraw their funds, by and with the consent of the President and Senate of the United States, and invest them in such a manner as they may deem most proper for their interest. The United States also agree and stipulate to pay to the Cherokee Council East, sixty thousand dollars, and to expend thirty thousand dollars in the erection of such mills, council and school-houses in their country west of the Mississippi as their Council shall designate. The sum of ten thousand dollars shall be expended for the introduction of improved breeds of the different domestic animals, as horses, hogs, cattle, and sheep, which shall be placed under the direction of the Agent of the Tribe; and who, by and with the advice of the Council, shall distribute them to the best advantage for the general benefit of the whole people. They shall also pay to the Council five thousand dollars towards procuring materials for a printing press, to enable them to print a public newspaper, and books in the Cherokee language for gratuitous distribution.

Art. 12. The sum of two hundred and fifty thousand dollars is hereby set apart to satisfy and liquidate all claims of every kind and nature whatever of the Cherokees, upon the United States, and such claims of the citizens of the United States against the Cherokees as come within the provisions of the intercourse act of 1802, and as existed in either of the States of Georgia, Alabama, North Carolina, and Tennessee, prior to the extension of the laws of either such States over them. All claims of the Indians shall first be examined by the Council of the Nation, and then reported to the Commissioner appointed to adjudicate the same; and the claims of the United States shall first be examined by the Agent and Council of the Nation, and then referred to the Commissioner, who shall finally decide upon them; and on his certificate of the amount due in favor of the several claimants, they shall be paid. If the above claims do not amount to the sum of two hundred and fifty thousand dollars, the amount unexpended shall be added to the orphans' and school funds.

Art. 13. The Cherokee Nation of Indians, believing it will be for the interest of their people to have all their funds and annuities under their own direction and future disposition, hereby agree to commute their permanent annuity of ten thousand dollars for the sum of two hundred and fourteen thousand dollars, the same to be invested by the President of the United States as a part of the general fund of the Nation: and their present school fund, amounting to forty-eight thousand two hundred and fifty-one dollars and seventy-six cents, shall be invested in the same manner as the school fund provided in this treaty, and constitute a part of the same; and both of them to be subject to the same disposal as the other part of these funds by their National Council.

Art. 14. Those individuals and families of the Cherokee Nation that are averse to a removal to the Cherokee country west of the Mississippi, and are desirous to become citizens of the States, where they reside, and such as, in the opinion of the Agent, are qualified to take care of themselves and their property, shall be entitled to receive their due portion of all the personal benefits accruing under this treaty, for their claims, improvements, ferries, removal, and subsistence; but they shall not be entitled to any share or portion of the funds vested or to be expended for the common benefit of the Nation.

Art. 15. It is also agreed on the part of the United States, that such warriors of the Cherokee Nation as were engaged on the side of the United States, in the late wars with Great Britain and the southern tribes of Indians, and who were wounded in such service, shall be entitled to such pensions as shall be allowed them by the Congress of the United States, to commence from the period of their disability.

Art. 16. The United States hereby agree to protect and defend the Cherokees in their possessions and property, by all legal and proper means, after their enrolment, or the ratification of this treaty, until the time fixed upon for their removal; and if they are left unprotected, the United States shall pay the Cherokees for the losses and damages sustained by them in consequence thereof.

Art. 17. The expenditures, payments and investments, agreed to be made by the United States, in the foregoing articles of this treaty, it is understood, are to be paid out of the sum of four millions five hundred thousand dollars, agreed to be given to the Cherokee Nation for the cession of their lands, and in full for all their claims, of every kind, now existing against the United States.

Art. 18. The annexed schedule contains the estimate for carrying into effect the several pecuniary stipulations and agreements contained in this treaty; and if the sums affixed for any specific object shall be more or less than is requisite to carry the same into effect, the excess for such estimate shall be applied to make up the deficiency, if any occur, for the other objects of expenditure; and if, in the aggregate, the payments and expenditures shall exceed or fall short of the several sums appropriated for them, the same shall be taken from or added to, (as the case may be,) the funds to be vested for the benefit of the Cherokee Nation, according to the relative amounts intended to be invested for each specific fund, by this treaty: but the sum of two hundred and fourteen thousand dollars commuted for their permanent annuity, and their present school fund, already invested, shall not be considered as any part of the above sum of four millions and five hundred thousand dollars, the full amount agreed to be paid by the United States for all claims and demands against the same, and for the cession of their lands; and in no case shall the amount agreed to be paid and invested in the aforesaid articles of this treaty exceed this sum.

SCHEDULE.

For Removal	-	-	$255,000 00
Subsistence	-	-	400,000 00
Improvements and ferries	-	1,000,000 00
Claims and spoliations	-	250,000 00
Domestic animals	-	-	10,000 00
National debts	-	-	60,000 00
Public buildings	-	-	30,000 00
Printing press, &c.	-	-	5,000 00
Blankets	-	-	36,000 00
Rifles	-	-	37,000 00
Kettles	-	-	7,000 00
Per capita allowance	-	1,800,000 00
General fund	-	-	400,000 00
School fund	-	-	160,000 00
Orphan's fund	-	-	50,000 00
Additional territory	-	500,000 00
			$5,000,000 00
School fund already invested	-	48,251 76
Commutation of perpetual annuity	-	-	214,000 00
			$5,262,251 76

ART. 19. This treaty, when it shall have been approved and signed by a majority of the Chiefs, Headmen, and Warriors, of the Cherokee Nation of Indians, and ratified by the President, by and with the advice and consent of the Senate of the United States, shall be binding on the contracting parties.

In testimony whereof the said John F. Schermerhorn, authorized as aforesaid, and the said Cherokee Delegation, have set their hands and seals the day and year above written.

John F. Schermerhorn,	[Seal.]
John Ridge,	[Seal.]
Archilla Smith,	[Seal.]
Elias Boudinot.	[Seal.]
S. W. Bell,	[Seal.]
John West,	[Seal.]
Wm. A. Davis,	[Seal.]
Ezekiel West,	[Seal.]

Witness present:

Alex. Macomb, Maj. Gen. U. S. A.
Geo. Gibson, Com. Gen.
William Allen.
Hudson M. Garland.
Sherman Page.
John Garland, Maj. U. S. A.
Ben. F. Currey, Sup. Cher. remov. &c.
A. Van Buren, U. S. A.
Dyer Castor.

To the Senate and House of Representatives of the United States in Congress assembled,

THE UNDERSIGNED MEMORIALISTS,

CITIZENS OF PENNSYLVANIA,

Beg leave respectfully to represent :——

That, although in the Bill authorizing the President to procure, and provide for, the removal of the Indians residing within the limits of the states of Georgia, Mississippi, and Alabama, a proviso is subjoined; that nothing therein, shall authorize a violation of existing treaties; your memorialists apprehend, that the said Bill may be the means of encouraging a gross violation of the treaties existing between the United States and the Cherokees.

Your memorialists believe that the following questions would be answered in the affirmative by the most

Independently of the acts of those whom they may justly consider as foreigners and invaders of their country, would not the Cherokees be an independent sovereign people, and the rightful inheritors of the lands on which they reside?

Have not the lands, which they now hold, been solemnly guaranteed to them by treaties with our national government, more especially by the treaty of Holston?

Are not treaties made by the national government with a sovereign and independent people, the supreme law of the United States agreeably to the constitution?

Assuming that affirmative answers would be given to the foregoing queries, your memorialists infer, that it must be conceded; that so far only as the most sacred rights of a people can, without their own consent, be abrogated by the ability of others to oppress them, and the precedents afforded by the long established practice of oppression: and so far only as the Cherokees could, by these extraneous means, be deprived of their claims to be treated as a sovereign people, can it be legal, forcibly to eject them from their patrimony.

Your memorialists conceive, that with the power to make treaties, the discretionary power of deciding on the question of the existence of a competent degree of sovereignty in any people, with whom a treaty might be made, was necessarily associated; and that it would not be justifiable for the people of any state, in our great confederation, to evade the obligations arising under a treaty, by alleging that, in their opinion, the party with whom the treaty had been made, had not a competent degree of sovereignty.

But as in the case of the Indians, the exclusive right to treat with them, whether within the geographical limits of a state, or otherwise situated, was specifically given to the national government, it were evidently irrational to question the constitutionality of any treaty made with them by that government.

Your memorialists conceive that nothing can be more irreconcilable with law, reason, or national honour, than that a treaty, solemnly ratified by the first, best, and wisest of our presidents, to which the people of the several states were parties under the constitution, and which they sanctioned by their acquiescence, is now to be questioned upon the pretence, that Washington and the senate, with whose advice and assistance he acted, were so ignorant of the constitution, and the relation in which the aborigines stood to the people of the United States, as to make with the former a treaty, to be violated whenever it should become the interest of a state to treat it as illegal.

To the annals of our country, your memorialists would turn in order to demonstrate, that not only by Washington, but by his successors, by the British government, and even by the government of Georgia, has the sovereignty of the Cherokees been deemed adequate to the treaty making power.

Your memorialists conceive that the sacred obligations arising from the treaties of the United States, ought to be a sufficient protection to the Cherokees, in the possession of their lands, had they been intruders: but viewing them as those who would be the *undisturbed legitimate* owners, independently of the superior power of the invaders of their country, and the sanction for the exercise of that power furnished by similar wrongs heretofore elsewhere committed, your memorialists feel an increased repugnance at the anticipated breach of our national faith.

They are penetrated with sentiments of disapprobation, and sorrow, when they hear from distinguished politicians, a recital of instances of injustice towards the aborigines, not with the intention of deprecating a continuance of that course of iniquity, but in order to make it an excuse for the perpetration of another wrong, in which our character, as a nation and as republicans, will be more deeply, and more generally implicated.

The only pretence which could be set up to the lands of the Cherokees, supposing them unprotected by their treaties with our national government, would, in the opinion of your memorialists, be that claim of the strong to the possessions of the weak, which has been miscalled the right of conquest. But if obtained by conquest, those lands were won by the disinterested soldiers of our revolution, who inspired by genuine patriotism, a love of liberty and of virtuous fame, hazarded, or sacrificed, wealth, health, blood, and life itself, in that perilous struggle. Your memorialists observe, therefore, with pain that those territorial acquisitions have been, by a promised distribution, held up as the means of influencing a portion of our countrymen, to forget what is believed due, to the national character, to humanity, and to those rights of man, which are so well portrayed in our Declaration of Independence.

Your memorialists admit that there may be plausible ground for the opinion expressed by the Secretary of War, and other eminent men, that the ultimate happiness of the red men, would be best consulted by their removal beyond the reach of the cupidity of the whites, if such a spot can be found for them on this side of the grave; and it would diminish the mortification of the undersigned at the contemplated evasion of our national engagements, agreeably to the reprobated principle that the end justifies the means, did facts allow them to suppose, that the ultimate happiness of the red men and their neighbours was the incentive of this policy.

But had such been the incentive, instead of projected lotteries, and other methods of effecting a promiscuous partition of the Cherokee lands, among the adjoining population, your memorialists would expect to read of a plan for the sale of those lands, in order to create a fund for the benefit of a people, expatriated for the common good. In that case, your memorialists would not have had to complain, that with respect to the territory acquired, and the national reputation established, by the impoverishment of the heroes of the revolution, the one is to be tarnished, in order that the other may be employed for the enrichment of a multitude, happening to reside within the geographical boundaries, unjustly, and injudiciously assigned, by a foreign monarch, to one of *his* provinces.

Your memorialists are indignant that in a republican country, which has spurned the previously legitimate control of British kings, the illegitimate charters and proclamations of those monarchs, should be considered competent to authorize the seizure of a territory, in despite of a solemn guarantee.

Nor is there, agreeably to the opinion of the memorialists, less cause for regret, that at a moment when we are universally rejoicing on account of the liberty gained by a nation in the eastern hemisphere, we should, in our own country, sanction the worst of all tyranny—that of one nation over another.

Heretofore the acts of Congress have been considered as pre-eminently the law of the land, unless declared unconstitutional by the Supreme Court of the United States; your memorialists are therefore surprised to observe, that the act of Congress of 1802, for the protection of the Indian tribes, which derives additional claims to a faithful observance, from its incorporation in more than one compact with them, should be treated as void, upon the plea of its unconstitutionality; without any decision, authorizing this view of it, by the only competent tribunal.

In the provincial history of some of the states of our Union, there may be sufficient instances of fraud and violence towards the aborigines to furnish precedents for the course which the Indian bill has been made to sanction, but your memorialists are under the impression, that in our national history no instance of ill faith, cruelty, or injustice, can be adduced prior to the proceedings in relation to the southern Indians. Our national character will be looked for, not in times anterior to our existence as a nation, but in the period which has succeeded the formation of our general government. Your memorialists trust that the Senate, and House of Representatives, of the United States, will not consider the *crimes* of our provincial times, as worthy of imitation; but will rather endeavour to wipe off any stain which may thence arise, by a rigid performance of national obligations, and scrupulous adherence to the path of justice and humanity.

Document 43b. Memorial of Pennsylvanians opposed to Indian removal, January 10, 1830. [National Archives]

ORDERS. *No.* 25.

Head Quarters, Eastern Division. Cherokee Agency, Ten. May 17, 1838.

MAJOR GENERAL SCOTT, of the United States' Army, announces to the troops assembled and assembling in this country, that, with them, he has been charged by the President to cause the Cherokee Indians yet remaining in North Carolina, Georgia, Tennessee and Alabama, to remove to the West, according to the terms of the Treaty of 1835. His Staff will be as follows:

LIEUTENANT COLONEL W. J. WORTH, acting Adjutant General, Chief of the Staff.

MAJOR M. M. PAYNE, acting Inspector General.

LIEUTENANTS R. ANDERSON, & E. D. KEYES, regular Aids-de-camp.

COLONEL A. H. KENAN & LIEUTENANT H. B. SHAW, volunteer Aids-de-camp.

Any order given orally, or in writing, by either of those officers, in the name of the Major General, will be respected and obeyed as if given by himself.

The Chiefs of Ordnance, of the Quarter-Master's Department and of the Commissariat, as also the Medical Director of this Army, will, as soon as they can be ascertained, be announced in orders.

To carry out the general object with the greatest promptitude and certainty, and with the least possible distress to the Indians, the country they are to evacuate is divided into three principal Military Districts, under as many officers of high rank, to command the troops serving therein, subject to the instructions of the Major General.

Eastern District, to be commanded by BRIGADIER GENERAL EUSTIS, of the United States' Army or the highest officer in rank serving therein:—North Carolina, the part of Tennessee lying north of Gilmer county, Georgia, and the counties of Gilmer, Union, and Lumpkin, in Georgia. Head Quarters, in the first instance, say, at Fort Butler.

Western District, to be commanded by COLONEL LINDSAY, of the United States' Army, or the highest officer in rank serving therein:—Alabama, the residue of Tennessee and Dade county, in Georgia. Head quarters, in the first instance, say, at Ross' Landing.

Middle District, to be commanded by BRIGADIER GENERAL ARMISTEAD of the United States' Army, or the highest officer in rank, serving therein:—All that part of the Cherokee country, lying within the State of Georgia, and which is not comprised in the two other districts. Head Quarters, in the first instance, say, at New Echota.

It is not intended that the foregoing boundaries between the principal commanders shall be strictly observed. Either, when carried near the district of another, will not hesitate to extend his operations, according to the necessities of the case, but with all practicable harmony, into the adjoining district. And, among his principal objects, in case of actual or apprehended hostilities, will be that of affording adequate protection to our white people in and around the Cherokee country.

The senior officer actually present in each district will receive instructions from the Major General as to the time of commencing the removal, and every thing that may occur interesting to the service, in the district, will be promptly reported to the same source. The Major General will endeavour to visit in a short time all parts of the Cherokee country occupied by the troops.

The duties devolved on the army, through the orders of the Major General & those of the commanders of districts, under him, are of a highly important and critical nature.

The Cherokees, by the advances which they have made in christianity and civilization, are by far the most interesting tribe of Indians in the territorial limits of the United States. Of the 15,000 of those people who are now to be removed—(and the time within which a voluntary emigration was stipulated, will expire on the 23rd instant—) it is understood that about four fifths are opposed, or have become averse to a distant emigration; and altho' none are in actual hostilities with the United States, or threaten a resistance by arms, yet the troops will probably be obliged to cover the whole country they inhabit, in order to make prisoners and to march or to transport the prisoners, by families, either to this place, to Ross' Landing or Gunter's Landing, where they are to be finally delivered over to the Superintendant of Cherokee Emigration.

Considering the number and temper of the mass to be removed, together with the extent and fastnesses of the country occupied, it will readily occur, that simple indiscretions—acts of harshness and cruelty, on the part of our troops, may lead, step by step, to delays, to impatience and exasperation, and in the end, to a general war and carnage—a result, in the case of those particular Indians, utterly abhorrent to the generous sympathies of the whole American people. Every possible kindness, compatible with the necessity of removal, must, therefore, be shown by the troops; and, if, in the ranks, a despicable individual should be found, capable of inflicting a wanton injury or insult on any Cherokee man, woman or child, it is hereby made the special duty of the nearest good officer or man, instantly to interpose, and to seize and consign the guilty wretch to the severest penalty of the laws. The Major General is fully persuaded that this injunction will not be neglected by the brave men under his command, who cannot be otherwise than jealous of their own honor and that of their country.

By early and persevering acts of kindness and humanity, it is impossible to doubt that the Indians may soon be induced to confide in the Army, and instead of fleeing to mountains and forests, flock to us for food and clothing. If, however, through false apprehensions, individuals, or a party, here and there, should seek to hide themselves, they must be pursued and invited to surrender, but not fired upon unless they should make a stand to resist. Even in such cases, mild remedies may sometimes better succeed than violence; and it cannot be doubted that if we get possession of the women and children first, or first capture the men, that, in either case, the outstanding members of the same families will readily come in on the assurance of forgiveness and kind treatment.

Every captured man, as well as all who surrender themselves, must be disarmed, with the assurance that their weapons will be carefully preserved and restored at, or beyond the Mississippi. In either case, the men will be guarded and escorted, except it may be, where their women and children are safely secured as hostages; but, in general, families, in our possession, will not be separated, unless it be to send men, as runners, to invite others to come in.

It may happen that Indians will be found too sick, in the opinion of the nearest Surgeon, to be removed to one of the depots indicated above. In every such case, one or more of the family, or the friends of the sick person, will be left in attendance, with simple subsistence and remedies, and the remainder of the family removed by the troops. Infants, superannuated persons, lunatics and women in a helpless condition, will all, in the removal, require peculiar attention, which the brave and humane will seek to adapt to the necessities of the several cases.

All strong men, women, boys & girls, will be made to march under proper escorts. For the feeble, Indian horses and ponies will furnish a ready resource, as well as for bedding and light cooking utensils—all of which, as intimated in the Treaty, will be necessary to the emigrants both in going to, and after arrival at, their new homes. Such, and all other light articles of property, the Indians will be allowed to collect and to take with them, as also their slaves, who will be treated in like manner with the Indians themselves.

If the horses and ponies be not adequate to the above purposes, wagons must be supplied.

Corn, oats, fodder and other forage, also beef cattle, belonging to the Indians to be removed, will be taken possession of by the proper departments of the Staff, as wanted, for the regular consumption of the Army, and certificates given to the owners, specifying in every case, the amount of forage and the weight of beef, so taken, in order that the owners may be paid for the same on their arrival at one of the depots mentioned above.

All other moveable or personal property, left or abandoned by the Indians, will be collected by agents appointed for the purpose, by the Superintendant of Cherokee Emigration, under a system of accountability, for the benefit of the Indian owners, which he will devise. The Army will give to those agents, in their operations, all reasonable countenance, aid and support.

White men and widows, citizens of the United States, who are, or have been intermarried with Indians, and thence commonly termed, *Indian countrymen*; also such Indians as have been made denizens of particular States by special legislation, together with the families and property of all such persons, will not be molested or removed by the troops until a decision, on the principles involved, can be obtained from the War Department.

A like indulgence, but only for a limited time, and until further orders, is extended to the families and property of certain Chiefs and head-men of the two great Indian parties, (on the subject of emigration) now understood to be absent in the direction of Washington on the business of their respective parties.

This order will be carefully read at the head of every company in the Army.

By Command:

W. J. Worth Colonel
Chief of the Staff

Winfield Scott.

Washington City
Jany. 27. 1838

Sir,

I write these lines in order to let you hear of
your delegation at Washington. We are all well, also
the delegation that was sent to the Seminoles is in
good health. We are all together at one place. We
hear news of this kind, that you are informed that
we cannot do any thing nor make any alterations —
whatever, but we do not think it the case ourselves.
We are here with some encouragement. You are told
these things at home in order to dishearten you, but
it will not do to believe such news as that, for if
we believe we cannot do any thing we will let you
know, for we will not be silent. It is done in order
to outwit you, and get you to acknowledge the Treaty.
They know that we have the Question before the Senate
that is the reason they are so uneasy and work so
hard against us. Their proceedings will be done away,
and that makes them restless, and that is the reason
you hear so many false reports. But the answer
will not be hard to make them — just tell them you
have sent on a delegation, and you are waiting for
them to come home, and tell you the Secretary of War
and the man he appointed to have an interview with
us, did disappoint us. They did it for one reason, it
was for this. They want to get something to help
them on with some news they send to dishearten you.

Cherokee Agency East,
March 15, 1838.)

Hon. C. A. Harris,
    Com'. Ind. Affairs.

                    Sir

              In order that you may know what
measures are resorted to here to prevent emigration, I have
the honor to enclose herewith a translated Copy of a letter
written in Cherokee, and purporting to be from White Path
to Thomas Manning, a near neighbour of M' Jn' Ross. — White
Path is a very old man, and can neither read nor write
Cherokee. This is another plan invented by the Delegation
at Washington to keep the Indians here, and (having been
Copied and sent through the Nation by runners to Leading
Men in all the towns, who called meetings and read it)
it has had considerable effect in stopping emigration.

        This, with no doubt numbers of other measures that are
practised, accounts for the delay and disappointment to
which I am subjected in getting these miserable and deluded people started for their Country West.

        I am extremely mortified at not being able to do more
towards their removal, on account of such heavy and daily
expenses that are incurred. But I assure you their delay
here is caused by only a few of their leading men, who
are now misleading their people with their eyes open.
                    Very Respectfully
                    Yr. Mo. Obt. Sert.)

                    N. Smith
                    Sup'. Che. Removal

they know very well that the President alone could not break the Treaty that was made by Jackson or by his order. That is the way the President got his seat, and he is at this time afraid to interfere with Jackson proceedings. That was the reason why he wanted us to lay the Case before the Senate, then if the Senate will say that the Treaty was made by unauthorized power, that would give the President a chance to make a new Treaty, for we have already given them evidence that there was a fraud put on the Nation, and we have laid in our Memorial before the Senate, and it is not long before they will let it be known. We have given up all our papers to the person who will present them, and we are in great hopes that there will be some alteration in that which they strive so hard for us to acknowledge. That is one of the most hurtful thing to us, but just bear it, the time will not be long before you can hear how it was determined. They tell you they will drive you off by force, it is very doubtful about us being drove. No more, when you receive this show and let the people of Ellijay hear it it.

Signed, White Path

[illegible]

Document 45d. Letter from Nathanial Smith to C.A. Harris with enclosures in Cherokee, March 15, 1838. [National Archives]

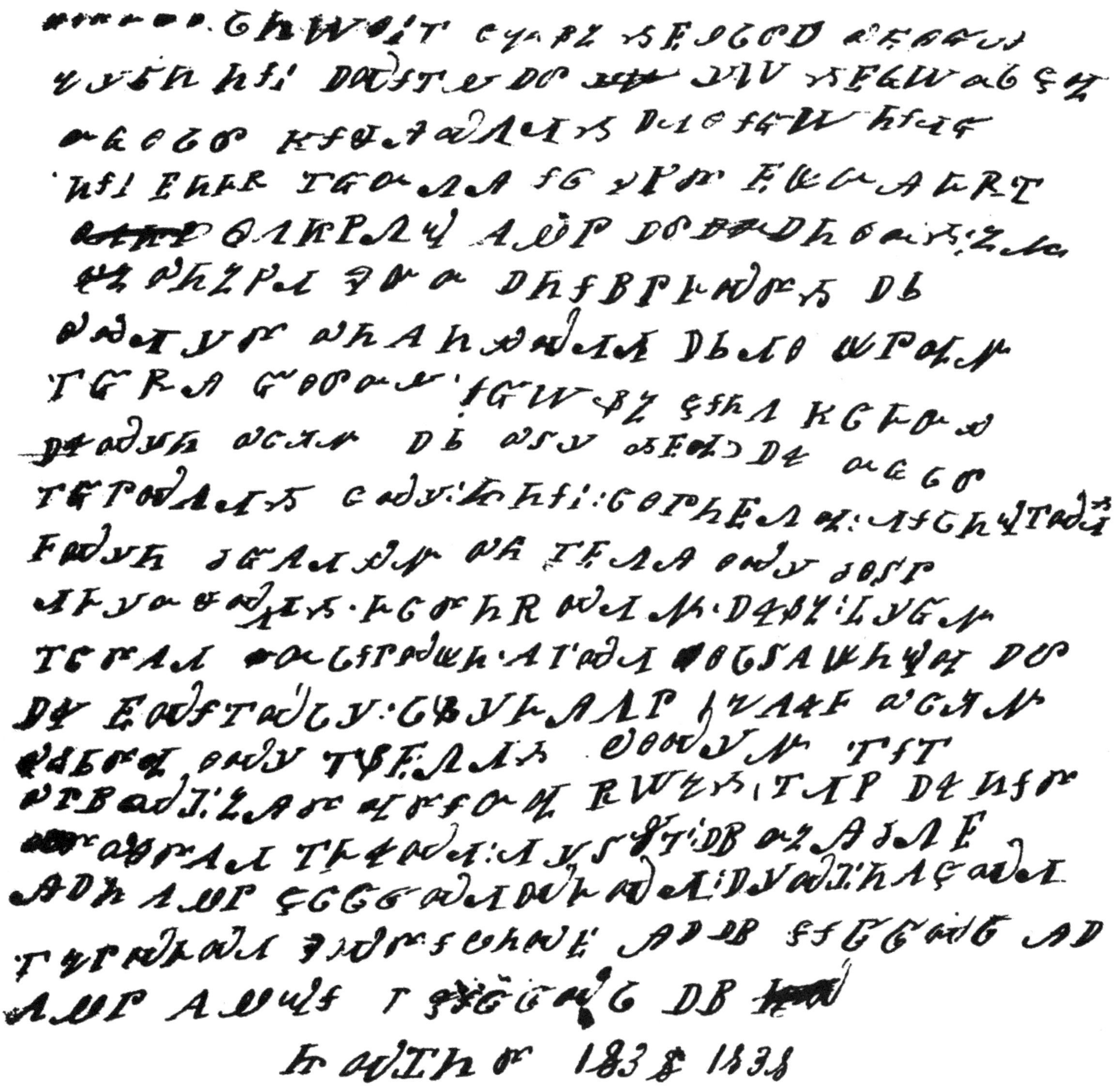

Document 45e. Letter from Nathanial Smith to C.A. Harris with enclosures in Cherokee, March 15, 1838. [National Archives]

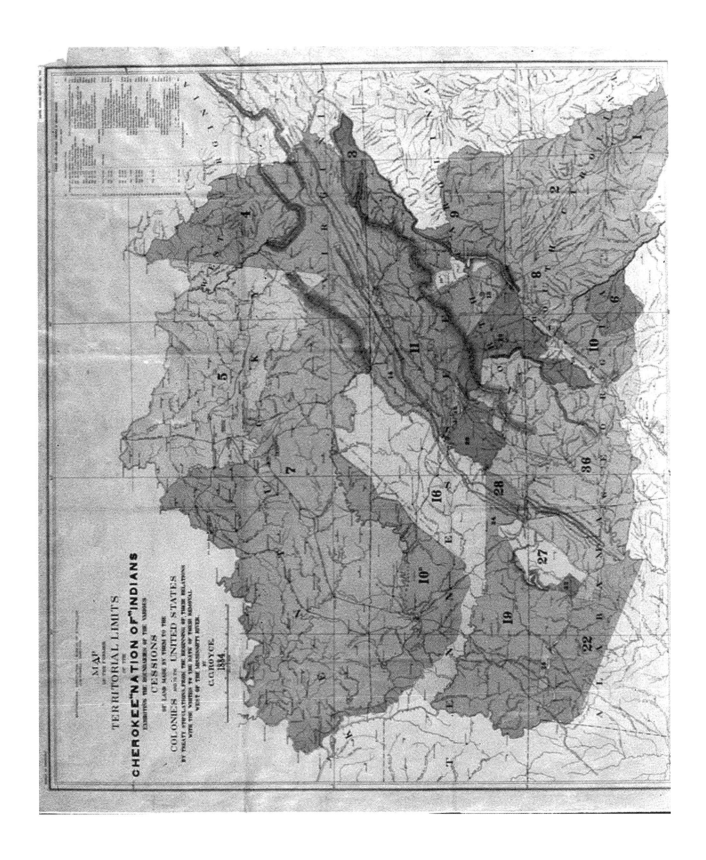

Slide A. Cherokee Treaty Map, Eastern lands, 1884. [National Archives]

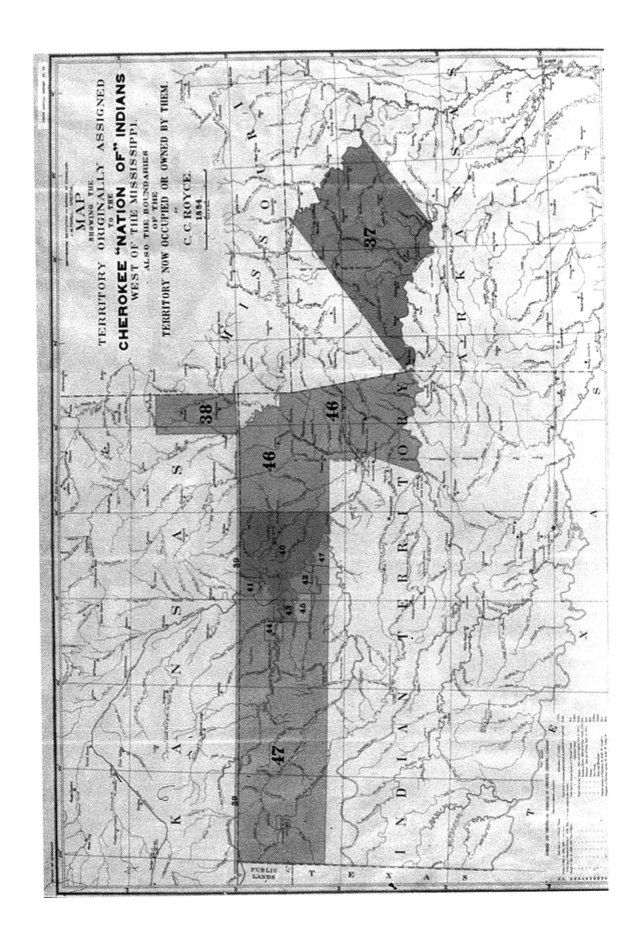

Slide B. Cherokee treaty map, Western lands, 1884. [National Archives]

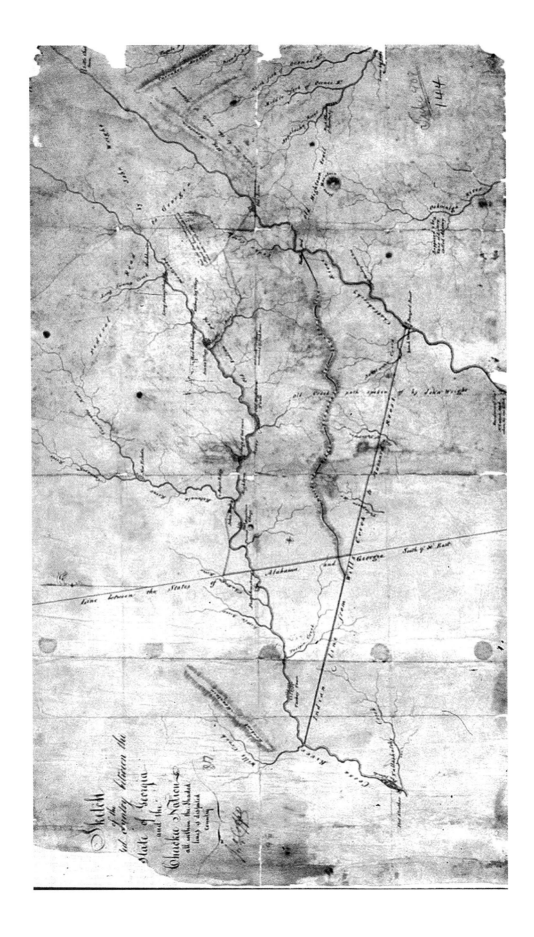

Slide C. Map of territories disputed between Georgia and the Cherokee, ca. 1830. [National Archives]

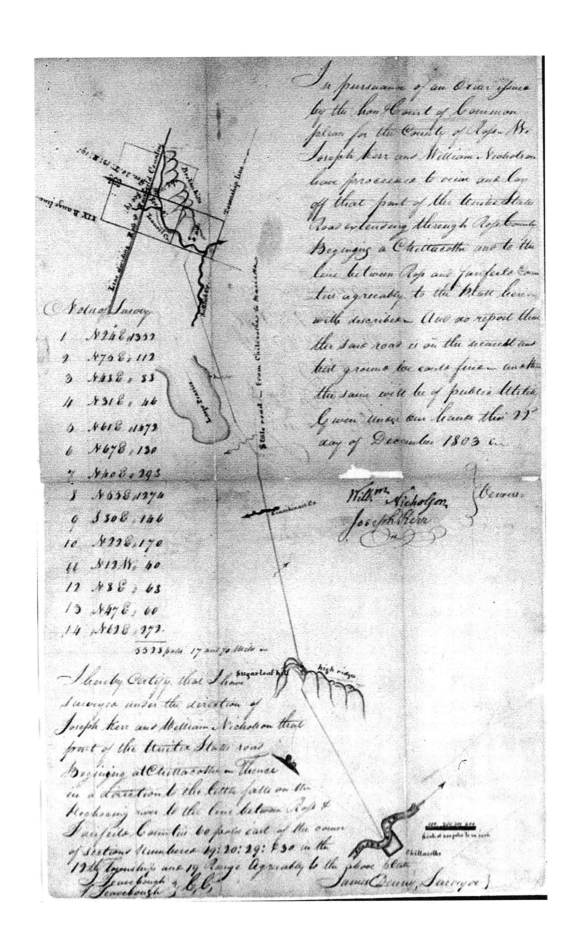

Slide D. Map of the National Road, December 22, 1803. [National Archives]

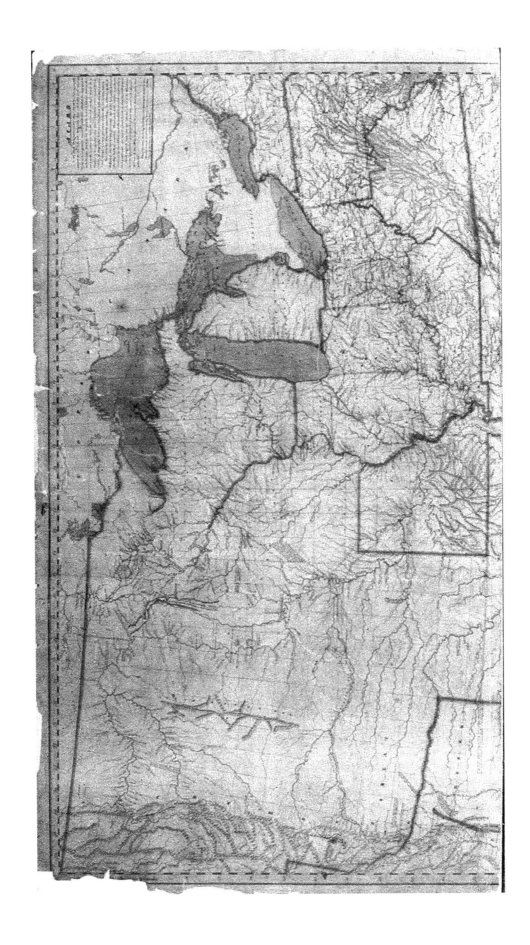

Slide E1. Map produced by the Long Expedition, 1820-1821. [National Archives]

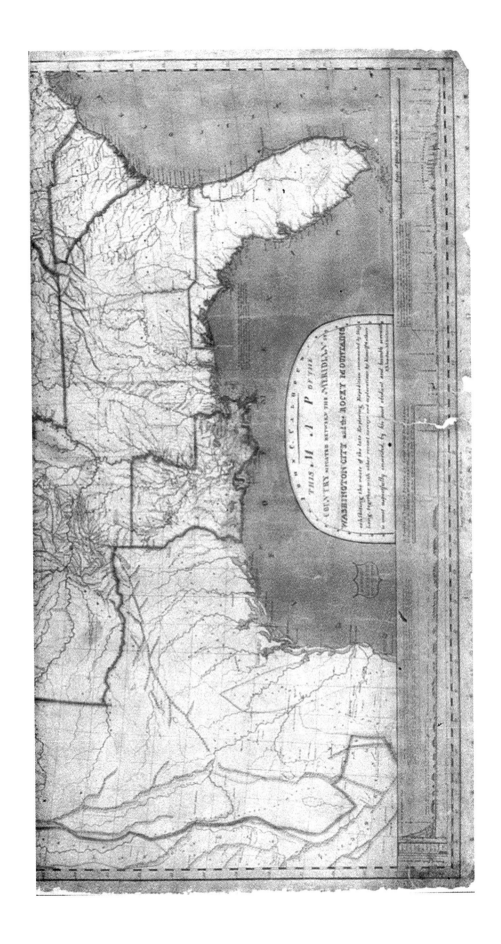

Slide E2. Map produced by the Long Expedition, 1820-1821. [National Archives]

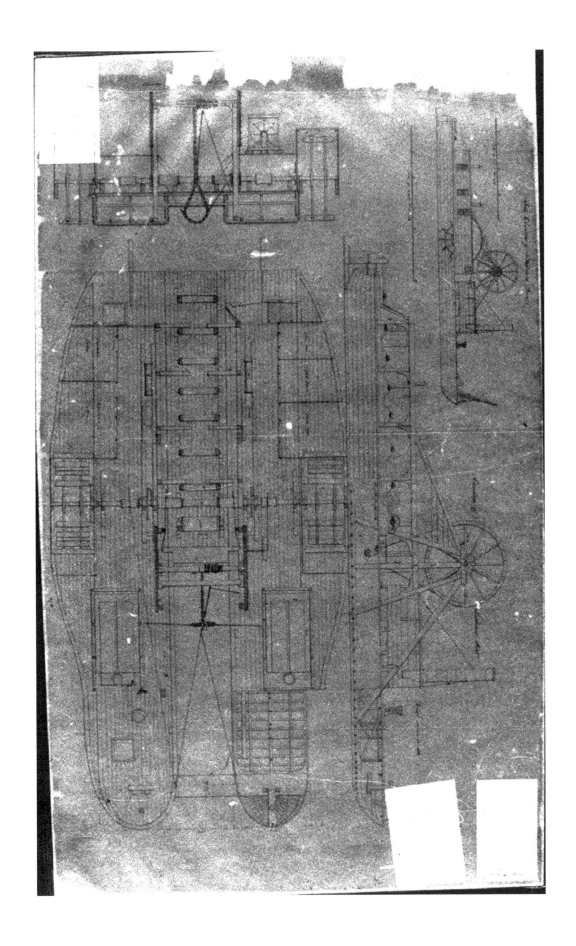

Slide F. Snag boat design, ca. 1838. [National Archives]

No. 913

The United States of America

TO ALL TO WHOM THESE LETTERS PATENT SHALL COME:

Whereas Henry M. Shreve, of St Louis, Mo

has alleged that he has invented a new and useful Improved machine for removing snags and sawyers from the beds of rivers

which he states has not been known or used before his application has made oath that he is a citizen of the United States that he does verily believe that he is the original and first inventor or discoverer of the said Improvement and that the same hath not to the best of his knowledge and belief been previously known or used has paid into the treasury of the **United States** the sum of Thirty dollars and presented a petition to the **COMMISSIONER** of **PATENTS** signifying a desire of obtaining an exclusive property in the said Improvement and praying that a patent may be granted for that purpose

These are Therefore to grant according to law to the said Henry M. Shreve his heirs administrators or assigns for the term of fourteen years from the twelfth day of September one thousand eight hundred and thirty-eight the full and exclusive right and liberty of making constructing using and vending to others to be used the said Improvement a description whereof is given in the words of the said Henry M. Shreve in the schedule hereunto annexed and is made a part of these presents

In Testimony whereof I have caused these letters to be made Patent and the seal of the **PATENT OFFICE** has been hereunto affixed GIVEN under my hand at the City of Washington, this twelfth day of September in the year of our Lord one thousand eight hundred and thirty-eight and of the **INDEPENDENCE** of the United States of America the sixty-third

John Forsyth, Secretary of State

Countersigned and Sealed with the Seal of the Patent Office

Henry L. Ellsworth, Commissioner of Patents

Slide G. Patent issued to Henry Shreve for snag boat, September 12, 1838. [National Archives]

Slide H. Patent drawing of the cotton gin, 1794. [National Archives]

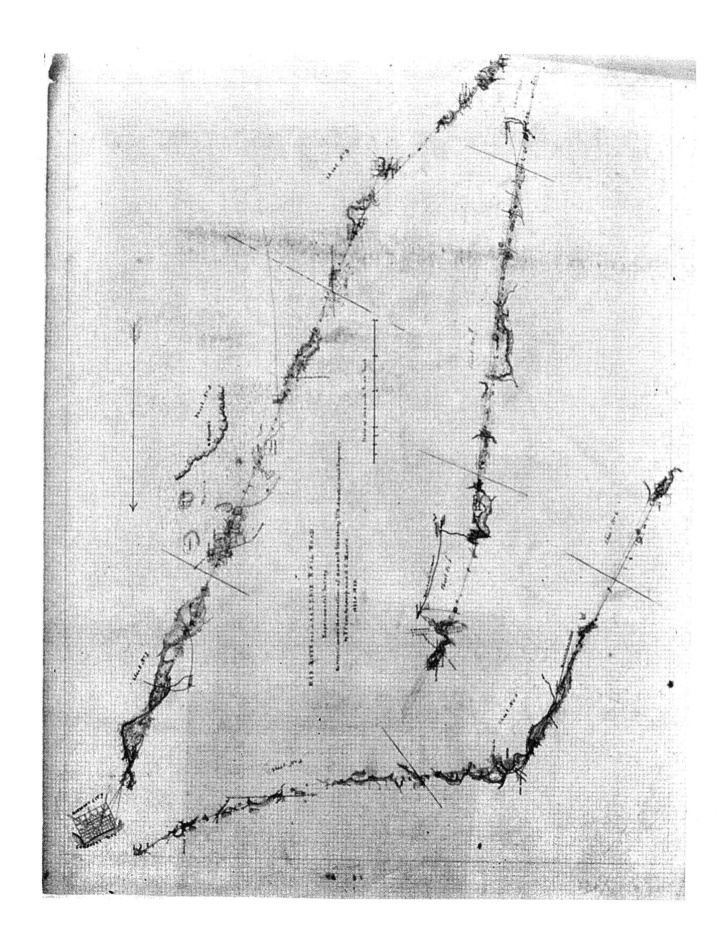

Slide I. Erie Railroad map, 1832-1833. [National Archives]

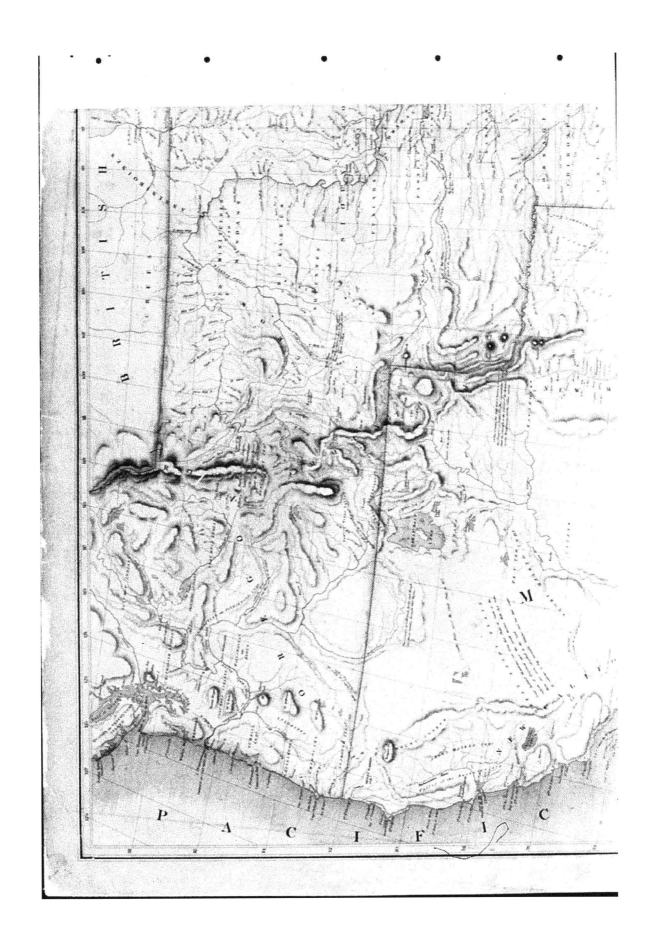

Slide J. Burr's Postal Atlas, 1839. [National Archives]

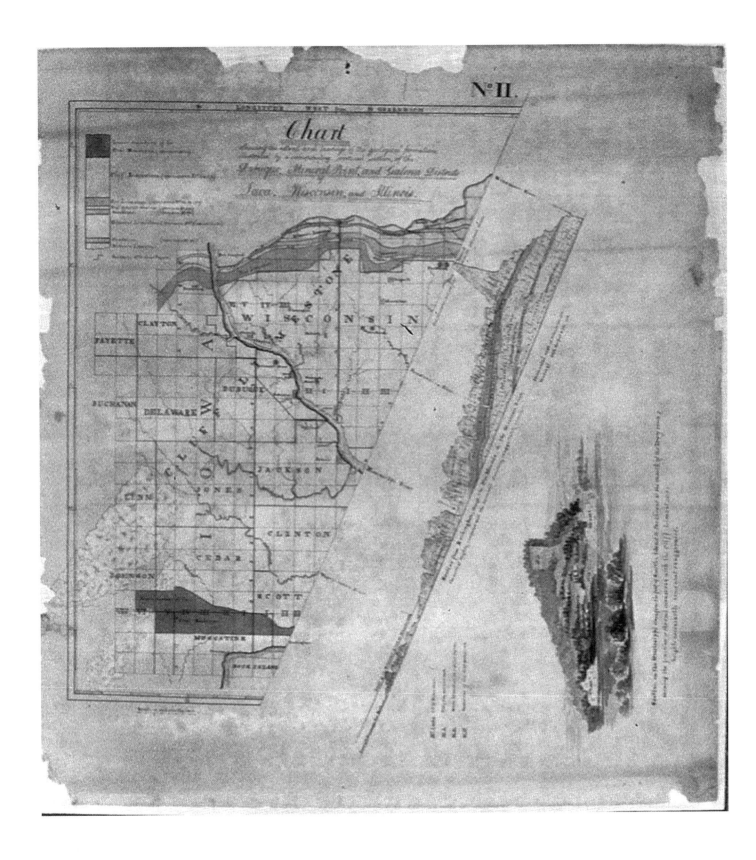

Slide K. Minerals map, 1839-1841. [National Archives]

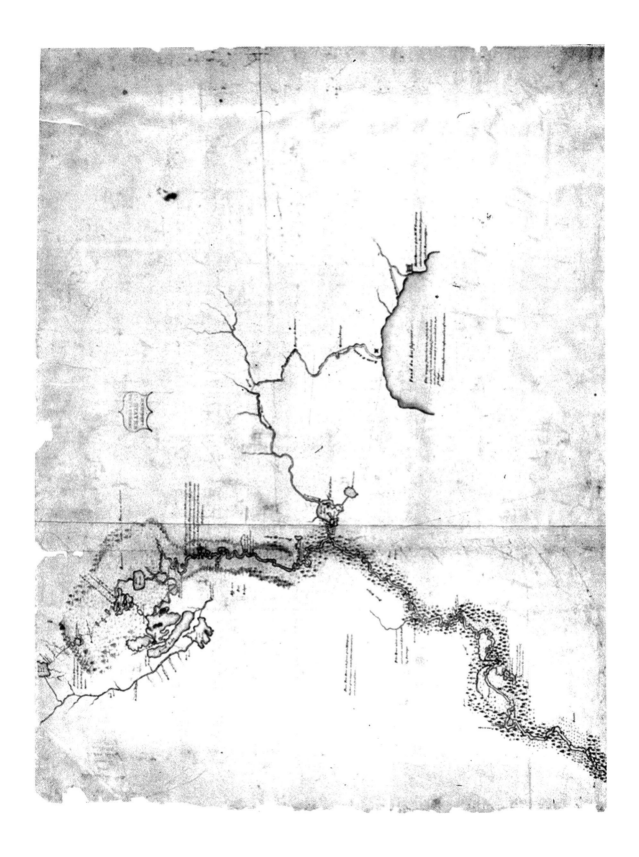

Slide L1. Map produced by the Pike Expedition, 1805-1806. [National Archives]

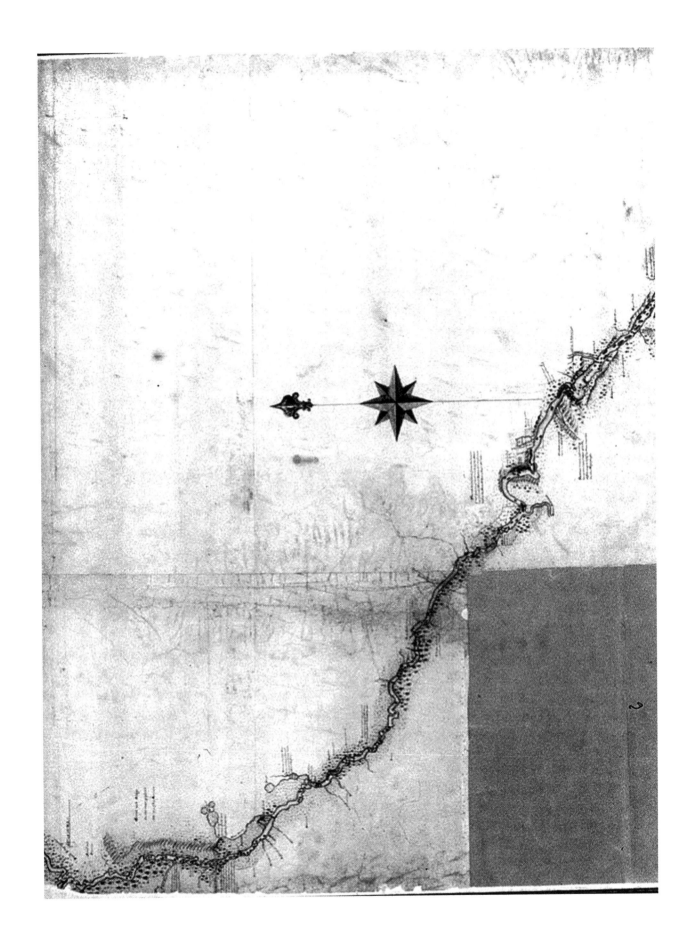

Slide L2. Map produced by the Pike Expedition, 1805-1806. [National Archives]

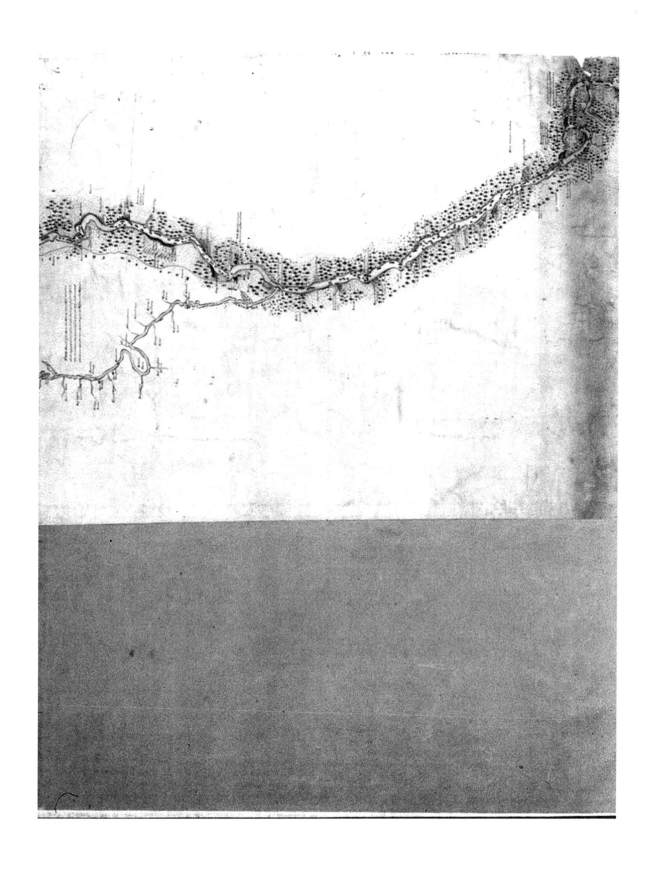

Slide L3. Map produced by the Pike Expedition, 1805-1806. [National Archives]

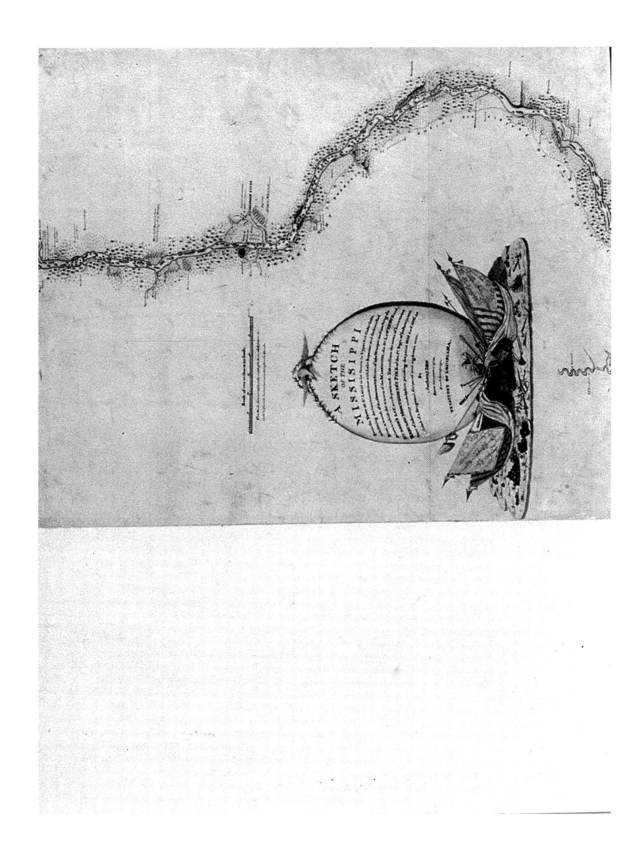

Slide L4. Map produced by the Pike Expedition, 1805-1806. [National Archives]

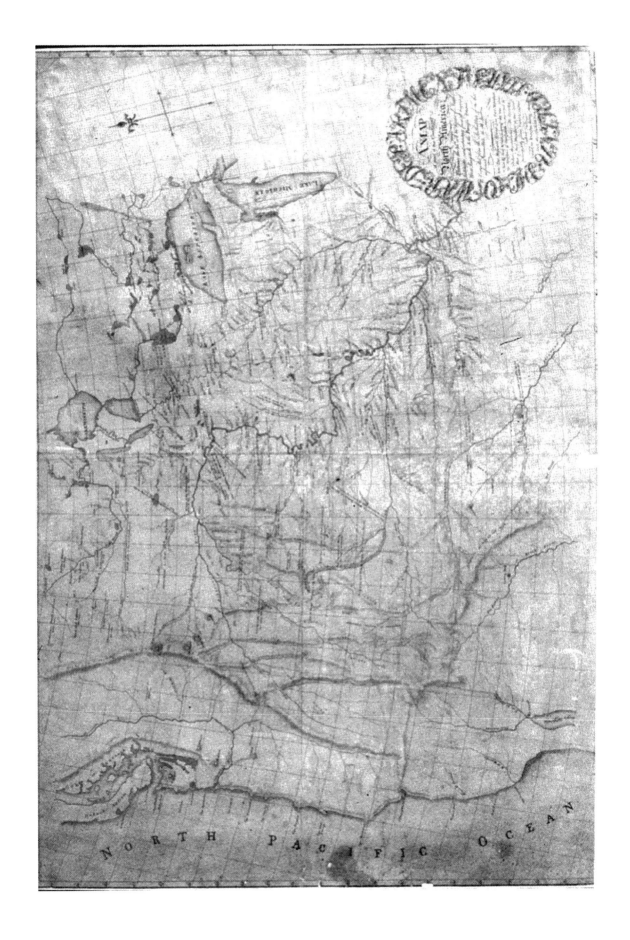

Slide M. Map based on the Lewis and Clark Expedition, 1806. [National Archives]

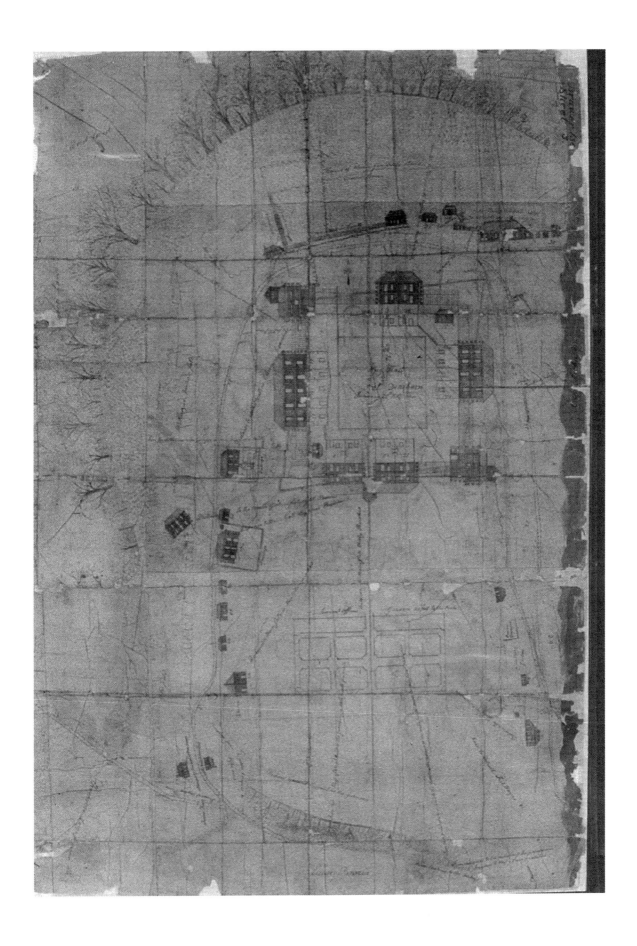

Slide N. Fort Dearborn groundplan and elevation, January 25, 1808. [National Archives]

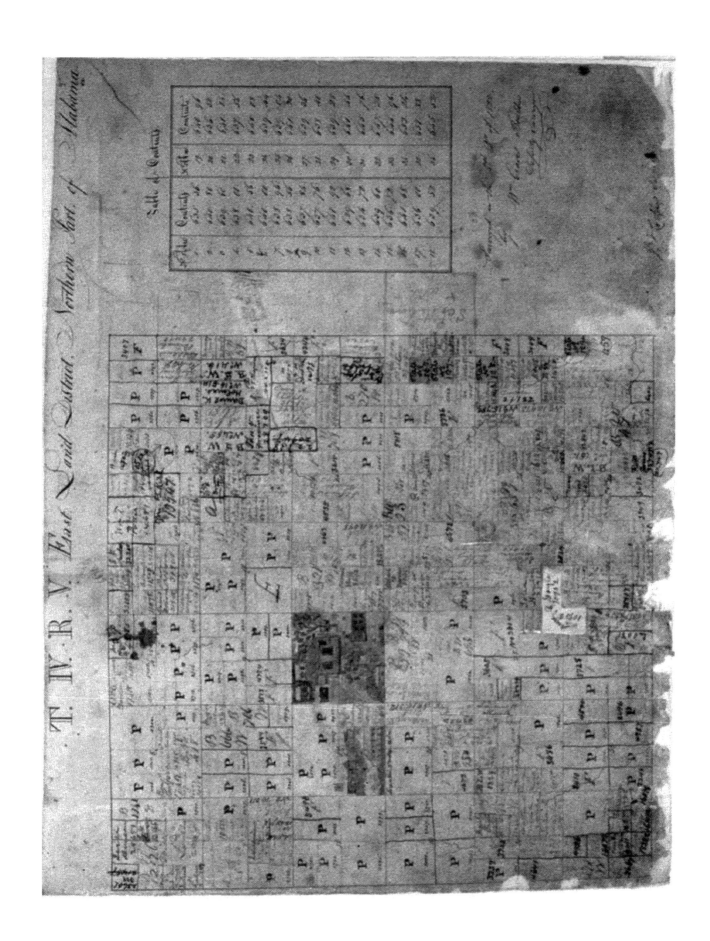

Slide O. Township plat, Alabama, Huntsville Meridian,
Township 4 South, Range 5 East, 1822. [National Archives]

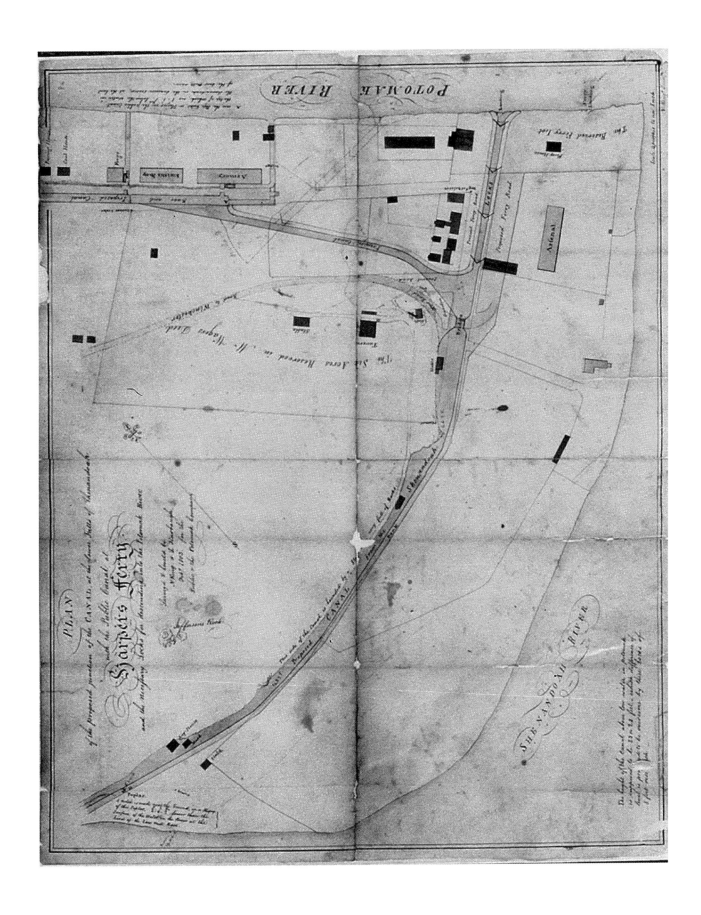

Slide P. Proposed canal at Harper's Ferry, February 1803. [National Archives]

Slide Q. *Buffalo Dance of the Mandans*, artwork by Karl Bodmer, 1833-1834. [National Archives]

3123.

Slide R. *Osceola*, artwork by George Catlin, ca. 1837. [National Archives]

Teaching With Documents Order Form

The United States Expands West: 1785-1842

You may order copies of the following documents in their original size:

Document	Price	Qty.	Total
Document 5. *(17x22, b/w, 2-sided)* The Kentucky Gazette, newspaper, October 8, 1819.	$45.00		
Document 8. *(17x22, b/w)* Chart of Chesapeake and Ohio Canal toll rates, July 1, 1857.	$24.00		
Document 24. *(11x17, b/w)* Proclamation about territorial elections, July 26, 1805.	$14.00		
Document 31. *(17x22, b/w, 2-sided)* The Missouri Compromise, March 6, 1820.	$45.00		
Document 38. *(11x17, b/w)* Statement of the Protestant Episcopal Mission at Green Bay, September 30, 1833.	$14.00		
Document 40. *(17x22, b/w)* Enrolled Cherokee immigrants, March 31, 1832.	$24.00		
Add 5% MD Sales Tax (if applicable)			
Shipping & Handling (Ground Shipping: $10.00, Air Shipping: $22.00)			
Total			

Billing Address:

_____

_____

_____

_____

Shipping Address: (if different from Billing Address)

_____

_____

_____

_____

☐ Check Enclosed payable to Graphic Visions Associates

☐ VISA   ☐ Mastercard   ☐ American Express

_____/_____/_____/_____/   _____/_____/

Credit Card Number   Exp. Date   Authorized Signature

(_____)_____   (_____)_____

Telephone   Fax

Mail Order To: Graphic Visions
640 East Diamond Avenue, Ste. F
Gaithersburg, MD 20877